M000169030

Calvin

CALVIN

A Brief Guide to His Life and Thought

Willem van 't Spijker

TRANSLATED BY
Lyle D. Bierma

 WESTMINSTER
JOHN KNOX PRESS
LOUISVILLE · KENTUCKY

© 2009 Westminster John Knox Press

English translation of the unpublished Dutch manuscript of Willem van 't Spijker; also published in Germany: *Calvin: Biographie und Theologie,* trans. Hinrich Stoevesandt, Die Kirche in ihrer Geschichte, ed. Bernd Moeller (Göttingen, Germany: Vandenhoeck & Ruprecht, 2001); © Vandenhoeck & Ruprecht GmbH & Co. KG, Willem van 't Spijker: *Calvin. Biographie und Theologie,* 1. Aufl., Göttingen, 2001.

First English edition
Westminster John Knox Press
Louisville, Kentucky

09 10 11 12 13 14 15 16 17 18—10 9 8 7 6 5 4 3 2 1

All rights reserved. No part of this book may be reproduced or transmitted in any form or by any means, electronic or mechanical, including photocopying, recording, or by any information storage or retrieval system, without permission in writing from the publisher. For information, address Westminster John Knox Press, 100 Witherspoon Street, Louisville, Kentucky 40202-1396. Or contact us online at www.wjkbooks.com.

Scripture quotations from the New Revised Standard Version of the Bible are copyright © 1989 by the Division of Christian Education of the National Council of the Churches of Christ in the U.S.A. and are used by permission.

Book design by Sharon Adams
Cover design by Night & Day Design
Cover art: Portrait de John Calvin © *Stefano Bianchetti/CORBIS*

Library of Congress Cataloging-in-Publication Data
Spijker, W. van 't.
  [Calvin. English]
  Calvin : a brief guide to his life and thought / Willem van 't Spijker ; translated by Lyle D. Bierma.—1st ed.
       p. cm.
  Includes bibliographical references (p.) and index.
  ISBN 978–0-664–23225-2 (alk. paper)
  1. Calvin, Jean, 1509–1564.   2. Reformed Church—Clergy—Biography.   3. Reformation—Switzerland.   4. Reformed Church—Doctrines—History—16th century.   I. Title.
  BX9418.S655 2009
  284′.2092—dc22
  [B]   2008030394

PRINTED IN THE UNITED STATES OF AMERICA

♾ The paper used in this publication meets the minimum requirements of the American National Standard for Information Sciences—Permanence of Paper for Printed Library Materials, ANSI Z39.48-1992.

Westminster John Knox Press advocates the responsible use of our natural resources. The text paper of this book is made from at least 30% post-consumer waste.

Contents

Translator's Acknowledgments

I am indebted to a number of people for their assistance with this project. In particular I would like to thank Paul W. Fields, Theological Librarian and curator of the H. Henry Meeter Center for Calvin Studies at Calvin College and Calvin Theological Seminary, who formatted all the bibliographies, and Todd Rester, a PhD student at Calvin Seminary, who prepared the index. I am also grateful to Willem van 't Spijker, the author of the book, from whose unpublished Dutch manuscript I prepared this English translation; John Bolt, Carl Bosma, Henry De Moor, Arie Leder, and Pieter Tuit, Dutch-speaking colleagues of mine at Calvin Seminary who answered many translation questions; Donald K. McKim, Executive Editor for Theology and Reference at Westminster John Knox Press; and Daniel Braden, Associate Managing Editor at Westminster John Knox Press. Final responsibility for the translation, of course, remains mine alone.

Lyle D. Bierma

Abbreviations

CO   *Ioannis Calvini opera quae supersunt omnia* (Corpus refor-
              matorum, vols. 29–87)

Herminjard,   Aimé-Louis Herminjard, *Correspondance des réformateurs*
  Correspondance   *dans les pays de langue française* (Geneva: Georg, 1866–97)

OS   *Johannis Calvini opera selecta*, ed. Peter Barth, Wilhelm
              Niesel, and Dora Scheuner

TRE   *Theologische Realenzyklopädie*, ed. Gerhard Krause et al.
              (New York: W. de Gruyter, 1981)

ZW   *Huldreich Zwinglis sämtliche Werke*, ed. Emil Egli, Georg
              Finsler, and Walther Köhler (Corpus reformatorum,
              vols. 88–)

1

France at the Beginning
of the Sixteenth Century

THE POLITICAL SITUATION

The history of the reformation in France was determined in large part by developments in the foreign policy of King Francis I (1515–47). This history was connected most closely with the particular situation of the French Roman Catholic Church and was shaped especially by the evangelical and reform movements that arose in France at the beginning of the sixteenth century.

Already upon his accession to office, Francis I had raised high expectations. All his efforts were directed toward the unity of the kingdom. At the same time, however, the kingship was moving in the direction of monarchical absolutism, which would eventually come to full blossom under Louis XIV. The king's victory in the Battle of Marignano (1515), where the Swiss forces were badly defeated, gave him possession of the Duchy of Milan, and Pope Leo X was forced into the Concordat of Bologna, by which Francis was enabled to exercise a direct influence on the French church.

In 1519 Francis I became a candidate for the imperial throne of the Holy Roman Empire. The electors, however, preferred the young king of Spain, who as Charles V became the natural rival of the French king. To the latter would fall the role of potential protector of the German Protestants.[1] From that point on, the question of who would gain hegemony over Europe dominated the ambition for power in Madrid and Paris. The rivalry between king and emperor led to intense diplomatic activity and provoked several wars between 1519 and 1558. The rising power of capital also played a significant role. The solicitation

---

1. Alfred Kohler, *Quellen zur Geschichte Karls V.* (Darmstadt: Wissenschaftliche Buchgesellschaft, 1990), 44–58.

1

of the emperorship required huge financial sacrifices of both Charles and Francis, and the many wars that followed further drained their resources.

The position of the papal see changed repeatedly, depending on how the prospects for the outcome of the struggle were assessed in Rome. For a while it was the king who won the pope's favor. The emperor then found himself more limited in what he could do against those inclined toward reformation in the empire. Conversely, the chances of the evangelical movement in France improved when Francis suffered defeat in the Battle of Pavia (1525) and was taken as a prisoner of war to Madrid. While the Peasants' War was raging in Germany, the theological faculty, the Sorbonne, and the Parlement of Paris felt strong enough in the absence of the king to take measures against the young evangelical movement.

In the mid-1530s, Francis sought to win over the German Protestant princes by inviting Philipp Melanchthon to Paris as a theological adviser. At the same time, however, the heat of persecution was rising there, which made Francis's "open letter" of February 1, 1535, to the estates of the German Empire appear disingenuous. Particularly the secret and open contacts that Francis was pursuing with the Turks made clear that this "most Christian king" was not guided by genuine religious motives.[2] His foreign policy made it impossible for him to hold a credible position with respect to the Reformation. It was determined too much by ambition for power in the great scales of European events, and his concern for the unity of the church in France was too limited.

The same was true of his position on resolving the religious question by means of an ecumenical council. While Charles V (also from personal religious motives) was a proponent of a council at which questions about the unity of the church could be resolved, Francis opposed any such plans, fearing Charles's influence. When the pope showed the same reluctance, Charles tried to settle the matter inside the empire on his own initiative by means of religious colloquies. When it came to the church and religion in France, however, European politics dictated Francis's agenda.

CROWN AND CHURCH

Francis I's attitude toward the Reformation was closely connected with the situation of the French church since the late Middle Ages. At a French synod under Charles VII in 1438, the French clergy had adopted the Pragmatic Sanction of Bourges, which gave the king the right to appoint bishops.[3] This not

2. Hubert Jedin, *Geschichte des Konzils von Trent*, 2nd ed. (Freiburg: Herder, 1951), 1:182–83.
3. Carl Mirbt and Kurt Aland, *Quellen zur Geschichte des Papsttums und des römischen Katholizismus*, vol. 1, *Von den Anfängen bis zum Tridentinum*, 6th ed. (Tübingen: Mohr, 1967), 481–82.

only represented a support of conciliarism over against curialism, in line with French policy since the Council of Basel,[4] but it also granted to the prince the authority to levy taxes on benefices. This Gallicanism made the French church more or less independent of the papal see. Therefore, measures similar to those later taken by Henry VIII of England were wholly unnecessary.

In 1516, after the victory at Marignano, Francis I entered into the Concordat of Bologna with Pope Leo X. In this agreement, the rights of the kings of France and the independence of the French church were once again confirmed. Francis I would make ample use of these rights to appoint friends and cronies to ecclesiastical posts and thus expand his influence. The church became an instrument of power in the hands of the monarchy. It is an interesting question how this power related to the rights of the parlement and the university, both of which were very active in defending religious orthodoxy. At times Francis I acted quite independently as an autonomous prince over against both the Parlement of Paris and the theological faculty of the university, the Sorbonne. These two often joined hands in the struggle against the new doctrinal ideas. A condemnation of Martin Luther's theses appeared on April 15, 1521, naming 104 of them in particular. At the same time, the Parlement of Paris, with the approval of the king, decided that no book about Scripture or the Christian religion might be published without the consent of the faculty. In June 1523 the theological doctors sent a delegation to the chancellor to demand the public burning of Luther's writings.[5]

In defending pure doctrine, the Sorbonne had an air about it of near infallibility. From 1520 to 1534 Noel Beda acted as the leader of the theological faculty—antihumanist and sharply antagonistic toward the exegetical methods of the evangelical movement, which energetically pursued the study of the original text of Scripture. He battled hard against those who sympathized with Erasmus and Luther, leading the opposition against Louis Berquin, who in 1529 was burned at the stake as an Erasmian. Already a year before, he had to prepare the condemnation of Erasmus. But Beda was not able to prevent the establishment of the *Collège de France*, where the *lecteurs royaux* taught the classics on the model of the Three-Languages College in Leuven (Louvain). Francis I was not the founder of this institution, but he did support it, and in 1534, when Beda tried to forbid public instruction in biblical exegesis, he encountered resistance from the king. However, the opposition between the Sorbonne and the *Collège de France* had nothing to do with the controversy

4. Joseph Gill, *Konstanz und Basel-Florenz* (Mainz: Grünewald, 1967), 269–70.

5. James K. Farge, *Orthodoxy and Reform in Early Reformation France: The Faculty of Theology of Paris, 1500–1543* (Leiden: Brill, 1985), 125ff., 165ff.; Frans T. Bos, "Luther in het oordeel van de Sorbonne: Een onderzoek naar ontstaan, inhoud en werking van de Determinatio (1521) en naar haar verhouding tot de vroegere veroordelingen van Luther" (Amsterdam: Academische Pers, 1974).

between Rome and the Reformation. None of the royal professors opted for the Reformation. The liberty that Francis I took in his relation with the university had its basis in his well-known sympathy for the Renaissance, which had turned him into a patron of art and science and had, already in his own lifetime, led to his being called the "restorer of scholarship."[6]

The Parlement of Paris—one of eight provincial courts and the most important instrument of government with which the king was directly involved—also dealt with religious matters, although in most cases not directly, since heresy fell under the jurisdiction of ecclesiastical courts. As almost everywhere else, the church turned heretics over to the temporal judges for punishment. In 1525 the parlement took over the review of evangelical developments in Meaux. Bishop Briçonnet was considered responsible for the preaching of Pierre Caroli, Gérard Roussel, and others who took refuge in Strasbourg.[7] In 1535 the parlement took harsh action against heretics, burning thirty-five "Lutherans" in the month of January alone. This was around the same time that Francis I was trying to convince the German Protestant princes that his measures were directed only against revolutionary elements.

It is not easy to find a consistent pattern in the actions of Francis I. In some cases he used his personal authority to protect humanists and evangelical sympathizers. On the other hand, in the mid-1530s he showed himself to be harsh and intolerant. Sometimes family relationships played a role. His sister Marguerite (1492–1549), Queen of Navarre (1527–49), portrayed the relationship between mother, sister, and brother as that of a trinity. She herself granted asylum to those who could no longer tolerate the situation in Paris. Her influence can sometimes be detected in the way in which Francis I dealt with problems.

The king himself viewed the renewal of the church from the vantage point of the Renaissance, which he strongly wished to support in every way. It is that side of his character to which Zwingli and Calvin, as well as Sadoleto, appealed. Ulrich Zwingli dedicated his *De vera et falsa religione commentarius* (March 1525) to the French king, considering humanism as a bridge to France for the gospel itself.[8] John Calvin, too, tried to capitalize on the humanist-religious sensibilities that he assumed Francis I to have. In the "Epistola nuncupatoria" at the front of the 1536 *Institutes*, he tried to persuade the king to recognize the lies being told about those sympathetic to the Reformation and to convince him of the truth of the gospel as understood by the Reformation.[9] Jacopo Sadoleto dedicated his commentary on Paul's Epistle to the Romans in 1535

6. *TRE*, s.v. "Franz I."
7. Janine Garrisson, *A History of Sixteenth-Century France, 1483–1598: Renaissance, Reformation, and Rebellion*, trans. Richard Rex (New York: St. Martin's, 1995), 86.
8. ZW 3:590ff.; see Zwingli's "Verantwortung," 629.
9. CO 1:9ff.: "Prefatory Address to King Francis I of France."

to Francis I, "most Christian king of France."[10] His goal, however, was to urge the king to remain steadfast in the midst of the variety of views that had arisen.

Everyone, apparently, recognized in Francis I something of the ideal to which they thought they could appeal. Many saw him as a scholar who belonged to their circle, and he from his side did personally intervene to save humanist scholars from the authority of the Sorbonne and the parlement. The measures that he took in the 1530s can only be explained as the result of personal peevishness. This led to the persecution that finally forced Calvin to flee. From that moment on, the character of the evangelical movement, which had come into being already in the 1520s, was changed.

RELIGIOUS HUMANISM
AND THE EVANGELICAL MOVEMENT

The question whether the reformation in France originated by itself or should be viewed as a result of Luther's activity ignores the various aspects of the Renaissance and the fact that the Renaissance in France represented a wholly distinctive type. In a certain sense, the same was true of the diversity that arose within the broad European evangelical movement, in which fixed structures could be discerned only in the 1540s. Only after the religious colloquies broke off in 1541 (Regensburg) did the distinctions become recognizable.[11] Similarity, however, does not necessarily mean causality. The distinctive development of religious humanism in France can be distinguished from the early evangelical movement without assuming thereby that a path from both led directly to the Reformation. The influence of Desiderius Erasmus made its way to France from Basel, Strasbourg, and Antwerp, which were also centers of the early Reformation. Both Johann Oecolampadius in Basel and Martin Bucer in Strasbourg had been influenced by religious humanism, and both felt responsible for what happened in the neighboring country of France.

This influence, however, could not have been felt if humanism itself had not found a breeding ground in France. Louis de Berquin (ca. 1490–1529) belonged to a circle where Erasmus, Luther, and Melanchthon were being read, and he not only translated their writings but also helped spread a new view of the

10. *Iacobi Sadoleti, Episcopi Carpentoractis, In Pauli epistolam ad Romanos commentariorum libri tres* (Lugduni [Lyon]: Sebastianus Gryphius Germanus excudebat, 1536).

11. Jacques Pannier, *Les origines de la Confession de foi et de la discipline des Églises Réformées de France: Étude historique* (Paris: Alcan, 1936), 23ff.; Richard Stauffer, "Lefèvre d'Étaples, artisan ou spectateur de la Réforme?" in *Interprètes de la Bible: Études sur les réformateurs du XVIe siècle* (Paris: Beauchesne, 1980), 11–29; Francis Higman, *La diffusion de la réforme en France, 1520–1565* (Geneva: Labor & Fides, 1992), 19–20.

gospel through works of his own. On two occasions Francis I came to the rescue when the Sorbonne sought to have de Berquin condemned by a special court of theologians and parliamentarians. On a third occasion, however, de Berquin was condemned, and on April 17, 1529, he was burned at the stake—a move in a direction that the king at this point did not support.

In the early 1520s in Meaux, not far from Paris, a circle of evangelically minded parish clergy was formed under the leadership of Guillaume Briçonnet (ca. 1470–1534). They were primarily involved in preaching and pastoral care. Briçonnet corresponded extensively with Francis's sister, Marguerite d'Angoulême, who offered him her patronage. The bishop had been in the personal service of the king and had been involved in the settlement of the Concordat of Bologna. In Meaux he personally led the reform of the diocese, organized visitations, and saw to the preparation of preachers. He was supported in this by the Meaux group, which is usually considered to be a representation of the original French reformation.

Probably the best-known member of this group was Jacques Lefèvre d'Étaples (ca. 1460–1536), who, like Erasmus and de Berquin, advocated a return to the ancient sources. He did this initially by, among other things, editing, translating, and annotating the works of Aristotle. After that he turned his attention to the church fathers. His spirituality tended in the direction of mystical theology, in which he, along with others, found a basis for the inner renewal of the church. Eventually his interest turned primarily to translating and commenting on the Bible. In 1509 in Saint-Germain-des-Prés, he published his *Quintuplex Psalterium*, an edition of five parallel Latin translations of the Psalms. The fruit of his research was an interpretation of the Pauline Epistles, *S. Pauli Epistolae XIV ex vulgata adiecta intelligentia ex graeco, cum commentariis* (1512), in which some passages clearly teach justification by grace through faith (although a faith that is never without works). In 1521 he responded to Briçonnet's request to come to Meaux, where an evangelical working group assembled a collection of fifty-two homilies on texts from the Epistles and the Gospels (1532). There, too, he taught justification—in a double sense: justification through faith, which functions as the light that dispels the darkness; and justification as the fire that by its warmth makes the cold disappear.[12]

The circle of Meaux that was gathered around Briçonnet and Lefèvre also included several enthusiastic younger preachers, among them Gérard Roussel (d. 1555), Pierre Caroli (d. 1550), Martial Mazurier, and Guillaume Farel (1489–1565). Roussel had studied under Lefèvre in Paris and now enjoyed the special patronage of Marguerite d'Angoulême, who appointed him as her

---

12. Philip E. Hughes, *Lefèvre: Pioneer of Ecclesiastical Renewal in France* (Grand Rapids: Eerdmans, 1984), 74ff.

preacher because of his homiletical skill. His Passion sermons of 1533 were attended by thousands in Paris, which led to difficulties with the theological faculty.[13] In 1536 he became bishop of Oloron in the dominion of Marguerite. This occasioned Calvin's writing of his *Duae Epistolae* (1537), in which he reproached Roussel for a kind of Nicodemism. Caroli had followed Lefèvre to Meaux. He was accused by the Paris faculty of a variety of heresies, had to flee, and like others acquired a position with Marguerite as a priest in Alençon, where he remained until 1533. By the next year he had become a highly sought-after figure and left for Geneva, later becoming the first reformatory preacher in Lausanne, where he would come into conflict with Calvin and Farel. Farel, too, belonged to the circle of religious humanists in Meaux. In 1523 he headed for Basel because the reformation in Meaux was not radical enough for him.

Bishop Briçonnet discontinued his attempts at organizing the evangelical revival in Meaux when his efforts were frustrated by the authorities. Along with that was the fact that he was more interested in a somewhat elitist, ethical revival than a reformation that had clearly caught on with large sections of the common people. Briçonnet retired under pressure from the authorities when the population moved to radicalize the reformation with an outbreak of iconoclasm. In so doing they had crossed a line, and that meant the end of the movement in Meaux. The Parisian Parlement and the Sorbonne joined forces, while the king, who was in captivity in Madrid at the time, tried to intervene.[14]

Lefèvre and Roussel fled to Strasbourg, and the Meaux movement shifted in part to the territory of Marguerite d'Angoulême. Her spiritual development is outlined in Wolfgang Capito's dedication of his Hosea commentary to her: from vain and lofty philosophy to the true light that arises in Christ.[15] On that basis she ought to follow the way of the cross and promote the "Église naissante." "For experience teaches that the cruelest persecutions are the greatest consolations for the weakest Christians."[16] For her spiritual formation, Marguerite owed much to Briçonnet, Lefèvre, and Roussel. She had committed herself to the gospel and cultivated a piety that did not easily fit into ecclesiastical and confessional molds. Keeping company at her court were mystics, whom she prized very highly, as well as people whom Calvin would later characterize and attack as Libertines and Epicureans.

13. Aimé-Louis Herminjard, *Correspondance des réformateurs dans les pays de langue française* (Geneva: Georg, 1866–97), 3:54ff.; Charles Schmidt, *Gerard Roussel, predicateur de la reine Marguerite de Navarre* (1845; repr., Geneva: Slatkine, 1970).

14. Letter of Francis I to the Parlement of Paris (November 12, 1525), in Herminjard, *Correspondance*, 1:401–2.

15. Herminjard, *Correspondance*, 2:119ff.

16. Ibid., 2:122.

The 1520s, then, give us a picture of an evangelical movement whose sources should be sought primarily in the religious humanism of Erasmus. It fought hard against the scholastic theology being cultivated and defended in Paris, but at this stage it lacked the energy to persevere. The royal court was not categorically opposed to it, but the interests of an autonomous monarchy, supported by the ideals of the upper circles of society, prevailed. From time to time, the king's policy would change, often arbitrarily. The first decade of the history of the Reformation passed, therefore, without any essential change having occurred. But the 1530s would be of crucial importance.

CHAPTER BIBLIOGRAPHY

Beza, Theodore. *Histoire ecclésiastique des églises réformées au royaume de France: Édition nouvelle avec commentaire, notice bibliographique et table des faits et des noms propres.* 3 vols. Edited by G. Baum and A. Eduard Cunitz. Nieuwkoop: B. de Graaf, 1974.

Bos, Frans T. "Luther in het oordeel van de Sorbonne: Een onderzoek naar ontstaan, inhoud en werking van de Determinatio (1521) en naar haar verhouding tot de vroegere veroordelingen van Luther." PhD diss., Amsterdam: Academische Pers, 1974.

Bost, Charles. *Histoire des Protestants de France.* Carrières-sous-Poissy: La Cause, 1996.

Chambon, Joseph. *Der französische Protestantismus. Sein Weg bis zur französischen Revolution.* Munich: C. Kaiser Verlag, 1937.

Crouzet, Denis. *Genèse de la Réforme française 1520–1562.* Paris: SEDES, 1996.

Farge, James K. *Orthodoxy and Reform in Early Reformation France: The Faculty of Theology of Paris 1500–1543.* Leiden: Brill, 1985.

Gadoffre, Gilbert. *La révolution culturelle dans la France des humanistes: Guillaume Budé et François Ier.* Geneva: Droz, 1997.

Garrisson, Janine. *A History of Sixteenth-Century France 1483–1598: Renaissance, Reformation, and Rebellion.* Translated by Richard Rex. London: St. Martin's Press, 1995.

Gill, Joseph. *Konstanz und Basel-Florenz.* Mainz: Grünewald, 1967.

Heller, Henry. *The Conquest of Poverty: The Calvinist Revolt in Sixteenth Century France.* Leiden: Brill, 1986.

Herminjard, Aimé-Louis. *Correspondance des réformateurs dans les pays de langue française.* Geneva: Georg, 1866–97.

Higman, Francis. *La diffusion de la réforme en France 1520–1565.* Geneva: Labor & Fides, 1992.

Hughes, Philip E. *Lefèvre: Pioneer of Ecclesiastical Renewal in France.* Grand Rapids: Eerdmans, 1984.

Imbart de la Tour, Pierre. *Les origines de la réforme.* Vol. 3, *L'évangélisme (1521–1538).* Paris: Librairie Hachette, 1914.

Jedin, Hubert. *Geschichte des Konzils von Trent.* 2nd ed. Freiburg: Herder, 1951.

Kingdon, Robert M. "Pamphlet Literature of the French Reformation." In *Reformation Europe: A Guide to Research*, edited by Steven Ozment, 233–48. St. Louis: Center for Reformation Research, 1982.

Knecht, Robert J. *Renaissance Warrior and Patron: The Reign of Francis I.* Cambridge: Cambridge University Press, 1994.

Kohler, Alfred. *Quellen zur Geschichte Karls V.* Darmstadt: Wissenschaftliche Buchge-sellschaft, 1990.

Léonard, Émile G. *Histoire générale du protestantisme.* Vol. 1, *La réformation.* Paris: Presses universitaires de France, 1961.

Mirbt, Carl, and Kurt Aland. *Quellen zur Geschichte des Papsttums und des römischen Katholizismus.* Vol. 1, *Von den Anfängen bis zum Tridentinum.* 6th ed. Tübingen: Mohr, 1967.

Moreau, Edouard de, P. Jourda, and P. Janelle. *La crise religieuse de XVI siècle.* Paris: Bloud & Gay, 1950.

Mours, Samuel. *Le protestantisme en France au XVI siècle.* Paris: Librairie Protestante, 1959.

Pannier, Jacques. *Les origins de la Confession de foi et de la discipline des Églises Réformées de France: Étude historique.* Paris: Alcan, 1936.

Polenz, Gottlob von. *Geschichte des französischen Calvinismus bis zum Gnadenedikt von Nîmes im Jahre 1629.* Vols. 1–5. Gotha: F. A. Perthes, 1857–1869. Reprint, Aalen: Scientia Verlag, 1964.

Salmon, J. H. M. (John Hearsey McMillan). *Society in Crisis: France in the Sixteenth Century.* New York: St. Martin's Press, 1975.

Schmidt, Charles. *Gérard Roussel, prédicateur de la reine Marguerite de Navarre.* Geneva: Slatkine, 1970.

Soldan, Wilhelm G. *Geschichte des Protestantismus in Frankreich bis zum Tode Karl's IX.* Vol. 1, part 2. Leipzig: F. U. Brockhaus, 1855.

Stauffer, Richard. "Lefèvre d'Étaples, artisan ou spectateur de la Réforme?" In *Interprètes de la Bible: Études sur les réformateurs du XVIe siècle,* 11–29. Paris: Beauchesne, 1980.

Viénot, John. *Histoire de la réforme français.* Vol. 1, *Des origines à l'Édit de Nantes.* Paris: Fischbacher, 1926.

Wanegffelen, Thierry. *Ni Rome ni Genève: Des fidèles entre deux chaires en France zu XVI siècle.* Paris: H. Champion, 1997.

Wolf, G. P. "Luthers Beziehungen zu Frankreich." In *Leben und Werk Martin Luthers von 1526 bis 1546,* edited by Helmar Junghans, vol. 1, pages 663–75. Göttingen: Vandenhoeck & Ruprecht, 1983.

Wolff, Philippe. *Histoire des Protestants en France: De la Réforme à la Révolution.* 2nd ed. Toulouse: Privat: Diffusion SOFÉDIS, 2001.

2

Calvin's Early Development

John Calvin was born on July 10, 1509, in Noyon, a cathedral city in Picardy, France. His parents were Gérard Cauvin and Jeanne Lefranc. Calvin and his siblings—older brother, Charles; two younger brothers, Antoine and François; and two sisters, one of whom was named Marie—were raised primarily by their father. John's mother, according to tradition, was very beautiful and lived on in his memory, especially as a pious woman. When he was a small child, she would take him along to processions, and he later told how in Ourscamp, near Noyon, he once kissed a part of the body of St. Anne.[1] From his mother he learned the devotion that bound him to the church and its authority and that would later make it difficult for him to opt for the Reformation.

Calvin was also bound to the institution of the church in other ways. His father, who remarried after the death of his first wife, knew how to secure a financial base for his children that made it possible for young John to obtain an education. Gérard Cauvin procured for his twelve-year-old son a formal position as chaplain in the Chapel of La Gésine at the city cathedral. In 1527 Calvin was also appointed to the parish clergy of St. Martin de Marteville in the same diocese. The income from these benefices was more than adequate to cover the cost of his studies.

PREPARATORY EDUCATION

Calvin's father had intended his son for a spiritual office. Having come from a family of tradespeople, Gérard had worked his way up to being an administra-

1. CO 6:442.

tor and notary, the financial manager for the cathedral chapter. As secretary to the bishop, he had direct access to members of the noble family that usually occupied this high ecclesiastical office. His connections with the de Hangest family led to John's being educated along with the children of the Montmorts, a branch of the de Hangests. He first attended the Collège de Capettes, an educational institution under the auspices of the cathedral chapter of Noyon. Calvin was well aware of the difference in social standing between his family and the de Hangests. According to the dedication of his commentary on Seneca's *De clementia* to Claude de Hangest (1532), he regarded himself as of humble origin.[2] The interaction with this aristocratic family enhanced his natural gift for moving comfortably in higher circles.

In August 1523, after completing his elementary education in Noyon, Calvin and several of the Montmort children headed to Paris, where he found lodging with an uncle. There he began his training as a scholar—first at the Collège de la Marche, then at the Collège de Montaigu. Not all the stages of his study are chronologically clear, however, nor can it be established with certainty who made a substantial contribution to preparing him for his academic course of study.

Calvin attended the Collège de la Marche for only three months before the tutor of the Montmorts had him transferred to the Collège de Montaigu. But in Calvin's own opinion, those three months at la Marche were of great value. There he had been taught by Mathurin Cordier, who was known for his pedagogical innovations.[3] Calvin later highly praised the quality of Cordier's instruction, dedicating his commentary on 1 Thessalonians (February 17, 1550) to Cordier out of gratitude for his teaching, which had helped Calvin to make considerable progress in his study of Latin.[4] In 1536 Calvin was able to obtain a position for Cordier during the reorganization of education in Geneva, but in 1538 Cordier had to flee the city along with Calvin and Farel. After that, he worked in Neuchâtel and Lausanne until he obtained an executive post at the recently formed Academy of Geneva in 1562. Calvin valued Cordier not only as a pedagogue but also as a Christian, who sought to instill within his students a love for Christ. He combined the ideals of the *devotio moderna* with his teaching. Calvin considered it a blessing of God that he had met Cordier at the beginning of his studies.

2. Herminjard, *Correspondance*, 2:410; Ford L. Battles and André M. Hugo, eds., *Calvin's Commentary on Seneca's "De Clementia"* (Leiden: Brill, 1969), 4: "unus de plebe homuncio, mediocri, sue potius modica erutditione praeditus"; *Comm. in Psalmos*, CO 31:21: "ab obscuris tenuibusque principiis extractum."

3. Jean J. Lecoultre, *Maturin Cordier et les origines de la pédagogie protestante* (Neuchâtel: Secrétariat de l'Université, 1926); Charles É. Delormeau, *Mathurin Cordier: Un maître de Calvin, l'un des créateurs de l'enseignement secondaire moderne* (Neuchâtel: Messeiller, 1966).

4. CO 13:525.

At the end of 1523 or the beginning of 1524, Calvin was transferred to the Collège de Montaigu, where Erasmus and Rabelais had also studied. Their memories of this institution were extremely negative. The spirit of the place reflected little or nothing of the *devotio moderna* that John Standonck had introduced forty years earlier. Standonck had lived by the ideals of the Brethren of the Common Life, but over time this spirit had hardened into an orthodox moralism in which austerity and a heavy hand determined the rules. Designed to groom students for theological study, the school provided candidates for the conservative religious orders and prepared prospective priests for their spiritual office. Beza reports that Calvin received instruction from a Spanish teacher, but much of what happened during this period has to be left to conjecture. Noël Bedier, who would later cause quite a stir in a number of heresy trials, was no longer at the college. It is also unlikely that Calvin was taught by the Scottish theologian and philosopher John Major.[5]

The curriculum was largely defined by exercises in the art of disputation; theology as such was not taught at the Collège de Montaigu. Everything was directed toward mastery of the scholastic method, with an emphasis on rhetoric and logic. The licentiate in arts opened the way to more specialized study, and Calvin thoroughly mastered the fine points of this preparatory academic grooming. The dominating strictness of the school must have made an impression on him. The nickname that he acquired there, "the accusative case," leads one to suppose that he was at home in this system; it fit with his conception of ecclesiastical piety.[6] But he also showed himself to be a young man busily exploring life and at the same time comfortable only in a familiar circle of friends. Among them were his friends from Noyon and his cousin Pierre Robert Olivétan (Olivetanus). In addition, we know of early contacts with Nicolas Cop, who in 1533 would deliver the famous address as rector of the university. Calvin had his quarters in a boarding house for wealthy students, an indication that the benefices his father had procured for him were sufficient.

A DEDICATED STUDENT

As a student, Calvin was known not only for his sternness; he attracted attention especially because of his intellectual abilities and overall dedication to his

---

5. Alexandre Ganoczy, *Le jeune Calvin: Genèse et evolution de sa vocation réformatrice* (Wiesbaden: Steiner, 1966), 39; Heiko Oberman, "*Initia Calvini*: The Matrix of Calvin's Reformation," in *Calvinus Sacrae Scripturae Professor: Calvin as Confessor of Holy Scripture*, ed. Wilhelm H. Neuser (Grand Rapids: Eerdmans, 1994), 117ff.

6. Theodore Beza, *Ioannis Calvini Vita*, CO 21:121. On Calvin as "vitiorum censor," see Ernst Pfisterer, *Calvins Wirken in Genf*, 2nd ed. (Neukirchen: Buchhandlung des Erziehungsvereins, 1957), 46–53.

studies. His memory was well trained. Not only later at the University of Orléans but already now at Montaigu he must have worked very methodically at memorizing facts and information. He possessed the gift of a sharp and lucid judgment, which enabled him to analyze situations and problems clearly. Perhaps his greatest gift was that of assimilation, his ability to absorb material. In his cognitive work, that automatically led to a natural selection of what seemed important to him.

Since his father had destined him for ecclesiastical office, and he had no disagreement with that, Calvin considered his literary studies at the Collège de Montaigu as preparation for theological study.[7] Before he actually embarked on this advanced study, however, his father changed his mind: Calvin would now study jurisprudence, as he reports in the preface to his Psalms commentary.[8] The emphasis there is on the obedience that Calvin showed to his father, whose stated motive was that the study of law would offer better financial prospects.[9] This change in field of study was no doubt also related to the fact that his father had come into conflict with the chapter of Noyon, which ultimately led to his excommunication. Out of respect for his father, therefore, Calvin earnestly devoted himself to the study of law, as he himself relates, and at the end of 1527 or the beginning of 1528 he headed to Orléans. But this change in direction might also have been inspired by the fact that Calvin himself was no longer attracted to theological study in the way it was being done at the university. Both Beza and Colladon link Calvin's motives to his cousin Olivétan, who would have introduced him to the *vera religio*. According to those two biographers, that is what led Calvin already then to turn from the superstitions of the church.[10]

Again at this point the chronology is not entirely clear. Calvin probably remained in Orléans until the spring of 1529. After the summer break, he moved on to Bourges to study law there as well. In Orléans, Pierre de l'Étoile was teaching in the traditional style, but in Bourges, Andreas Alciati had revived the spirit of the Renaissance in the study of ancient texts. However, not everyone appreciated the Latin that he spoke in his lectures; students expected him to explain the law in an elegant, literary manner. Calvin shared this criticism,

7. Nicolas Colladon, CO 21:54: "Quant à ses moeurs, il estoit sur tout fort consciencieux, ennemi des vices, et fort adonné au service de Dieu qu'on appelloit pour lors: tellement que son coeur tendoit entierement à la Theologie, et son pere pretendoit de l'y faire employer."
8. CO 31:21.
9. CO 31:21: "Theologiae me pater tenellum adhuc puerum destinaverat. Sed quum videret legum scientiam passim augere suos cultores opibus, spes illa repente eum impulit ad mutandum consilium. Ita factum est, ut revocatus a philosophiae studio, ad leges discendas traherer, quibus tametsi ut patris voluntati obsequerer fidelem operam impendere conatus sum, Deus tamen arcano providentiae suae fraeno cursum meum alio tandem reflexit."
10. Ganoczy, *Le jeune Calvin*, 43–44; cf. CO 21:29, 54, 121.

as can be seen from the preface he wrote for a work by a university friend, Nicolas Duchemin, entitled *Antapologia*. This is the first publication that we have from Calvin's hand (1531). There he defends Pierre de l'Étoile, whom Alciati had attacked rather rudely. Calvin appreciated the lectures of de l'Étoile more than those of Alciati, for de l'Étoile stuck more closely to the text of the law. However, Calvin's own hermeneutical method would differ from those of both of these teachers by its use of practical criteria in the interpretation of texts.[11]

Calvin was able to satisfy his thirst for knowledge without interruption. According to Beza's account, he worked very hard, sometimes studying until midnight. His self-discipline was such that he often skipped meals. He used the morning hours to recollect and review as fully as possible what he had been reading. In doing this work, he did not like to be disturbed. Through ongoing nighttime study, he acquired a basic store of knowledge and an especially sharp memory. Then again, this probably also seriously weakened his body, which "was plagued by many illnesses that finally led to his early death."[12] In Orléans he was regarded more as one of the teachers than as a student. He often taught classes and was offered the doctorate because he had rendered such great service to the university.[13]

Calvin took the study of law very seriously, and later he would be able to use his knowledge of this area in his reforming work in Geneva.[14] But he did not find any real satisfaction in this study. He had been motivated by obedience to his father, but his heart kept tugging him in the direction of the litterae humaniores, which were being rigorously studied in Orléans and Bourges. Michael Wolmar, a German humanist, assisted him there in the study of Greek, and in 1546 Calvin dedicated his commentary on 2 Corinthians to him. Earlier Wolmar had had to leave Paris because he belonged to the religious humanists who had been positively influenced by Luther's ideas. It cannot be inferred from Calvin's letters, however, that he was influenced by Wolmar in a religious sense. He was grateful for the instruction he received in Greek literature while he was studying law. This way he could combine studies of civil law and the classical authors. We can deduce from Calvin's dedicatory preface that he had only learned the basics of Greek from Wolmar when the death of his father on May 26, 1531, completely changed the course of his life.[15] Calvin now felt free to devote himself entirely to his humanistic training.

11. Michael L. Monheit, "Young Calvin: Textual Interpretation and Roman Law," *BHR* 59 (1997): 263–82.
12. CO 21:122.
13. Colladon, CO 21:54.
14. Patrick Le Gal, *Le droit canonique dans la pensée dialectique de Jean Calvin* (Fribourg: Éditions universitaires, 1984).
15. CO 12:365.

After a short stay in Orléans, he made his way to Paris, where he studied at the Collège Royal. This institution, which specialized in Latin, Greek, and Hebrew, had been founded by Budé, Cop, and others; it enjoyed the personal patronage of Francis I. Here Calvin moved in the circles of religious humanists who were inspired by the spirit of Lefèvre's biblical thought, though he did not loosen ties with his friends in Orléans. He remained in Paris for a good part of 1532 and until the end of October 1533. There he rubbed shoulders with friends and fellow students, and in the summer of 1533 he was appointed substitute attorney of the "nation picarde," a representative function for this group of students. Colladon reports that already during this time Calvin was serving as a highly regarded preacher in the area around Orléans and Bourges.[16]

"THE DIE IS CAST"

Calvin also used his time in Paris to publish his first major work, the commentary on Seneca's *De clementia* (April 4, 1532), which his friends had encouraged him to do. That he covered the costs himself says something about his financial position but also about the high hopes he had for this publication. "The die is cast," he wrote to François Daniel, a friend in Orléans.[17] The book was supposed to represent his entrance into the guild of scholarly humanists. He urged some of the professors in Paris to use it in their lectures, and he was prepared to send a hundred copies for distribution in Orléans. But the effort was all in vain. Calvin was hoping for a brilliant humanistic career, but the commentary, at any rate, did not start him on his way.

What we can learn from the commentary is something of Calvin's hermeneutic. We catch a sense of his respect for the text, his wish to do it justice. With the help of a surprisingly wide knowledge of the classics, he provides an exposition of the work through which Seneca had pressed for clemency from Nero. It is going too far, however, to suppose that in the antievangelical atmosphere in Paris, Calvin was pleading here for tolerance from Francis I. At this point, Calvin still stood outside the threatening religious conflict, as is apparent from the preface addressed to a friend from his youth, the abbot of Saint Eloy. What he provides in the commentary is a study that is purely literary in nature. If it gives some indication already of a religious tendency, it consists in Calvin's attempt to bridge the Christian faith and the ethics of the Stoics. One may look upon the work as a sign that with this publication, Calvin the scholar had established a

16. CO 21:55.
17. Herminjard, *Correspondance*, 2:417.

place in the humanistic circles that claimed so many representatives in Paris, Orléans, and Bourges.

All the same, it is quite clear that at this very time a radical change was occurring in Calvin. His concentration on the classical authors, from whom he had acquired an enormous store of knowledge, slowly but surely gave way to a great interest first in the reading and study of the Bible and then of the church fathers.[18] This shift in interest was part of a process that cannot be analyzed in all its particulars. Calvin later called it his conversion.

CHAPTER BIBLIOGRAPHY

Battles, Ford L. "Calvin's Humanistic Education." In *Interpreting John Calvin—Ford Lewis Battles*, edited by Robert Benedetto, 47–64. Grand Rapids: Baker, 1996.

Battles, Ford L., and André M. Hugo, eds. *Calvin's Commentary on Seneca's De Clementia*. Leiden: Brill, 1969.

Bohatec, Josef. *Budé und Calvin: Studien zur Gedankenwelt des französischen Frühhumanismus*. Graz: Böhlau, 1950.

Bourrilly, E. *Calvin et la Réforme en France*. Aix-en-Provence: Faculté libre de Théologie Protestante d'Aix-en-Provence, 1959.

Breen, Quirinus. *John Calvin: A Study in French Humanism*. 2nd ed. Hamden, CT: Archon Books, 1968.

Delormeau, Charles É. *Mathurin Cordier: Un maître de Calvin, l'un des créateurs de l'enseignement secondaire modern*. Neuchâtel: Messeiller, 1966.

Ganoczy, Alexandre. *Le jeune Calvin: Genèse et evolution de sa vocation réformatrice*. Wiesbaden: F. Steiner, 1966.

Herminjard, Aimé-Louis. *Correspondance des réformateurs dans les pays de langue français*. Geneva: Georg, 1866–97.

Le Gal, Patrick. *Le droit canonique dans la pensée dialectique de Jean Calvin*. Fribourg: Editions universitaires, 1984.

Lecoultre, Jean J. *Maturin Cordier et les origines de la pédagogie protestante*. Neuchâtel: Secrétariat de l'Université, 1926.

M'Crie, Thomas. *The Early Years of John Calvin: A Fragment 1509–1536*. Edinburgh: D. Douglas, 1880.

Monheit, Michael L. "Young Calvin: Textual Interpretation and Roman Law." *Bibliothèque d'Humanisme de Renaissance* 59, no. 2 (1997): 263–82.

Oberman, Heiko A. "Initia Calvini: The Matrix of Calvin's Reformation." In *Calvinus Sacrae Scripturae Professor*, edited by Wilhelm Neuser, 113–54. Grand Rapids: Eerdmans, 1994.

Pannier, Jacques. *Recherches sur la formation intellectuelle de Calvin*. Paris: Librairie Alcan, 1931.

18. Remko J. Mooi, *Het kerk- en dogmahistorisch element in de werken van Johannes Calvijn* (Wageningen: Veenman & Zonen, 1965), 365–66; Quirinus Breen, *John Calvin: A Study in French Humanism*, 2nd ed. (Hamden, CT: Archon, 1968), 93ff.; André M. Hugo, *Calvijn en Seneca: Een inleidende studie van Calvijns Commentaar op Seneca's "De Clementia," anno 1532* (Groningen: Wolters, 1957), 58–59; Ford L. Battles, "The Sources of Calvin's Seneca Commentary," in *Interpreting John Calvin—Ford Lewis Battles*, ed. Robert Benedetto (Grand Rapids: Baker, 1996), 65–89.

————. *Recherches sur l'évolution religieuse de Calvin jusqu'à sa conversion*. Strasbourg: Istra, 1924.

Pfisterer, Ernst. "Achtundfünfzig Hinrichtungen und sechsundsiebzig Ausweisungen in fünf Jahren." In *Calvins Wirken in Genf*, 2nd ed., 46–53. Neukirchen: Buchhandlung des Erziehungsvereins, 1957.

3

Calvin's Conversion

Calvin's testimony about his conversion is, in contrast to that of Luther, highly restrained. "I don't like to talk about myself," he once said.[1] We have available three texts that can be connected to the decisive change that took place in his life around this time. Best known is the biographical sketch with which he prefaced his commentary on the Psalms (1557). There he draws a parallel between David's call to lead the nation of Israel and his own past, in which he saw, as in a mirror, the beginning and continuation of his own *vocatio*.[2]

Calvin was granted the honorable office of preacher and minister of the gospel. Although his father had intended him for a career in theology when Calvin was still a child, his plan changed, and theology was replaced by the study of law:

> Thus it came to pass that I was withdrawn from the study of philosophy, and was put to the study of law. To this pursuit I endeavored faithfully to apply myself, in obedience to the will of my father; but God, by the secret guidance of his providence, at length gave a different direction to my course. And first, since I was too obstinately devoted to the superstitions of popery to be easily extricated from so profound an abyss of mire, God by a sudden conversion subdued and brought my mind to a teachable frame, which was more hardened in such matters than might have been expected from one at my early period of life. Having thus received some taste and knowledge of true godliness, I was immediately inflamed with so intense a desire to make progress therein, that although I did not altogether leave off other studies, I yet

1. "De me non libenter loquor" (CO 5:389).
2. CO 31:21ff. See Heiko Oberman's analysis in "*Initia Calvini*: The Matrix of Calvin's Reformation," in *Calvinus Sacrae Scripturae Professor: Calvin as Confessor of Holy Scripture*, ed. Wilhelm H. Neuser (Grand Rapids: Eerdmans, 1994), 114 n. 3.

pursued them with less ardor. I was quite surprised to find that before a year had elapsed, all who had any desire after purer doctrine were continually coming to me to learn, although I myself was as yet but a mere novice and tyro.

"SUDDEN CONVERSION" (*SUBITA CONVERSIO*)

Calvin was apparently following the wishes of his father out of obedience when God, by a secret bridle of his providence, reined him in. His conversion was guided by God himself. What is striking is the openness with which Calvin describes how "obstinately devoted" he was "to the superstitions of popery," so that he could not "be easily extricated from so profound an abyss of mire." Even considering his age, he was already "hardened in such matters." Only by a "sudden conversion" was he "subdued and brought . . . to a teachable frame." Calvin indicates by the term "sudden" (*subita*) that this was not only a decisive change but also an unexpected, gracious conversion that could really only be explained as the gracious intervention of God himself.[3] Thereby he became a disciple who, "having thus received some taste and knowledge of true godliness," now became receptive to the "purer doctrine." Within a year all who desired such doctrine were coming to him to learn. A radical change had occurred.

Apparently we should think of the *subita conversio* as a theological concept that Calvin employed in 1557, when his position in Geneva was secure, to express the conviction of his calling. It is not, therefore, intended first of all as a chronological term. The *conversio* led to a *vocatio* that he could not shirk. He was subdued into conversion by virtue of the fact that his search for true godliness found satisfaction in the *purior doctrina*. Reined in by divine providence, he finally gave in.

The question of what had held him back until this point is answered by Calvin himself in his letter to Sadoleto: reverence for the church (*ecclesiae reverentia*).[4] We may assume that Calvin is speaking very personally here about the resistance that he showed to the purified doctrine, to which he hardly listened. When he opened his ears and allowed himself to be taught, however, he realized that this fear of insufficient reverence for the church had no basis.[5]

---

3. *Institutes* 1.8.11 (CO 2:67): "Paulus vero non tantum ex professo hoste, sed etiam saevo et sanguinario, conversus in novum hominem, subita et insperata mutatione ostendit coelesti imperio se compulsum doctrinam quam oppugnaverat asserere."
4. CO 5:412.
5. Ibid. "Verum ubi aliquando aures aperui, meque doceri passus sum, supervacuum fuisse timorem illum intellexi, ne quid ecclesiae maiestati decederet."

What had earlier seemed to him as an affront to dignity, now looked like superstition. Reverence for the church must be accompanied by reverence for Scripture.[6] For Calvin, this turn toward Scripture was connected with the fact that he found true peace of conscience nowhere else than in biblical preaching. He was not one for writing his "confessions," like Augustine. He also did not speak with the same openness about his experience of faith that Luther usually did. In the letter to Sadoleto, however, he lets us see something of his inner struggle: "For whenever I descended into myself, or raised my heart to You, extreme terror seized me—terror that no expiations or satisfactions could cure." To this affliction of conscience, the gospel, which had come to him in an entirely new form as *doctrina*, finally brought rest when he allowed himself to be taught. In its content this passage from the letter to Sadoleto agrees with the autobiographical note in the introduction to the commentary on the Psalms. Perhaps in both documents, Calvin is describing the motives that led him to choose the evangelical movement, even when by doing so a break with Rome had become unavoidable.

The *subita conversio*, then, provides a snapshot of what was in fact a longer development toward a definitive decision that had begun earlier. In yet another place, Calvin speaks of a time in which he had tried just a little taste of the sound doctrine that began to free him from the darkness of the papacy. It was at the beginning of the Lord's Supper controversy, even before the Marburg Colloquy.[7] This detail agrees with what Beza reports in his biography of Calvin, where we read that in Orléans, Calvin again encountered his cousin Pierre Robert Olivétan (Olivetanus), who was also born in Noyon. He is most likely the one who brought Calvin into contact with the Reformation.[8] According to this same information, at the time of his studies in Orléans and Bourges, Calvin was regularly preaching in the area. This was all still taking place, however, within the context of the religious humanism of the circle around Lefèvre, which could also be found at this time in Orléans. Beza relates that it was after Calvin's stay in Paris that he decided to devote himself entirely to God.[9] We can assume that this definitive decision coincided with the *subita conversio* mentioned in the Psalms commentary.

---

6. Cf. *Institutes* 1.8.11 (CO 2:67).

7. CO 9:51: "Quum enim a tenebris papatus emergere incipiens, tenui sanae doctrinae gustu concepto. . . ."

8. CO 21:29–30, 54ff., 121–22: Calvin would also have abandoned the study of theology because Olivetanus placed him on the path of true religion, "ayant desia par le moyen d'un sien parent et ami, nommé Pierre Robert, autrement Olivetanus, . . . gousté quelque chose de la pure religion, commençoit à se distraire des superstitions Papales."

9. CO 21:56: "Calvin donc de sa part prenant dés lors resolution de se dedier du tout à Dieu, travailloit avec grand fruit."

THE EVENTS IN PARIS

The question now is whether we can date this event and whether we can more precisely determine its character. So far as the former is concerned, the only light shed on the question is from letters that Calvin wrote to his friends. On June 27, 1531, Calvin and Nicolas Cop visited a sister of François Daniel in Paris. At François' request, Calvin spoke with her about her decision to enter a convent. He did not wish to dissuade her from her intentions, but he urged her to rely not on her own strength but on the power of God and not to act rashly.[10] Apparently, Calvin's thinking went no further than was common at this time in the Lefèvre circle. The tone of his letters does not essentially change before October 1533.

In August of the same year he was in Noyon, where, as a chaplain, he led discussions with other members of the chapter about a prayer campaign against the plague, which had broken out there. It can be assumed that he remained there during the holiday break. At the end of October, he wrote to Daniel and his other friends in Orléans about the events in Paris, where students had put on a play highly critical of the evangelical ideas of Marguerite of Navarre. Nicolas Cop, the new rector, took action against the students and thereby found himself at odds with the *factiosi theologi* of the Sorbonne. Calvin was very concerned about what had happened and provided a detailed account of what he regarded as a conspiracy against the queen of Navarre, "a woman endowed with holy manners and the pure religion."[11]

Calvin's next letter to Daniel was composed in mid-March 1534 in Angoulème, where he had fled and where, in spite of the way things looked, he considered himself safe under the providence of the Lord. There he wrote:

> I have learned that we cannot see into the distant future. Whenever I promised myself peace, something happened that I least expected. On the other hand, whenever I thought I had arrived at an unpleasant place, a nest of peace awaited me beyond all expectation. It is all the hand of the Lord. If we commit ourselves to him, he will watch over us.[12]

The event that Calvin was alluding to in this letter took place sometime between October 1533 and the next spring: his escape from Paris following the address on All Saints' Day, November 1, 1533, by Nicolas Cop, the rector of the university. The address had an unmistakable evangelical character, and

---

10. Herminjard, *Correspondance*, 2:347.
11. Ibid., 3:106ff.
12. Ibid., 3:156ff.

Calvin was at least jointly responsible for it.[13] In the address we encounter elements that can be traced to Erasmus and Luther. The introduction is an encomium to the gospel, which is characterized as *philosophia christiana*. The text itself deals with the meaning of the beatitudes (Matthew 5:3–8), and the perspective there on law and gospel is reminiscent of Luther. One can recognize the influence of both Erasmus's preface to the New Testament and a sermon by Luther from his *Kirchenpostille*, which was used for the address in a Latin translation by Bucer.[14] The situation at the university was tense after the imbroglio surrounding the student play in October. In these circumstances, Cop's appeal to fight with the Word of truth rather than to threaten with persecution and the sword was inflammatory. Charges were brought against him, but he managed to escape to Basel.

Calvin, too, found it necessary to leave Paris, and that began a period of travel for him. It is difficult to track all his movements during this time, but one thing that stands out is that on May 4, 1534, he renounced his benefices in Noyon. This step can only be explained as the result of his decision not to serve the church as an ordained priest under any circumstances. This would have been necessary otherwise, since canon law required a decision upon reaching the age of twenty-five. One need not necessarily regard this step yet as Calvin's break with Rome, although inwardly that had already happened at the end of 1533 or the beginning of 1534. The gospel could also work inside the church— but in a wholly different manner than through the hierarchy. Nevertheless, it is clear that, in effect, the matter had been settled. The die had been cast. However, it landed quite differently than when he had introduced the world to his commentary on Seneca's *De clementia*. Calvin had experienced this course of events as a *subita conversio*, an unexpected turnabout in his life. He adjusted to the yoke under which God had put him and sought instruction from the Scriptures, which from that point onward he also began to explain to others.

VIA MEDIA

Calvin found respite in Angoulème at the home of a friend whom he had probably come to know in Paris, the learned canon from Claix, Louis du Tillet. There

13. Jean Rott, "Documents strasbourgeois concernant Calvin: Un manuscrit autographe; La harangue du recteur Nicolas Cop," in *Regards contemporains sur Jean Calvin: Actes du Colloque Calvin, Strasbourg 1964* (Paris: Presses universitaires de France, 1965), 28–49; also in *Investigationes historicae: Gesammelte Aufsätze zur Kirchen- und Sozialgeschichte*, ed. Marijn De Kroon and Marc Lienhard (Strasbourg: Oberlin, 1986), 2:266–87.

14. The text of the address (*Concio academica*) can be found in CO 10:30ff. (OS 1:4ff.) and Eberhard Busch et al., eds., *Calvin-Studienausgabe* (Neukirchen-Vluyn: Neukirchener Verlag, 1994–), 1.1:1–25.

Calvin had access to an outstanding library, and he spent his time in studying, thus laying the groundwork for the writing of the book that would make him famous, the *Institutes*. During this time, he also made a trip to Nerac to visit Lefèvre, who was under the patronage of Marguerite of Navarre. According to Florimond de Raemond, Calvin was preaching in Poitiers in 1534, and there he gathered the first Reformed congregation of France around a new celebration of the Lord's Supper. That same year Calvin made an appointment to meet Michael Servetus in Paris, but Servetus never showed up.

The relative peace that Calvin enjoyed during this time enabled him to compose a work showing that his decision for the Reformation had nothing to do with Anabaptist or revolutionary tendencies. His encounter with a few sectarians in Paris or Orléans led him to challenge the doctrine of soul sleep in *Psychopannychia*.[15] He wrote the foreword in 1534, but on the advice of Capito in Strasbourg left it unpublished for the time being. It was finally published in Strasbourg in 1542. In this first reformational treatise by Calvin, his insight into Scripture is evident. At the same time it represents a choice that would characterize his work from then on: his way was a via media between Rome and Anabaptism. This became for him the royal road, that is, the way of the kingdom of God (*regnum Dei*), which already in this first treatise he traces in broad salvation-historical strokes.

Calvin's choice was thus firmly established in 1534. It was not a choice against the church; on the contrary, the church had forced him to launch a reformation of itself according to the Word, the meaning of which was opening up to him more and more. Once he was on this path, it was impossible to turn back. In fact, this *conversio* was not only a break with Rome; it also implied a renunciation of religious humanism. In his conversion, Calvin had become aware of the overpowering force of God's providence. God himself had taken hold of the reins that from now on would direct his life. He actually experienced his conversion. His conscience, gripped by sin, found freedom in the grace of forgiveness.

When Calvin in his commentary on the Psalms relates the idea of *conversio* directly to his *vocatio* confirmed in Geneva in 1557 (like that of David in his day), what he is doing is looking back. It is possible that he is giving *conversio* a more comprehensive meaning here than in 1533–34. But present from the very beginning was this sense that we do not exist for ourselves. God had constrained him in his providence, but that providence gradually deepened into election, the foundation of which lies in the grace of forgiveness. That marked the essence of Calvin's conversion: it is nothing other than obedience in faith and trust in God himself, to whose voice he had learned to listen.

---

15. CO 5:162–232; Jung-Uck Hwang, *Der junge Calvin und seine Psychopannychia* (Frankfurt: Lang, 1991).

CHAPTER BIBLIOGRAPHY

Cadier, Jean. "Conversion de Calvin." *Bulletin de la Société de l'Histoire du Protestantisme Français* 116, no. 2 (1970): 142–51.

Calvin, John. "Concio academica." In *Calvin-Studienausgabe.* Edited by Eberhard Busch et al., 1.1:1–25. Neukirchen-Vluyn: Neukirchener Verlag, 1994.

Ganoczy, Alexandre. *Le jeune Calvin: Genèse et évolution de sa vocation réformatrice.* Wiesbaden: F. Steiner, 1966.

Herminjard, Aimé-Louis. *Correspondance des réformateurs dans les pays de langue français.* Geneva: Georg, 1866–97.

Hwang, Jung-Uck. *Der junge Calvin und seine Psychopannychia.* Frankfurt: Lang, 1991.

Lang, August. *Die Bekehrung Johannes Calvins.* Leipzig: A. Deichert, 1897.

Müller, Karl. "Calvins Bekehrung." In *Nachrichten der Königliche Gesellschaft der Wissenschaften zu Göttingen [NGWG], Philologisch-Historische Klasse,* 188–257, 463–64. Göttingen: Dieterich'schen Verlagsbuch, 1905.

Nijenhuis, Willem. "Calvijns 'subita conversion': Notities bij een hypothese." *Nederlands theologisch tijdschrift* 26, nos. 3 & 4 (1972): 248–69.

Oberman, Heiko A. "Initia Calvini: The Matrix of Calvin's Reformation." In *Calvinus Sacrae Scripturae Professor,* edited by Wilhelm H. Neuser, 113–54. Grand Rapids: Eerdmans, 1994.

Rott, Jean. "Documents strasbourgeois concernant Calvin: Un manuscrit autographe; La harangue du recteur Nicolas Cop." In *Regards contemporains sur Jean Calvin: Actes du Colloque Calvin, Strasbourg 1964,* 28–49. Paris: Presses universitaires de France, 1965.

———. "Documents strasbourgeois concernant Calvin: Un manuscrit autographe; La harangue du recteur Nicolas Cop." In *Investigationes historicae: Gesammelte Aufsätze zur Kirchen- und Sozialgeschichte.* Edited by Marijn De Kroon and Marc Lienhard, 2:226–87. Strasbourg: Oberlin, 1986.

Sprenger, Paul. *Das Rätsel um die Bekehrung Calvins.* Neukirchen: Kreis Moers, 1960.

Tinsley, Barbara S. *History and Polemics in the French Reformation: Florimond de Raemond, Defender of the Church.* Selinsgrove: Susquehanna University Press, 1992.

Wernle, Paul. "Noch einmal die Bekehrung Calvins." *Zeitschrift für Kirchengeschicte* 27 (1906): 84–99.

———. "Zu Calvins Bekehrung." *Zeitschrift für Kirchengeschicte* 31 (1910): 556–83.

4

The *Institutes of the Christian Religion*

The prospects for a breakthrough of the evangelical movement in Paris had seemed favorable at the time that Cop delivered his address. The reactions to his speech, however, were vehement. Toward the end of November 1533 numerous arrests were made. The theological faculty warned the king about the growing influence of the Lutherans, and he took measures to purge the capital of heresy. However, his foreign policy, which had forced him into partnership with the German Protestant princes, moderated the situation somewhat. Beda, who had instigated the suppression of the evangelical movement, was himself banished, and the movement appeared to have gained some breathing space.

A turning point came, however, when a radical French preacher from Neuchâtel, Antoine Marcourt, did something that was supposed to bring about a breakthrough but instead caused a traumatic stir in Parisian public opinion. In a number of public places, even outside of Paris, placards were put up condemning the mass as an intolerable abuse.[1] One was even found on the door of the king's bedchamber in Amboise, where he was staying. Within twenty-four hours, a procession was organized in Paris, and one on an even larger scale took place a couple of months later (January 21, 1535).

If Cop's address was considered an academic matter, the "affair of the placards" (October 18, 1534) was seen as a challenge to the personal authority of Francis I and an attack on the religion of France as a nation. It was much more than an expression of an evangelical disposition, which was still tolerable. This was an attack upon the king's leadership in the defense of the faith. He interpreted it as a form of revolutionary rebellion, comparable to the Anabaptist

---

1. "Articles veritables sur les horribles, grandz & importables abuz de la messe papalle," in Herminjard, *Correspondance*, 3:224–29.

revolt in Münster. That is the way he explained his counteraction to the German princes.[2] The selective tolerance that Francis had practiced up to this point had come to an end.[3]

The ensuing persecution claimed a large number of victims, among them Calvin's friend Étienne de la Forge, with whom he had boarded in Paris.[4] Calvin decided to leave France and go into voluntary exile, "because from there were exiled the truth of the gospel, pure religion, and the unadulterated worship of God."[5] Early in January 1535 he arrived with Louis du Tillet in Basel, where he took up residence in the suburb of St. Alban under the pseudonym Martianus Lucianus.[6]

BASEL

Basel had been *Basilea reformata* ever since April 1, 1529, but on January 21, 1534, the city clearly declared itself on the side of evangelical doctrine with the First Basel Confession. Erasmus, along with the cathedral chapter and a large number of students, had distanced himself from the movement and retreated to the neighboring city of Freiburg (Germany). Oecolampadius, who with Zwingli led the Swiss reformation, pleaded not only for an open proclamation of the gospel but also for an ecclesiastical structure in which the independent jurisdiction of the church with its own discipline would be recognized.[7] The congregation was viewed as a community centered in the Lord's Supper, in which the citizens were expected to participate. The guilds had played a significant role in carrying out the reformation, and they were in charge of monitoring citizen attendance at the Lord's Supper. Calvin would later have in view

2. Ibid., 3:249–54.

3. Robert J. Knecht, *Renaissance Warrior and Patron: The Reign of Francis I* (Cambridge: Cambridge University Press, 1994), 313–21.

4. Calvin, *Contre la secte des libertins*, in CO 7:160: "Estienne de la Forge, duquel la memoire doit estre beniste entre les fideles comme d'un sainct Martyr de Iésus Christ."

5. From Calvin's dedication of his Jeremiah commentary to Frederick III of the Palatinate, in CO 20:78.

6. Petrus Ramus, *Basilea: Eine Rede an die Stadt Basel aus dem Jahre 1570*, ed. Hans Fleig (Basel: Basilisk-Verlag, 1944), 53: "Sed inter academiae Basiliensis hospites Joannes Calvinus praecipue commemorandus est: lumen Galliae, lumen Christianae per orbem terrarum ecclesiae, lumen in hoc ipso (in quo haec meditor commentorque) hospitio praecipue perspectum." Calvin lived there at the home of Catharina Klein. "Hic illustres illae Christianae Institutionis, caelestesque vigiliae, sunt exaratae et elaboratae."

7. Ernst Staehelin, *Das theologische Lebenswerk Johannes Oekolampads* (1939; repr., New York: Johnson, 1971), 506ff. The "Oratio de reducenda excommunicatione" before the magistrate on June 8, 1530, can be found in Staehelin, *Briefe und Akten zum Leben Oekolampads* (1934; repr., New York: Johnson, 1971), 2:448–61.

a similar massive introduction of the Reformation in Geneva in his attempt to create a confessional commonwealth there.

In Basel, Calvin again encountered Nicolas Cop, whose presence there might have been what drew him to the city. Since Basel was not far from France, Calvin could follow events there and contribute from nearby in his own way to the spread of the Reformation. There were also a number of good book printers in Basel with whom he would establish a relationship: among them was Platter, who published his *Institutes*. Here, too, Calvin again experienced what had so captivated him in Paris, an interest in the three languages (Hebrew, Greek, Latin). Beza recounts that in Basel, Calvin attended lectures by the Hebrew professor Sebastian Münster (1480–1553). Simon Grynaeus (1493–1541), who was deeply involved in the reformation in Basel and with Oswald Myconius (1488–1552) led the church there after the death of Oecolampadius in 1531, was also a Greek scholar almost without peer. He made a deep impression on Calvin, as evidenced by the dedication that Calvin wrote on October 18, 1539, in his first commentary on a book of the Bible, the Letter to the Romans. Both Calvin and Grynaeus were convinced that a *perspicua brevitas* was essential to the exegesis of Scripture.[8]

Among the friends that Calvin met or made in Basel was also Bonifacius Amerbach (1495–1562), who by 1535 had established a reputation as a competent lawyer. His extensive correspondence provides insights not only into the reformation in Basel but also into the spread of the movement across Switzerland and France. The reformation of the university in Basel, which was legally secured in 1532, came about primarily under his leadership.[9]

It is not likely that Calvin encountered Erasmus, who returned to Basel in 1535, old and sick, and died a year later. We do know, however, that he had contacts with others who played a role in the reformation in Switzerland: Pierre Toussain (1499–1573), who would be involved in the reformation of Montbéliard; Guillaume Farel (1489–1565), who was from the reform circle in Meaux and would recruit Calvin for Geneva; Pierre Viret (1511–1571), a future coworker in French Switzerland; Joachim Vadian (1484–1551), reformer of St. Gall; and Heinrich Bullinger (1504–1575), Zwingli's successor (but more than just his disciple), with whom Calvin would bring about the unity of the Swiss reformation. In Basel, Calvin also got to know Leo Jud (1482–1542), who worked closely with Bullinger, and he met Martin Bucer (1491–1551) and Wolfgang Capito (1478–1541), both influential leaders of the church in Strasbourg.

8. Richard C. Gamble, "*Brevitas et Facilitas*: Toward an Understanding of Calvin's Hermeneutic," in *Calvin and Hermeneutics*, vol. 6 of *Articles on Calvin and Calvinism*, ed. Richard C. Gamble (New York: Garland, 1992), 33–49.

9. Edgar Bonjour, *Die Universität Basel von den Anfängen bis zur Gegenwart, 1460–1960* (Basel: Helbing & Lichtenhahn, 1971), 117ff.

With many of these men, Calvin would have future contacts that would be of critical importance for the history of the Reformation.

While in Basel, Calvin worked on two important writings: the *Praefatio* to the French translation of the Bible by Olivetanus, and an introduction to the New Testament part of that translation (1535). Various Bible translations were coming on the market in the 1530s, including a 1534 revised edition of the New Testament translation by Lefèvre d'Étaples, of which there would be twenty-three editions in all. This edition was published despite opposition from the Parlement of Paris. Olivetanus provided a translation that was more from the original languages, and Calvin worked on a revision of this translation and added a foreword addressing emperors, kings, princes, and all those subject to the rule of Christ. There he responds to the argument that the Bible is not suitable for the illiterate masses: God turned shepherds into prophets and fishermen into apostles; there are pupils in his school from every rank and station. That does not mean, however, that the calling of teaching and learning from the church should fall into disuse. One ought to regard the prophets, teachers, and interpreters sent by God himself as signs of the splendid goodness of God, through whom people can hear God himself speaking "and [can] learn from him as he teaches."[10] The *doctrina* of the Word will unfailingly bring about the learning of the truth. The Word itself will do the actual work.

In the introduction to the New Testament, which was intended for all "lovers of Jesus Christ and his gospel," Calvin provides a salvation-historical theology in brief, with Christ at the center. This does not function as a theological principle; it is pastoral in nature:

> All without distinction are called to the inheritance of Christ. . . . No one is excluded here who receive Christ only as he is offered by the Father as salvation for all and who embrace him as he is offered. . . . Remove the gospel, and all human righteousness, when judged in the tribunal of God, will come to nothing. But conversely, through the knowledge of the gospel we become children of God, brothers of Christ, fellow saints. This must be searched for in Scripture, that in truth we know Christ and the benefits that the Father offers us in him.[11]

FIRST EDITION OF THE *INSTITUTES* (1536)

In Basel, Calvin also put the finishing touches on the first edition of the book that would make him famous. We can assume that he had collected material for the book while staying in du Tillet's parsonage in France. By studying there

10. CO 9:788.
11. CO 9:808.

on his own, he had expanded his theological knowledge enormously in a short span of time. In du Tillet's library he was able to consult the works that he would need for the *Institutes*, but he also had a photographic memory, which enabled him to quote sources almost perfectly. In his defense against Pighius, he wrote that he kept his sources in his head.[12]

Calvin introduced the *Institutes* with an address to the French king dated August 23, 1535. Events in France had compelled him to write. Francis had accused the evangelicals of treason and revolutionary disturbances, and he had put them in the same camp as the Münster Anabaptists, who had been defeated by the German princes. Calvin rejected this argument as slander. His apology for the reformation in France is a masterpiece of classical rhetoric, modeled on Cicero. The language of the second-century apologists seems to have come back to life. Personal friends of Calvin had been victims of the cruel persecution, and Calvin defended them with all the gifts and powers at his disposal: "To the most mighty and illustrious monarch Francis, most Christian king of France, his esteemed prince John Calvin sends peace and greeting in Christ."

Calvin knew the arguments against the doctrine of the gospel: it was new, only recently on the scene, not supported by the testimony of the ancients; a dubious doctrine, not authenticated by signs and wonders, in conflict with the unanimous testimony of the fathers, and schismatic in nature. It was not only unfruitful; it also stirred up all kinds of sects and fomented rebellion. Calvin refuted these accusations, one after the other, with clear and cogent arguments, calling upon the Lord, who would bear witness to the truth.

This apology appeared in all subsequent editions of the *Institutes*. It is one of the strongest defenses that the Protestant Reformation produced. Every sentence and word appeals to the common sense that the king must surely possess, but Calvin wants even more to reach the king's heart. There must be room for the gospel not only in the heart of Francis I but also in the entire territory that he rules and that is so dear to Calvin's own heart.[13]

When the *Institutes* first appeared, it was seen as a catechism—in a treatise rather than a question-and-answer form. A preacher from Basel reported that in March 1536 "a catechism had been published by a certain Frenchman for the king of France."[14] Farel thought so highly of the work that he did not see the need for a new edition of his own *Sommaire et breifve declaration* (1529). The power of the work lay in the direct manner in which Calvin tried

---

12. CO 6:336, where Calvin indicates that when he was writing the *Institutes*, he did not have a single book in front of him except for a work by Augustine, "quod mihi commodatum datum erat." Indeed, he had to do it with citations "quod memoria tenebam."

13. Ford L. Battles, "The First Edition of the *Institutes of the Christian Religion* (1536)," in *Interpreting John Calvin—Ford Lewis Battles*, ed. Robert Benedetto (Grand Rapids: Baker, 1996), 100ff.

14. Herminjard, *Correspondance*, 4:23, n. 9.

to promote piety. He had no goal other than to identify those first principles by which those who were affected by a certain zeal for religion would be molded into a true piety. He especially had in mind here his fellow country-men. Many of them hungered and thirsted after Christ, but only a few had even a mediocre knowledge of him. That is why Calvin was designing his book as a simple manual of instruction.

In the structure of the work, Calvin follows Luther's catechism, treating in order the law, faith, and prayer. A fourth chapter discusses the significance of baptism and the Lord's Supper, and a fifth examines and rejects the five so-called sacraments. The last chapter is devoted to the discussion of Christian freedom, ecclesiastical power, and civil government. It is obvious that Calvin composed the final two chapters with special care. The tone here is also dif-ferent than in the preceding discussions, more like that of the apologist. Here he challenges the deformed church and tyrannical state as he had come to know them firsthand in France. The first part of his work is dominated by a more pastoral tone that resounds in all the editions of the *Institutes* to follow.

REPRODUCTION AND TRANSFORMATION

Calvin was a second-generation reformer, which enabled him to assimilate the writings of Luther, Zwingli, Bucer, Oecolampadius, and many others into his own thinking and transform these ideas into something new. It has been said that Calvin was not original, and in a certain sense that is true. In presenta-tion, form, and method of instruction, however, he was unique. Without ben-efit of a theological training in the strict sense, he had the ability to assimilate a classical tradition and reproduce it in a harmonious and fundamentally uni-fied fashion. His basic approach was common property of the Reformation: "Nearly the whole of sacred doctrine consists of these two parts: knowledge of God and of ourselves," a passage which would later be expanded.[15] One comes across this same idea in Luther, Zwingli, and Bucer, but in Calvin it functions not as a starting point but as an existential reality integrated into every part of doctrine. This living correlation between God and humanity gave the book a place among the works of the deepest thinkers, while at the same time determining its character as a devotional piece focused on the promotion of true spirituality: piety as "reverence joined with love of God, which the

15. CO 1:27 (OS 1:37): "Summa fere sacrae doctrinae duabus his partibus constat: Cognitione Dei ac nostri." From the 1539 edition onward, the sentence read: "Tota fere sapientiae nostrae summa, quae vera demum ac solida sapientia censeri debeat, duabus partibus constat, Dei cogni-tione et nostri."

by us?"[27] Calvin bypassed the question in dispute by raising it to a higher level, a quality that would also later enable him to reconcile different traditions with each other.

Calvin's treatment of the sacraments led him to several practical suggestions for the administration of baptism and the Eucharist, including a plea for a weekly administration of the Lord's Supper.[28] The eucharistic liturgy that he proposed begins with prayer and a sermon, followed by the minister repeating the words of institution, reciting the promises to be sealed, and admonishing those who ought to be excluded, according to God's command, not to partake. Before the administration itself, there is a special prayer, after which the bread is broken and the cup passed during a reading of Scripture or singing of a psalm. Next the congregation is exhorted to profess their faith sincerely in an upright Christian life. The ceremony then concludes with a prayer of thanksgiving, a psalm, and a blessing.

Calvin here was guided by material that he had gleaned from the early church. He designed his liturgical plan in the study and perhaps used it himself in the meetings he led when he was still roving about in France. In later editions of the *Institutes*, he hardly changed these sections at all. His liturgical views underwent no fundamental changes, although Geneva did not practice all that he had prescribed. That shows us that for Calvin liturgy as such was not so crucial. What really mattered for him was the spiritual service of God, worship in spirit and in truth.

When Platter brought the *Institutes* on the market in 1536, Calvin (under the pseudonym Charles d'Esperville) had already left with du Tillet for Ferrara. There he hoped to actively devote himself to the French reformation. Renata (1510–1575), the Duchess of Ferrara and daughter of Louis XII, was known for her sympathy for the evangelical movement. Raised in the court of Francis I and a disciple of Lefèvre d'Étaples, she maintained ties with Marguerite d'Angoulême in Nérac. Calvin saw a possibility here for the French aristocracy to help the French churches. He stayed in Ferrara only a short time, but he developed a lasting friendship with the duchess, which was reflected later in a number of letters that he wrote her.[29] In her court he also encountered Clémont Marot (1496–1544), who would seek accommodation in Geneva in 1542.

---

27. "Si haec vis sacramenti pro dignitate excussa expensaque esset, satis superque habebat, unde nobis satis fieret, nec excitatae essent horribiles istae dissensiones, quibus tum olim, tum nostra etiamnun memoria, ecclesia misere vexata est"; CO 1:120 (OS 1:139).

28. CO 1:139f. (OS 1:161).

29. Florence W. Barton, *Calvin and the Duchess* (Louisville, KY: Westminster John Knox Press, 1989).

LETTERS FROM FERRARA

According to Colladon, while Calvin was in Ferrara, he wrote two letters that were published by Platter in Basel in 1537.[30] On this occasion he calls himself "Professor of Holy Scripture in Geneva."

The first letter was intended for his earlier friend, Nicolas du Chemin, who had asked his advice about attending services in which the mass was celebrated. Calvin delved into a problem that would frequently engage him later on. His view, shared by Bucer, Peter Martyr, and Melanchthon, was that one should flee the defilements of Babylon as quickly as possible. With an appeal to the word of Christ, Calvin called upon his friend not to be ashamed to confess Christ: "We sin when we make God's command a matter of fearful debate. Nothing good can be expected from those who make fear and anxiety their advisers. From such feelings only malformed children are born." Calvin writes that this view is not only the result of meditation in the shade of peace and quiet; it is also the view of the martyrs of God, who stood by it in the midst of cross, fire, and oppression.[31]

Calvin addressed the second letter to Gerard Roussel, who, having come out of the circle of Bishop Briçonnet, had devoted himself to preaching the gospel. Calvin had probably been influenced by him in Paris. Roussel was appointed by Marguerite as bishop of Oloron and had accepted the appointment, precisely the opposite of what Calvin himself had done. This led to a rift between them, as can be seen already in the salutation of the letter: "John Calvin to an *old* friend, currently a prelate." The tone is not so friendly. Calvin gives his view of office, according to which it is not the status of the "order" and the worthiness of the office-bearer that should be central but the loftiness of the work.

There is no reason to doubt that Roussel, too, regarded preaching the gospel as the chief task of the bishop. Therefore, he probably let the letter containing Calvin's appeal go unanswered. He remained a bishop and led a pious life, confessing a doctrine that became more and more evangelical. For that, however, he chose a place inside the church that Calvin had left. Calvin, of course, never became a bishop, but in this letter he offers a felicitous description of the office that he held his entire life: pastoral episcopate by virtue of instruction from the Scriptures.[32]

---

30. CO 21:60; CO 5:239–312 (OS 1:284–362): *Epistolae duae de rebus hoc saeculo cognitu apprime necessariis. Prior, De fugiendis impiorum illicitis sacris, et puritate Christianae religionis observanda; Altera, De Christiani hominis officio in sacerdotiis Papalis ecclesiae vel administrandis, vel abiicendis.*

31. CO 5:278 (OS 1:228).

32. Roussel died in 1555 as the result of an attack intended to make it impossible for him to preach. He should not be regarded as a Nicodemite.

From Ferrara, Calvin and du Tillet returned to Basel, and du Tillet traveled on to Geneva. Calvin proceeded to Paris to put some affairs in order and then left France, accompanied by his brother and sister, to settle in either Basel or Strasbourg. His desire was to help spread the evangelical movement in France through study and publication. Because of troop movements connected with the conflict between Charles V and Francis I, the way through Lotharingia (Lorraine) was blocked. They instead traveled through the territory of the duke of Savoy via Geneva, where they arrived on an evening in early July 1536. Through du Tillet, word of Calvin's presence and identity got out among du Tillet's circle of friends, and Farel immediately seized the opportunity to recruit Calvin for the work of the reformation in Geneva. Farel broke down Calvin's resistance with a dreadful curse—according to Calvin, it was "as if God had from heaven laid his mighty hand upon me."[33] Calvin heard the will of God resounding in Farel's voice. Just as in his *subita conversio*, God himself "by the hidden reins of his providence" had steered Calvin's course in a different direction. Seized by the fear of God, therefore, he abandoned his travel plans. He realized that God had subdued him a second time. But in the city of Geneva, where the papacy had been overthrown through the work of Farel and Viret just a short time before, the two factions were bitterly opposed to each other.[34]

CHAPTER BIBLIOGRAPHY

Barton, Florence W. *Calvin and the Duchess.* Louisville, KY: Westminster John Knox Press, 1989.

Battles, Ford Lewis. *Analysis of the Institutes of the Christian Religion of John Calvin.* Grand Rapids: Baker, 1980. Reprint, Phillipsburg: P. & R. Publishing, 2001.

———. "The First Edition of the *Institutes of the Christian Religion* (1536)." In *Interpreting John Calvin—Ford Lewis Battles,* edited by Robert Benedetto, 91–116. Grand Rapids: Baker, 1996.

———. *Interpreting John Calvin—Ford Lewis Battles.* Edited by Robert Benedetto. Grand Rapids: Baker, 1996.

Benoît, Jean-Daniel. "The History and Development of the *Institutio*: How Calvin Worked." In *John Calvin,* edited by G. E. Duffield, 102–17. Grand Rapids: Eerdmans, 1968.

Bonjour, Edgar. *Die Universität Basel von den Anfängen bis zur Gegenwart, 1460–1960.* Basel: Helbing & Lichtenhahn, 1971.

---

33. CO 31:23; 31:25: "Et quum privatis et occultis studiis me intelligeret esse deditum, ubi se vidit rogando nihil proficere, usque ad exsercrationem descendit, ut Deus otio meo malediceret, si me a ferendis subsidiis in tanta necessitate subducerem. Quo terrore perculsus susceptum iter omisi, ut mihi et verecundiae et timiditatis meae conscius obeundo certo muneri fidem meam non obstringeram."

34. CO 31:25: "Paulo ante huius optimi viri et Petri Vireti opera profligatus erat papatus: sed res adhuc incompositae et urbs in pravas et noxias factiones divisa."

Calvin, John. *Institutes of the Christian Religion, 1536 Edition.* Translated by Ford Lewis Battles. Grand Rapids: Erdmans, 1986.

Gamble, Richard C. *"Brevitas et Facilitas*: Toward an Understanding of Calvin's Hermeneutic." In *Articles on Calvin and Calvinism,* vol. 6, *Calvin and Hermeneutics,* edited by Richard C. Gamble, 33–49. New York: Garland, 1992.

Gerdes, Daniel. "De Johannis Calvini Institutione Relig. Historia Litteraria." In *Scrinium Antiquarium sive Miscelleana Groningana* 2:451–77. Groningen & Bremen: Spandaw & G. W. Rump, 1750.

Herminjard, Aimé-Louis. *Correspondance des réformateurs dans les pays de langue français.* Geneva: Georg, 1866–97.

Knecht, Robert J. *Renaissance Warrior and Patron: The Reign of Francis I.* Cambridge: Cambridge University Press, 1994.

Marmelstein, Johan Wilhelm. *Étude comparative des texts latins et français de l'Institution de la religion Chréstienne par Jean Calvin.* Groningen: J. B. Wolters, 1923.

Ramus, Petrus. *Basilea: Eine Rede an die Stadt Basel aus dem Jahre 1570.* Edited by Hans Fleig. Basel: Basilisk-Verlag, 1944.

Staehelin, Ernst. *Das theologische Lebenswerk Johannes Oekolampads.* New York: Johnson, 1971.

———. "Oratio de reducenda excommunicatione." In *Briefe und Akten zum Leben Oekolampads.* 2:448–61. New York: Johnson, 1971.

Warfield, Benjamin B. "On the Literary History of Calvin's 'Institutes.'" In *Calvin and Calvinism,* 371–428. New York: Oxford University Press, 1931.

5

Geneva, 1536–1538

BACKGROUND

The history of the reformation of Geneva is closely interwoven with the political events that led to the liberation of the city from the rule of the duke of Savoy. The bishop of Geneva, whose position depended largely on the support of Savoy, also played a role. In large measure, the balance of power was also determined by an alliance formed in 1526 between the Swiss cities of Bern, Fribourg, and Geneva. This *combourgeoisie* was a thorn in the side of the bishop. Bern had joined the Reformation following a disputation in early 1528 (January 6–26), in which the leaders of the evangelical movement from south Germany and Switzerland had participated. The mandate of February 7, 1528, formed the basis for the organization of the church in the canton of Bern. The authority of the bishop came to an end, and Roman Catholic worship was abolished. After the defeat at Kappel (1531), the situation in Bern recovered under the leadership of Capito, who led the synod of January 9–14, 1532. The authority of the civil government in ecclesiastical affairs was established, whereas the gospel was entrusted to the preachers under the leadership of the magistracy, which was to regulate the outward proclamation. The decisions of 1532 were reflected in the organization of the state church in Bern. The city tried very hard to extend its influence to the west. As a part of these efforts, Farel was authorized to proclaim the gospel in all the territories under Bern's control.

Farel had been trained in the circle around Lefèvre, and there he was won for the gospel.[1] He had a fiery spirit, and because of his radical approach, he could not feel at home in the circle of Meaux. In Basel he organized a

---

1. Herminjard, *Correspondance*, 2:43.

disputation that prompted the magistracy to expel him from the city. He also worked in Metz, Strasbourg, and Aigle, which at that time was under the authority of Bern. He then moved through western Switzerland and succeeded in getting the citizens of Neuchâtel to choose for the Reformation in 1530. In a number of other places, too, he became the initiator of their reformation. In 1524 he wrote the first French treatise of the Reformation, *Pater noster et le Credo en français*,[2] and the first detailed handbook on Reformed doctrine, *Sommaire et brève declaration* (1515).[3]

Farel's evangelistic campaign brought him to Geneva for the first time in 1532. He was soon ordered out of the city, however, on the ground that he was a Lutheran. The tensions that forced him to leave Geneva at that time were related in part to the political party formation that had occurred there. Everyone was familiar with the "Eidgnots," who were supporters of a strong alliance with Fribourg and Bern, which could weaken the power of Savoy. The name alludes to an oath of loyalty that bound people together against a common enemy, and the term was later taken over by the Swiss cantons. It is not clear whether it also later led to the name of the French Protestants, the Huguenots.

The other party in Geneva was designated by its opponents as the Mammelukes, an allusion to the mercenaries of an Egyptian sultan. It was used to refer to the supporters of Savoy, who believed that a relationship with the duke would protect their religion and freedom. The parties had existed for a long time and played a role when matters came to a head. The alliance with Bern and Fribourg received its strongest support from the tradespeople. The clergy, especially the bishop, sided with Savoy.

THE SIGNIFICANCE OF THE ALLIANCE

The mixture of religious matters with political factors in Geneva was highly complex. The Reformation had not bypassed Geneva entirely, but there was little sign of it in the seven parish churches. Saint Peter's Church (Saint Pierre) was the cathedral where the bishop had his seat. When the reformation took place in Bern, the functioning of the alliance became significant for what happened in Geneva. Bern could not stand off to the side even though Geneva was relatively isolated from it. At first Bern hesitated about whether to play a role in a city more oriented toward France. But when in difficult straits Geneva began to turn its eyes westward (toward France), Bern stepped in. In February 1536 Bern freed Geneva from the power that had influenced the city for so long.

2. Edited by Francis Higman (Geneva: Droz, 1982).
3. Edited by Arthur-L. Hofer (Neuchâtel: Editions Belle-Rivière, 1980).

The conditions were now in place for a real reformation in Geneva. Further, the form of government that had developed in the city took on importance, because it was within those structures that relationships in the city were reflected also in the religious area. At the head of the government (*Seigneurie*) was a quadrumvirate of four mayors, called syndics, who were elected each year in January by the citizenry. They made up part of the Small Council of twenty-five members, which constituted the daily government, met at least three times a week, and regulated the important ongoing affairs. A large council comprising two hundred members carried out its business in monthly meetings and in February elected members of the Small Council. Twice a year there was a meeting of the *commune*, the general assembly in which the male citizens were consulted about important economic, political, and religious matters. As in practically all free cities where the Reformation gained a firm foothold, Geneva tried to maintain a balance between the powers of the magistracy on the one hand, and the demands of the ecclesiastical leaders on the other.[4]

Already on October 1, 1531, Farel had written Zwingli (who just ten days later would die at Kappel) how matters stood in Geneva: "It has become clear to me that the inhabitants of Geneva are beginning to think about Christ and that if the Fribourgers would allow it, they would accept the gospel without hesitation. Bern—for the glory of Christ—is not as accommodating to the wishes of the papacy as Fribourg is."[5] During this time sympathy for the gospel was on the rise in Geneva, but the magistracy hesitated for quite some time.

A letter of papal indulgence was removed from the church and replaced by an announcement of a general pardon for anyone who believed in Christ. This document in turn was removed by a canon from Fribourg, who was injured in the ensuing tumult. Fribourg lodged a formal protest that embarrassed the council, who did not wish to break the alliance but even less to take strong measures against the evangelical sympathizers. On July 8, 1532, the papal nuncio complained to the council of Geneva about the fact that Lutheran doctrine was being openly taught "in homes, churches, and schools."

Farel maintained close contact with the evangelicals in Geneva, despite the fact that he had to flee the violence there in September 1532. He encouraged them by letter and sent a young man to the city, Antoine Froment, who made it known that he wished to open a school for both men and women so that they would be able to read and write the French language within a month. He began his lessons and also proclaimed the gospel. On January 1, 1533, he began to preach in public, which was followed by a government order that forbade preaching in houses and public places without permission. The atmosphere

4. William E. Monter, *Calvin's Geneva* (New York: Wiley, 1967).
5. Herminjard, *Correspondance*, 3:364f.

became tense; citizens carried arms even when they went to church. Fribourg complained again about Lutheran preaching, and the council of Geneva responded that they had been poorly informed: there was no Lutheran preacher in Geneva. The evangelicals appealed to Bern for support, whereupon the council of Bern complained to the council of Geneva about the treatment of "their beloved William" and protested against the persecution of those who confessed the gospel. They demanded space for the truth, "so that those in your city who wish to speak and live according to the holy gospel of Jesus Christ shall be able to do so without being harassed or persecuted, and so that the Word of God shall be proclaimed in freedom."

On April 8, 1533, a Dominican monk made himself available for a disputation, but the council prohibited it. Bern insisted that such a disputation be held and wanted to send Farel to Geneva to participate. On May 5 the evangelical sympathizers in Geneva appealed to Farel himself to plead with the council of Bern. The reason was that on the day before, a group of armed priests had taken the law into their own hands and come to blows with their opponents. A few of the leaders were imprisoned, which only made things worse. The Catholic bishop left the city on July 14, 1533, never to return. Froment, meanwhile, was interrupting the anti-Reformation preaching in St. Peter's by a professor from the Sorbonne, Guy Furbity, who was attacking Bern as well. The council of Bern complained once again and insisted upon a disputation. Their letter was delivered by a messenger accompanied by Farel and Viret. As soon as they arrived, Farel began to preach. The disputation on which Bern had been insisting took place on January 27–30, 1534, with Furbity crossing swords with Farel. Although Farel was convinced that he had won, the encounter produced no decisive change. The council broke off the discussion because "enough had been disputed."

BREAKTHROUGH OF THE REFORMATION

In the elections of February 1534, however, it became clear what the mood of the city was: three of the four syndics were convinced supporters of the gospel. The cause of the Reformation was significantly enhanced during the summer when Bishop Pierre de la Baume recruited an army with which, along with the duke of Savoy, he hoped to take up the struggle against Geneva. In point of fact, this marked the end of his power. A nighttime surprise attack on the city failed. Even then, however, the council still refused to make a decision. The bishop was regarded as a vassal of the duke, so that a break with him did not yet represent a definitive break with the past. Bern, however, intervened by force of arms, and Farel worked up his courage, for Bern now insisted that a church be made available for the preaching of the gospel. On March 1 a crowd took possession of the convent of the Rive, where, with the silent consent of the council, Farel preached from a pulpit for the first time and for the entire period of Lent, amid the ringing of bells.

The elections of 1535 confirmed the reform party's efforts. The clergy were challenged to a disputation but refused. When the magistracy wanted to proceed with the disputation anyway, two clergymen who would take on the Roman Catholic defense were found: Jean Chapuis and Pierre Caroli, both already known for their sympathy for the evangelicals. The disputation was held from May 30 through June 24, 1535, and covered a number of topics.[6] Chapuis was recalled by his superiors after a few days, and Caroli—who had belonged to the Meaux circle in France, had fled Paris in 1534, and after the disputation found a position as a preacher in Lausanne—went over to the Reformation.

The one conclusion that for Farel went without saying was that the tide of the Reformation could now no longer be stemmed. On August 8, 1535, he preached under the protection of the people in St. Peter's Church. The images were removed, because "these things were fashioned in conflict with the Word of God." The magistracy decreed that the celebration of the mass be abolished, a definitive sign that Geneva had switched to the Reformation. In December of the same year, the council declared that anyone who did not wish to listen to the preaching would be better off leaving the city. New coins were minted, a right of the bishop that was now taken over by the magistracy. The legend on the coins read: *Post tenebras lux* (After the darkness, light).

When in 1536 all the syndics appeared to be supporters of the Reformation, the time had come to give expression to the change through a decision about the "manner of life." On May 21, 1536, an unusual public meeting was held: citizens testified by a show of hands to their agreement with the change, which meant "that we unanimously promised and swore with the help of God to want to live by this holy, evangelical law and the Word of God as it is preached to us; and that we abolished the mass and other ceremonies and papal abuses, images, superstitions, and everything related to them, in order to live in unity and obedience to the law."[7] This plebiscite officially ratified the decisions of the magistracy; Geneva now belonged to the Reformation camp.

Political factors, of course, played a major role in this important decision, particularly as they concerned Geneva's relationship to Bern, which had now taken the place of the bishop and the duke. In that regard, political factors also

---

6. Théophile Dufour, *Un opuscule inédit de Farel: Le résumé des Actes de la dispute de Rive* (Geneva: Schuchardt, 1885).

7. Comité Farel, *Guillaume Farel 1489–1565: Biographie nouvelle écrite d'après les documents originaux par un groupe d'historiens, professeurs et pasteurs de Suisse, de France et d'Italie* (Neuchâtel: Delachaux & Niestlé, 1930), 332.

led to friction within the old Genevan party groupings. Bern's expansion impulse related not only to the territory of the duke of Savoy in the Vaud region but also immediately to the interests that the city had there. The church of Geneva, too, would many times yet face off with Bern, which was oriented toward Zurich at a time when developments in Geneva were moving in another direction. There the Reformation would unfold in quite a different way than in Bern. Even before Calvin's arrival, the tinder was already present for the conflict that would bring his first stay in Geneva to a rather abrupt end.

CHAOS

It is an open question what the actual motivation was for the choice, with the help of God, to live according to the "holy, evangelical law." Was there unanimity on this point? For some this meant freedom from any law and all authority. Calvin would wage a fight against the libertines or epicureans, who would have trouble with any law, even the evangelical form. This was not a problem only in Geneva; it was also the case in Zurich, Basel, and Strasbourg. The reformation of a church is not the same as the renewal of a commonwealth. For Calvin, especially, it was a question of how law and gospel should function in a society that no longer had a pope, bishop, or duke, but did have a king. The problems that flowed from that were now fully exposed. Farel was the man of the hour at the beginning—impulsive, irrepressible, animated by an incredible courage. But was he also capable of actually organizing the church in Geneva? On his deathbed, Calvin recalled the situation he had encountered upon his arrival: "When I came to this church for the first time, it was as good as nothing. There was preaching, but that was all. People were hunting for images and burning them, but there was no set form of reformation. Everything was in chaos."[8]

In the midst of this tumult, Farel compelled Calvin to try his hand at constructing the reformation in Geneva. First, however, Farel had to allow him to travel to Basel to put his affairs in order there. On the journey to Basel, Calvin made contact with a number of congregations along the way, which invited him to stay. Apparently, his name had become well known. In the middle of August, he was back in Geneva, where for nine days he was not able to do a thing because of a cold, with several complications. When he recovered, he began lecturing on the Letters of Paul, which gave him the opportunity to apply his own exegetical method: use of the Greek text and literary-historical exegesis with wide use of the knowledge he had acquired in his reading of the

8. CO 9:891 (OS 2:401).

church fathers. On September 5, 1536, Farel made clear to the council how necessary these lectures were. The city clerk did not yet know Calvin's name; he mentioned the work of "that Frenchman" that ought to be paid for. Five months later it was decided to grant Calvin a salary of six golden crowns (February 13, 1537).

Upon his arrival Calvin had refused to assume a particular ecclesiastical office. He wanted to serve as an expositor of Scripture, a professor of theology. Beza reports that at the beginning Calvin did not exercise any pastoral office: "He agreed to remain there not to preach but to serve as a professor of theology."[9] It was not long, however, before he was also chosen as a pastor.[10] Beza writes, "When, therefore, he was appointed a teacher of this church by a lawful election and approbation, he drew up a brief confession of faith and church order, to provide a definite form for this recently established church."[11]

Within a short while, Calvin had taken over the initiative from Farel. His lectures on the Letter to the Romans enhanced his reputation, even outside of Geneva. Oporinus, a printer and publisher in Basel, asked Calvin for permission to publish the text.[12] He also informed Calvin that there was already demand for a second edition of the *Institutes*, of which only one copy remained in Basel. A revised and expanded edition would be welcome.

In October, however, Calvin had to interrupt his lectures because it was thought that he should be present at a disputation in Lausanne (October 1–8, 1536) that had been organized by Bern to introduce the Reformation in the Vaud region. Farel and Viret took the lead here, and Caroli was also present. Viret was originally from this area. He had attended lectures at the Collège de Montaigu, was won over to Reformation preaching by the sermons of Farel in his hometown of Orbe, preached his first sermon there as a nineteen-year-old on May 6, 1531, and since then had been an advocate of the new doctrine. He had assisted Farel in Geneva and was now working in Lausanne.

The disputation, for which Farel had prepared ten propositions, took as its starting point the authority of Scripture, which recognizes no other justification than through faith alone. Christ, who alone is head of the congregation, is in heaven and therefore cannot really be present in the Lord's Supper. Only ministers who preach the Word can be recognized as office-bearers. Civil authorities ought to be obeyed if they do not command anything contrary to the Word.

9. CO 21:30; cf. 21:126.
10. This must have been after August 1537, because the council of Bern wrote a letter on August 13 to "Maistre Guillaume Pharel, prescheur de l' Évangile, et Jehan Caulvin, Lecteur en la Saincte Escripture à Genève, nous bons amys"; Herminjard, *Correspondance*, 4:276.
11. CO 21:30f.
12. Herminjard, *Correspondance*, 4:207.

As in Geneva, it was difficult in Lausanne to interest any Roman Catholic theologians in the disputation. Calvin was present and for the most part stayed out of the discussion until a moment when he felt he had to correct a mistaken reference to the church fathers. In so doing, he won respect for his knowledge of the writings of Cyprian, Tertullian, and Augustine, which he could cite from memory, chapter and verse. When the disputation was over, Calvin informed a friend of his awareness that people everywhere were removing images from the churches: "May the Lord grant that idolatry disappear from the hearts of everyone!"[13]

After Lausanne, Calvin visited a synod that was held in Bern on October 16–18, 1536, in the context of a discussion of the Wittenberg Concord. Bucer and Capito were doing everything they could in trying to move the Swiss to a rapprochement with Luther that would have lasting significance. Bullinger did not entirely trust the enthusiasm coming out of Strasbourg; Zurich did not wish "to be led from light into darkness." During these discussions, Calvin must have made an impression on Bucer and Capito. Both wrote him on December 1, 1536, clearly with great expectations, inviting him to a discussion in either Basel, Bern, or Geneva, in which questions related to the "oeconomia Ecclesiae" (organization of the church) could be treated.[14] Both were convinced that the Lord wished to make him bear much fruit for his church.

CHURCH ORDER AND CATECHISM

After the synod of Bern, the real work in Geneva was waiting. Already toward the end of 1536, Calvin, in cooperation with Farel, must have finished the *Articles concernant l'organisation de l'église et du culte*. Along with that came the preparation of the *Instruction et confession de foy*, designed as a catechism for the youth. A shorter version, the *Confession de foy*, consisting of twenty-one articles, was intended as a summary by which the citizens of the city would express their Protestant faith. These documents not only testify to Calvin's capacity for work but also show that he could use his theology as a means to bring a whole society under the yoke of Christ.

The first document was a prototype of the church order whose traces would later be found within the broad stream of Reformed Protestantism. Calvin organized the congregation in its worship, and therefore also in its whole structure, around the Lord's Supper.

13. Ibid., 4:89.
14. Ibid., 4:115, 117.

A church cannot be well ordered and regulated if the Supper of the Lord is not frequently administered and attended, and indeed with such good supervision that no one dare participate except in a holy manner and with special reverence. Therefore, it is necessary, if the church is really to remain intact, that ecclesiastical discipline [excommunication] be exercised.[15]

With an appeal to Matthew 18, Calvin pleaded for the introduction of *disciplina* on three grounds: the honor of Christ, which may not be impugned; the mortification of the sinner, who must repent; and the protection of others, who ought not to be harmed by the sinner in the congregation.[16] What this regulation entailed was that in each district of the city certain persons of good repute would serve as monitors of the doctrine and life of the citizens. If someone strayed, one of the ministers would have to be informed, and if all pastoral admonitions proved futile, he would bring it to the attention of the congregation. If the person persisted in the sin, the congregation would have to excommunicate him until signs of repentance became evident. The Lord's Supper was off limits, but excommunicated persons were urged to attend preaching services, which could become a blessing for them.[17]

A second important aspect of the organization of the congregation was congregational singing. From the start, Calvin recognized the importance of church songs.[18] Third, he mentions catechesis: the youth must make profession of faith in the church. The congregation gathers around the Lord's Supper. The preservation of infant baptism requires a regulated ecclesiastical instruction of the youth. Finally, Calvin makes a plea for a thorough regulation of the marriage laws, which had become necessary because of bad mismanagement by the bishop.

Along with this church order, Farel and Calvin presented the catechism, which was a summary version of the *Institutes*. The material was arranged not in questions and answers but in short paragraphs. An abridgement of this catechism in twenty-one articles was intended as a statement of doctrine, to which all inhabitants of the city would be expected to subscribe under oath.

These documents were presented to the Small Council already on November 10, and then to the Council of Two Hundred on January 16, 1537. They were approved with the understanding that the Lord's Supper would be celebrated not weekly but, as had been the practice so far, four times a year. Marriage legislation was placed under the jurisdiction of the magistracy. Furthermore, public subscription to the confession of faith could not take place

15. CO 10:1.5 (OS 1:369); Herminjard, *Correspondance*, 4:154ff.
16. CO 10:1.9 (OS 1:372).
17. CO 10:1.10 (OS 1:373).
18. Calvin speaks of "chanter aulcungs pseaumes en forme d'oraysons publicqs."

immediately, since many people were still not sure about their decision for the Reformation. The form of church discipline set up by Calvin and Farel was viewed unfavorably by the civil magistracy, who more or less dragged their feet on the matter. It was known that there were Anti-trinitarians and Anabaptists in the city, or people that sympathized with them, and no immediate agreement could be expected, of course, from them. Therefore the public confession of faith that Farel and Calvin had insisted on was postponed. It finally took place on July 29, 1537, in a meeting in St. Peter's Church, with the district heads leading the way. Before that, the magistracy had distributed 1,500 copies of the confession. The turnout, however, left a lot to be desired. A good number of citizens refused to take the oath of subscription to the confession. Party loyalties divided the city.

PIERRE CAROLI

Meanwhile, unrest in the city was growing for other reasons. Appearing in Geneva were Anabaptist propagandists even though they were declared defeated after a public disputation on March 16 and 17, 1537, and were banished from the city. But their simple and direct approach to religious questions did strike a sympathetic chord here and there.[19]

A different sort of attack came from Caroli, who during Viret's absence from Lausanne took the opportunity to enhance his own profile. He argued for another approach to prayers for the dead, believing that he could act as a mediator between Rome and the Reformation. When Viret returned from Geneva and, at the insistence of the magistracy in Bern, again took over the leadership in Lausanne, Caroli charged Farel, Viret, and Calvin with denying the doctrine of the Trinity because terminology used by the ancient church could not be found in their writings. These reformers were being charged here with the most serious form of heresy, one that would place them outside the bounds of Christendom: Arianism. Calvin was afraid that this would remain as a blot on his work and did his best to remove it, even though he refused to oblige Caroli by subscribing to the three creeds of the ancient church.

Attempts were made to settle the dispute in meetings in Lausanne (May 14, 1537) and Bern (early June). Calvin's starting point was the conviction that the only way we can speak about God is with his own Word; we ought only to draw from the pure source of Scripture. Thus Calvin indicated in his *Confessio de*

---

19. Willem Balke, *Calvin and the Anabaptist Radicals*, trans. William J. Heynen (Grand Rapids: Eerdmans, 1981), 73–95.

trinitate, which was defended in Lausanne on behalf of the Genevan theologians.[20] This seemed to Calvin to remove the theological insinuations. Many people were still wondering, however, why he was not willing to adopt the terminology of the ancient church. All they would have needed to do was refer to the *Institutes*, for there one finds the heart of the Christian confession clearly expressed.

Calvin was left with a lifelong aversion to Caroli, whose position with respect to the Reformation was anything but clear. In 1545 Calvin composed a work in which he recounted once again his view of the events of 1537 and shed some light on the unstable character of Caroli.[21]

The situation in Geneva, meanwhile, left Calvin little room for tolerance as the differences sharpened. At the strong insistence of Farel and Calvin, another attempt was made to bring all citizens under the aegis of the confession. Those who refused would have to leave the city. After repeated entreaties by the preachers, the magistracy took a strong stance and decided on November 12 to ban any who were negligent. That number was so great, however, that the decision appeared unenforceable, which damaged the authority of the civil government and the prestige of Calvin and the others. The mood grew hostile, and the pulpit became a place where both government and citizenry came under sharp criticism. On November 25 there was a stormy meeting of the citizens, who reproached the magistracy for abandoning the freedom of the city and turning the citizens into slaves of Farel and his cohorts. The ministers, however, did not back down at all. They insisted more strongly than before that the oath-taking be carried out and church discipline maintained, including the use of excommunication. On January 4 the Council of Two Hundred decided that no one might be kept away from the Lord's Supper. That viewpoint betrayed the heart of the conflict. Calvin's view of the structure of the church had not yet fully matured at this stage, but the principle was clear. It was a question of the nature of spiritual jurisdiction and which bodies should exercise it. The magistracy opposed any attempts to portray it as purely ecclesiastical.

SHARP DIFFERENCES

The elections of February 3, 1538, brought victory to the opposition. The four syndics who were chosen belonged to those who had been protesting the actions of the preachers. The syndics pursued a cautious policy, using as a

20. CO 9:703.
21. CO 7:289–340.

model the church of Bern, which was heavily under the influence of the civil government. The syndics and council of Geneva were determined to maintain their rights over against the church. The magistracy there had an interest in the unity of civil administration and ecclesiastical practices, not only in the Vaud region but also in Geneva.

On orders from the government, Calvin and Farel attended a synod held in Lausanne at the end of March 1538. There it was decided that the entire region would adjust to the practices of the church in Bern. In the Lord's Supper, which should be administered also on Easter Sunday, they should again use the host, in this case unleavened bread, which was not to be broken.

The preachers protested vigorously against these measures. The reintroduction of several holy days and the use of a stone baptismal font placed in the chancel also stirred up opposition. These were points, of course, on which people could come to agreement. Nevertheless, Calvin believed that in the case involving these points, what was at stake was the very nature of ecclesiastical authority. One of the preachers, Elie Coraud (Courault), became so angry at the magistracy that he was forbidden to preach, and then he was imprisoned after he ascended the pulpit anyway. Under these circumstances, the preachers refused to administer the Lord's Supper on Easter Sunday, and they, too, were barred from preaching. In spite of the clear prohibition, however, they continued to preach—Calvin in St. Peter's and Farel in St. Gervais. They declared that in the midst of the confusion that reigned in Geneva among the magistracy and the people, it was impossible for them to administer the holy mystery of union with Christ.

The Small Council called the Council of Two Hundred together, whereupon a meeting of the General Council decided that Calvin and the other preachers who had refused to obey should be expelled. They were given three days to leave the city, but they had already left the following morning, April 23. Calvin remarked that they had been poorly rewarded for their service to people, "but we serve a great Master, who will reward us."

They tried to explain their position in Bern, which was partly successful. Following that, at a synod in Zurich (early May 1538), they tried to clarify the conditions under which they would return. Ceremonies were negotiable, but in the breaking of the bread a principle was at stake. If they should take up their work in Geneva again, however, one of the most important steps to be taken would be the introduction of church discipline: the city would have to be divided into districts, which would make supervision much easier. The practice of excommunication would also need to be restored.[22]

22. Herminjard, *Correspondance*, 5:3ff.

The citizens of Geneva were informed of these conditions. However, when the magistracy of Bern tried to mediate, since they were concerned about the political consequences of the expulsion as well (there was talk of a takeover by France), the mood in the city seemed to be totally against the reformers. When Calvin arrived on Genevan soil with the intention of explaining his proposals in the city in person, he was refused entry on no uncertain terms. Coraud left for Orbe, where he died within a few months. Farel and Calvin traveled to Basel, where they stayed at the home of Oporinus. Farel was then called to Neuchâtel, where he arrived in July 1538 and settled permanently. Calvin remained for awhile in Basel and found lodging at the home of Gryneaus. There he stayed until he responded to Bucer's invitation to move to Strasbourg.

CHAPTER BIBLIOGRAPHY

Balke, Willem. *Calvijn en de doperse radikalen*. Amsterdam: Van Bottenburg, 1973.
———. *Calvin and the Anabaptist Radicals*. Translated by William J. Heynen. Grand Rapids: Eerdmans, 1981.
Barthel, Pierre, Rémy Scheurer, and Richard Stauffer. *Actes du Colloque Guillaume Farel, Neuchâtel 29th Septembre–1st October 1980*. 2 vols. Geneva: Revue de théologie et de philosophie, 1983.
Bavaud, Georges. *Le réformateur Pierre Viret (1511–1571): Sa théologie*. Geneva: Labor & Fides, 1986.
Comité, Farel. *Guillaume Farel, 1489–1565: Biographie nouvelle écrite d'après les documents originaux par un groupe d'historiens, professeurs et pasteurs de Suisse, de France et d'Italie*. Neuchâtel: Delachaux & Niestlé, 1930.
Dufour, Théophile. *Un opuscule inédit de Farel: Le résumé des Actes de la dispute de Rive*. Geneva: Schuchardt, 1885.
Farel, Guillaume. *Le Pater noster et le Credo en françoys*. Edited by Francis Higman. Geneva: Droz, 1982.
———. *Sommaire et brève declaration* (1515). Edited by Arthur-L. Hofer. Neuchâtel: Éditions Belle-Rivière, 1980.
Froment, Anthoine. *Les actes et gestes merveilleux de la cité de Geneve*. Edited by Gustave Revilliod. Geneva: Iules Guillaume Fick, 1854.
Guggisbert, Kurt. *Bernische Kirchengeschichte*. Bern: P. Haupt, 1958.
Herminjard, Aimé-Louis. *Correspondance des réformateurs dans les pays de langue français*. Geneva: Georg, 1866–97.
Hesselink, I. John. *Calvin's First Catechism: A Commentary*. Louisville, KY: Westminster John Knox Press, 1997.
Junod, Eric, ed. *La dispute de Lausanne (1536): La théologie réformée après Zwingli et avant Calvin: Textes du Colloque international sur la Dispute de Lausanne 29 septembre–1er octobre 1986*. Lausanne: Presses Centrale Lausanne, 1988.
Linder, Robert D. *The Political Ideas of Pierre Viret*. Geneva: Droz, 1964.
Monter, William E. *Calvin's Geneva*. New York: Wiley, 1967.
Naef, Henri. *Les origines de la Réforme à Genève*. 2 vols. Geneva: Droz, 1968.
Nauta, Doede. *Guillaume Farel in leven en werken geschetst*. Amsterdam: Bolland, 1978.

———. *Pierre Viret (1511–1571): Medestander van Calvijn, in leven en werken geschetst.* Kampen: De Groot Goudriaan, 1988.

Piaget, Arthur, ed. *Les Actes de la Dispute de Lausanne 1536: Publiés intégralement d'après le manuscripte de Berne.* Neuchâatel: Secretariat de l'Université, 1928.

Vuilleumier, Henri. *Histoire de l'église réformée du pays de Vaud sous le régime Bernois.* Vol. 1, *L'âge de la réforme.* Lausanne: Editions la Concorde, 1927.

6

Strasbourg, 1538–1541

At the beginning of September 1538, Calvin made his way to Strasbourg, where at Bucer's urging he took responsibility for a small group of French refugees that under his leadership were organized into a congregation. Already in July of that year, he had, at Bucer's request, paid a visit to the city to get his bearings. At that time he would not yet comply with Bucer's and Capito's request. Bucer, however, laid down the law to convince Calvin that his calling did not consist in wide-open study but in the care of a congregation. Just as with Jonah in his day, God would manage to find him. Shaken by this example, Calvin finally gave in.[1] On September 8, 1538, he preached for the first time before the refugees, a large number of whom had come from the city of Metz.

BACKGROUND

The free imperial city of Strasbourg permanently joined the Reformation in 1529; pleas to abolish the mass had grown ever stronger since 1524, and the council finally complied. In an extensive consultation with the guilds, it was determined that for a long time already the mass had been nothing more than a lifeless duty, in conflict with the Word of God and the teaching of Christ. For the council, abolishing the mass was equivalent to accepting the Christian religion. The preachers came under the protection of the magistracy, who controlled a government operation in which, in the words of Erasmus, the discipline of Rome, the wisdom of Athens, and the modesty of Sparta went hand

---

1. CO 31:25.

in hand.[2] On a stopover on his way to Marburg in 1529, Zwingli considered the city as a place where true piety had been restored.[3] The evangelical movement experienced powerful growth within the balance of the structures prescribed by the form of government. The various instruments of government kept each other in balance and saw to it that the *publica pax* was not disturbed.[4] This political pattern played the most important role in guiding the new movement. The government allowed neither the old clergy nor the new preachers to take the helm. As in all imperial cities, leadership consisted primarily in the prevention of revolutions, and in Strasbourg, too, the government did not function as an engine of the Reformation. It guided the movement when it appeared that the preaching of the gospel could no longer be stopped.

Matthias Zell (1477–1548) began as the pioneer of the evangelical movement in 1521 with a series of sermons on the Letter to the Romans. In 1523 a trio of preachers entered the walls of the free city and, along with Zell, would set the tone for the reformation there: Wolfgang Capito (1478–1541) in March, Martin Bucer (1491–1551) in May, and Caspar Hedio (1495–1552) in the fall. Bucer became the undisputed leader of the reformation in Strasbourg.

BUCER AND THE PARISH WARDENS

When Calvin arrived in Strasbourg, the reformation there had already taken on a shape of its own. Most noticeable were the liturgical changes, which Bucer defended in his work *Grund und Ursach* (1524), in which he justified his critique of the mass.[5] It was also clear that he could no longer be satisfied with Luther's position. With respect to the question of baptism, the difference with the early Anabaptist movement was already becoming evident, a difference that would emerge more clearly in the 1530s. From the outset the Strasbourgers chose a position between Zurich and Wittenberg, always trying to act in a conciliatory, not polemical manner.

The reorganization of the large Strasbourg congregation came about at the synod held in June 1533. Preparations were made by the preachers and the *Kirchenpfleger* (church wardens), who drew up a confession of sixteen articles. This document already opposes Servetus's view of the Trinity and also men-

2. Desiderius Erasmus, *Opus epistolarum. Desiderii Erasmi Roterodami*, vol. 2, *1514–1517*, ed. P. S. Allen (Oxford: Clarendon, 1910), 19.

3. ZW 14:424.

4. Thomas A. Brady, *Ruling Class, Regime and Reformation at Strasbourg, 1520–1555* (Leiden: Brill, 1978), 163–68; Miriam U. Chrisman, *Strasbourg and the Reform: A Study in the Process of Change* (New Haven: Yale University Press, 1967), 14–31.

5. *Martin Bucers Deutsche Schriften*, vol. 1, *Frühschriften 1520–1524*, ed. Robert Stupperich (Gütersloh: Gütersloher Verlagshaus, 1960), 185–278.

tions and rejects Melchior Hoffmann's ideas about the incarnation and free will. It condemns the misuse of the ban, understanding the church's administration of the power of the keys as an exercise of the authority of Word and Spirit. Government and congregation ought to work together. The former is a servant of God and must do everything in its power to see to it that the name of God is hallowed by its subjects.[6] These sixteen articles are clearly directed against Anabaptists and spiritualists.

The synod also decided to draw up a church order. This document, however, did not appear until at least January 1535, along with a number of moral regulations by the council. Apparently the magistracy considered it part of its duty to keep a close watch on the moral level of the city. This led to tension between the government and the ministers of the church, which found expression in the way in which the church was organized. On October 30, 1531, the magistracy had decided that in each of the seven parishes, three "honorable and wise men" had to be named as *Kirchspielpfleger* (parish wardens): one from the council, one from the guilds, and one from the congregation. The appointment would be for life. It was their task to supervise the preachers and their assistants with respect to their doctrine, life, and preaching. Two times a year a synod would be held, in which the preachers and these parish wardens would deliberate on ecclesiastical matters. From their ranks a committee would be chosen that would manage day-to-day affairs. Every three months these parish wardens would meet with the preachers and their assistants to discuss the nurturing of the congregation. If ever someone wished to question the preachers about their doctrine or conduct, this was to be done in front of these functionaries.[7]

In addition to these regular meetings of the church wardens, there was also the *Kirchenconvent*, a weekly gathering of the preachers, where the unity of the ministers would be displayed. Bucer's most significant writings on the organization of the church of Strasbourg were published with the joint authorization of his colleagues.[8]

Behind this ecclesiastical organization stood an ideal not fully shared by the government. Bucer's theology had led him to the conviction that church discipline was indispensable for the well-being of the congregation. Although he had originally held another view, he came to adopt the position of Oecolampadius.

6. François Wendel, *L'église de Strasbourg, sa constitution et son organisation, 1532–1535* (Paris: Presses universitaires de France, 1942), 243–52.

7. Aemilius L. Richter, ed., *Die evangelischen Kirchenordnungen des sechszehnten Jahrhunderts* (1846; repr., Nieuwcoop: DeGraaf, 1967), 480f.; Walther Köhler, *Zürcher Ehegericht und Genfer Konsistorium*, vol. 2, *Das Ehe- und Sittengericht in den Süddeutschen Reichsstädten, den Herzogtum Württemberg und in Genf* (Leipzig: Heinsius, 1942), 408ff.; Bucer's proclamation is found in *Martin Bucers Deutsche Schriften*, vol. 7, *Schriften der Jahre 1538–1539*, ed. Robert Stupperich (Gütersloh: Gütersloher Verlagshaus, 1964), 244f.

8. For example, *Grund und Ursach* (1524) and *Von der waren Seelsorge* (1538).

The address that the Basel reformer delivered before the magistracy of his city in the spring of 1530 is well known. He urged the reintroduction of church discipline, which should be exercised under the authority of the congregation of Christ himself. For that to happen, the establishment of the office of elder would be necessary as an institution of the church, and Oecolampadius favored the reinstatement of the New Testament office of presbyter.[9] Bucer, too, was open to this idea, and the conflict with the Anabaptists only strengthened his conviction that the church itself should control the discipline. For him, a church without discipline was unimaginable. With this in mind Bucer penned one of his best-known works, *Von der waren Seelsorge und dem rechten Hirten-dienst* (1538), and with these same ideas he organized church life in Hesse at the behest of Landgrave Philip.[10] In Marburg, Bucer implemented what did not seem possible in Strasbourg.

The introduction of church discipline was one of the most important items on the ecclesiastical agenda when Calvin assumed leadership of the group of French refugees in the Alsace capital in September 1538. A month after his arrival in Strasbourg, he wrote to Farel about how carefully Bucer and his colleagues had gone about introducing ecclesiastical discipline.[11] He appreciated that all the more because connected with it was the freedom of the congregation in relation to the government, an issue that had played a major role in his banishment from Geneva. He followed the efforts of the Strasbourg preachers attentively, as his letters to Farel indicate. An increasingly warm friendship developed between him and especially Bucer, which is remarkable considering a letter he wrote to Bucer in early 1538 that contained strong accusations and was far too outspoken.[12] Regular contact with Bucer and the personal interest that Bucer showed in Calvin contributed to their relationship becoming like that of a father and son. Calvin experienced a lifelong bond with Bucer, something to which especially their congeniality in theology and view of the church and its practice also contributed. He was greatly influenced by Bucer, who also shaped him personally, while conversely, Calvin also served as an example to his older friend. Especially regarding the concept of church discipline can we speak of mutual influence.[13]

9. Olaf Kuhr, *Die Macht des Bannes und der Busse: Kirchenzucht und Erneuerung der Kirche bei Johannes Oekolampad (1482–1531)* (Bern: Lang, 1999).

10. *Ordnung der christlichen Kirchenzuchte: Für die Kirchen im Fürstenthumb Hessen*, in *Bucers Deutsche Schriften*, 7:247–318.

11. Herminjard, *Correspondance*, 5:144.

12. Ibid., 4:338–49; Cornelis Augustijn, "Calvin in Strasbourg," in *Calvinus Sacrae Scripturae Professor: Calvin as Confessor of Holy Scripture*, ed. Wilhelm H. Neuser (Grand Rapids: Eerdmans, 1994), 166–77.

13. Willem van 't Spijker, "Bucer und Calvin," in *Martin Bucer and Sixteenth Century Europe: Actes du colloque de Strasbourg (28–31 août 1991)*, ed. Christian Krieger and Marc Lienhard (Leiden: Brill, 1993), 1:461–70.

PREACHING AND PASTORAL CARE
AMONG THE FRENCH REFUGEES

The congregation entrusted to Calvin consisted of about five hundred members. During the years that Calvin led them, they met first in the Nicholas church, then in the Magdalene church, and finally in the chancel of the Dominican church. His salary during this time came largely from his friends. Only when he was appointed to teach at the academy was he awarded an annual allowance of fifty-two guilders, while Jacob Sturm tried to provide him with a chaplaincy income. Especially at the beginning, his financial situation was free of concern. The only real need he felt was to buy books. When a house of his own became available, the students who boarded with him helped to supplement his income.

In his congregation, Calvin concentrated especially on pastoral care. He preached twice every Sunday and was in charge of four services each week. The Lord's Supper was celebrated for the first time in October 1538. For that, Calvin employed the local liturgy and had in mind to administer the sacrament monthly.[14] Entrance to the Lord's Supper was originally unrestricted. Calvin believed, however, that a certain supervision of the celebration was necessary, and before Easter 1540 he announced that no one would be allowed at the table who had not first presented themselves for his approval; too many people just walk right up to the sacrament, he declared. Calvin complained to Farel about the rigid position of a few of the French, with whom his decision did not sit well.[15] Over against those who thought that this amounted to a reintroduction of Catholic confession, he defended his action by arguing that confession could really be set aside only if it were replaced by a pastoral conversation. In giving notice of the Lord's Supper, therefore, Calvin announced that those who wished to participate ought to apply with him. For Calvin, this was also about instruction, admonition, and comfort.[16] He judged that this could not be in conflict with Christian freedom because he would implement nothing other than what Christ himself had prescribed. It was Calvin's view of the congregation gathered around the Lord's Supper that led him to this pastorally conceived practice of church discipline. He put into practice what Bucer had envisioned in his *Von der waren Seelsorge*.

So far as the Lord's Supper was concerned, at least, Calvin concurred with the liturgical practices of the church of Strasbourg.[17] He also drafted a

14. CO 10:279.
15. CO 11:31.
16. CO 11:41.
17. CO 9:894.

baptismal form in this period in which people from many places were presenting children of Anabaptists to him. At his farewell to the preachers of Geneva on April 28, 1564, he would report that he had prepared this form without much preparation but hoped nevertheless that it would remain unchanged.[18] Although Calvin led an independent congregation, he obviously alienated himself as little as possible from the liturgical conventions in Strasbourg. Hence a large part of the Strasbourg reformation came into the Reformed tradition via Calvin.

A special aspect of Calvin's work in the Alsatian capital was his effort to promote congregational singing. The French congregation was singing psalms already toward the end of 1538, when Calvin himself was busy translating and rhyming the Psalms in French. It was a task that did not come easily to him. He had high regard for the German melodies, and he proceeded to set Psalms 46, 25, and a number of others to verse. He also carried on correspondence regarding this matter with his former colleagues;[19] apparently, the issue of congregational singing was of common concern among the French reformers. Here they followed their German colleagues, who had laid down some rules for their congregations.[20] When it came to congregational singing, the German reformation had actually taken the lead.

In the French reformation, the Psalms became the battle songs by which the movement spread. It all began with the psalmbook of the French congregation of Strasbourg, which appeared in 1539: *Aulcuns pseaulmes et cantiques mys en chant* (*Some Psalms and Songs Set to Music*). It contained eighteen psalms, the song of Simeon, the Ten Commandments, and the Apostles' Creed. Part of it was prepared by the well-known Clémont Marot, whom Calvin had met in 1536 in Ferrara; Calvin himself took the trouble to prepare some psalms. For these versifications he used Strasbourg melodies composed by Matthias Greiter.[21] Calvin let it be known that rhyming of psalms was not his area of strength, and he therefore did not participate in the later editions that appeared in Geneva. Beza and Marot were the poet-authors of the edition of 1562.[22] Their collection served as a model for the Reformed churches in France and the Netherlands.

18. Hughes Oliphant Old, *The Shaping of the Reformed Baptismal Rite in the Sixteenth Century* (Grand Rapids: Eerdmans, 1992).

19. Pierre Pidoux, *Le psautier huguenot du XVIe siecle: Melodies et documents* (Basel: Baerenreiter, 1962), 2:2ff.

20. Markus Jenny, *Luther, Zwingli, Calvin in ihren Liedern* (Zurich: Theologischer Verlag, 1983).

21. Théodore Gérold, *Les plus anciennes mélodies de l'Église protestante de Strasbourg et leurs auteurs* (Paris: Alcan, 1928).

22. Facsimile edition by Pierre Pidoux (Geneva: Droz, 1986).

EXEGETICAL ACTIVITY

Calvin's activity in Strasbourg was not limited to preaching and pastoral care in his own congregation. Jacob Sturm, well-known political leader, along with Bucer organized the educational system of the city and worked toward establishing a university. In 1538 Johannes Sturm from Paris was charged with the task of bringing the schools in Strasbourg under one organization. His ideal was the promotion of *sapiens et eloquens pietas* (wise and eloquent piety).

Bucer and Capito concentrated on the exegesis of the Old Testament, and at Capito's suggestion, Calvin and Hedio were appointed to lecture on the interpretation of the New Testament. In addition, Calvin participated in all the activities of the school. He led disputations and acquired a reputation that attracted students from all around to his classes. According to Sturm, he first gave exegetical lectures on the Gospel of John, then on the Letters to the Corinthians. This was possibly followed by his interpretation of Paul's Letter to the Philippians, and then the Letter to the Romans, on which he had already lectured in Geneva. Johannes Sturm praised Calvin's scholarly work in the highest terms.

There is no doubt that the publication of Calvin's commentary on Romans was partly the fruit of his study in Strasbourg. On October 16, 1539, he wrote the dedication of the work to Simon Grynaeus, in which he recalls discussions the two had carried on in Basel about the ideal principle of biblical interpretation: *perspicua brevitas* (brevity with clarity). He compares his work with that of Melanchthon, Bullinger, and Bucer. Bucer especially, in Calvin's view, was too wordy, although Calvin hastens to add that no one in his day had devoted himself to the interpretation of Scripture with more conscientious zeal.[23]

Calvin composed his commentaries on the other Letters of Paul between 1540 and 1551, and a revised edition appeared in 1556. His method was indeed that of brevity with clarity. Bucer had supplied his own commentary on the Letter to the Romans (1536) with digressions, excurses, and wide-ranging citations from the fathers.[24] He also included separate discussions of a number of dogmatic questions, so that his work provided a summary of his whole theology. Calvin was able to limit himself to the exposition of the text because he had already presented the dogmatic material in his *Institutes*. The second edition of the *Institutes*, which in many respects would turn out to be his most important work, had undergone significant change. It would no longer serve

23. CO 10:402–6.
24. *Metaphrases et enarrationes perpetuae epistolarum D. Pauli Apostoli: . . . Tomus primus, continens metaphrasim et enarrationem in Epistolam ad Romanos* (Strasbourg, 1536).

merely to elucidate the first principles by which true piety could be fostered, as was indicated in the first, 1536 edition. Calvin expressed the hope that his work would bear fruit for the church of the Lord, and above all that students of theology would use it so that in their reading of Scripture they could determine what really matters. At the same time he now felt relieved of the duty to devote detailed discourses to the commonplaces of theology. In his exegesis Calvin evidently wished to operate with free hand. His distinction between dogmatics and exegesis contributed to a proportional development in the Reformed tradition of biblical interpretation on the one hand, and a free-standing dogmatics on the other.

THE 1539 *INSTITUTES*

Out of the "small catechism," as the 1536 *Institutes* was called, there actually emerged a whole new doctrinal handbook, which, as the title indicates, could indeed be called an instruction manual in the Christian religion.[25] Calvin would continue working on the book right through to the last edition, and only then—also insofar as the order of topics was concerned—would it meet his ideal.[26]

The 1539 edition was a considerable expansion of the work. The form of 1536 was retained to a great extent; in nearly every later edition, large sections of the 1536 text can be found again. But every subsequent edition represented a further expansion, due to Calvin's ongoing study of Scripture and familiarization with the fathers, as well as to his increasingly stronger apologetic element. In no respect, however, did the expansions represent an alteration of the original concept. From 1543 onward, he concluded the preface with a quotation from Augustine: "I count myself one of the number of those who write as they progress and progress as they write." The "progress" that Calvin was making related to the expansion and shaping of the material. The first edition had already contained the opening "Nearly the whole of sacred doctrine consists in these two parts: knowledge of God and of ourselves." In the 1539 and all subsequent editions, it reads, "Nearly all the wisdom we possess, that is to say, true and sound wisdom, consists of two parts: the knowledge of God and of ourselves." The expansion from seven to seventeen chapters came about because, besides the catechetical material on law and faith and prayer, Calvin now devoted special attention also to the knowledge of God and ourselves (chapters 1 and 2), conversion (5), justification (6), the similarity and differ-

25. *Institutio christianae religionis nunc vere demum suo titulo respondens* (Strasbourg, 1539).
26. "Nunquam tamen mihi satisfeci, donec in hunc ordinem qui nunc proponitur digestum fuit"; CO 2:1–2.

ence between the Old and New Testaments (7), and predestination and providence (8). In the second edition, the sections on the sacraments are organized
into three chapters: sacraments in general (10), baptism (11), and the Lord's
Supper (12). The next three parts deal with Christian freedom (13), the power
of the church (14), and civil government (15), and the work ends with a sec-
tion on the five falsely termed sacraments (16) and the Christian life (17).[27]

In the foreword to the second edition, Calvin indicates that he might have
been able to produce a fuller version of the book if during the last two years
he had not been so busy. We know that during this time in Strasbourg, he did
not have a very extensive library available. However, he was able to make use
of what was firmly embedded in his memory, quoting Augustine and other
church fathers by heart.[28] Johannes Sturm could rightly say on the title page
of the 1543 *Institutes*, "In his *Institutes* John Calvin shows himself to be a man
of extraordinary discernment, massive learning, and superb memory. He is a
lucid writer, rich in profundity of thought."

TREATISE ON THE LORD'S SUPPER

Calvin's skill as a writer was certainly shown also in the little piece he composed while still in Strasbourg: *Short Treatise on the Holy Supper of Our Lord and
Only Savior Jesus Christ.*[29] He wrote the little book in French in order to bring
some clarity to questions that had arisen in the dispute about the Lord's Supper and had confused many simple believers. Calvin outlined the origin of the
dispute between Luther on the one hand, and Zwingli and Oecolampadius on
the other. Luther necessarily employed crude analogies, since he could not
explain his meaning in any other way: it was not easy to make so lofty a matter understandable. Zwingli and Oecolampadius used their powers of persuasion to defend a literal conception of the ascension of Christ. But they forgot
to show how one ought to understand the presence of Christ in the Lord's Supper. Both sides fell short: Luther overstepped his bounds, but the others gave
offense as well. Nevertheless, one ought not to forget the grace that God has
manifested to us through these men. Calvin then sums up his own view as follows: When we receive the sacrament in faith, we are made partakers of the
real substance of the body and blood of the Lord. How precisely this happens
some can explain better than others. What matters, however, is that we raise
our hearts on high to heaven and remember that this mystery is accomplished

27. See the "Synopsis" of the five editions in CO 1:li–lviii.
28. CO 6:336.
29. CO 6:537–88.

by the supernatural power of God. The Holy Spirit is the bond of this spiritual participation.

With this small treatise, Calvin wished to offer some direction to the French believers who were discomfited by the Lord's Supper controversy. At the same time, he appeared to take a conciliatory position toward Luther, whom he had characterized at the beginning of 1538 as a stubborn man. Calvin considered himself fortunate when he learned that Luther had greeted him via Bucer, and he indicated that he had read Luther's and Sturm's books with special pleasure.[30] Melanchthon let Calvin know that Luther held him in high esteem, which made Calvin so enthusiastic that he intended to give public testimony to Luther's brotherhood.[31] On Melanchthon's advice, however, he did not follow through.[32] Calvin never forgot Luther's friendliness, even when the evidence of it was no longer so visible around 1545.

In any case, Calvin was open to rapprochement with the Wittenbergers. At the end of February 1539, he personally sought contact with Melanchthon by traveling to Frankfurt on his own initiative. Bucer had been officially delegated to the colloquy there and had written Calvin that he had not succeeded in doing anything substantial for the persecuted French Protestants. Calvin traveled with Johannes Sturm to the meeting to try to persuade the German princes to intercede with Francis I. There he had the opportunity to speak with Melanchthon at length about the possibility of a real rapprochement between Luther and the Swiss. Melanchthon, however, saw no use in further human attempts; God would have to bring about unity in the truth itself. Calvin's plea for stricter church discipline also met with little response: the Wittenberger deplored the condition of the church but felt that there was not much that could be done to improve it.

Calvin must have made a very positive impression on Melanchthon on this occasion, for when the religious colloquies seeking rapprochement between Roman Catholics and Protestants needed to be organized, Melanchthon made a strong plea that Calvin be included. One of the things that motivated Calvin to participate in these meetings was his hope that the German princes would be willing to devote themselves to the cause of the church in France.

For a delegation to Paris, Calvin drafted a set of instructions in which he pressed for freedom for the Word of God. This freedom must be given room to work. Just judges should be appointed, and whoever is accused ought to have the opportunity to give an explanation. What Calvin had stressed in his letter to Francis I at the beginning of the *Institutes* now reappeared in these instructions in abbreviated form: freedom for the gospel.

---

30. CO 10:402.
31. CO 10:432.
32. Herminjard, *Correspondance*, 6:132–37.

HAGENAU, WORMS, AND REGENSBURG

The Strasbourgers saw in Calvin more than just an advocate for the reformation in France. They also valued his presence at the colloquies, as Melanchthon had attested, because of his knowledge of the Bible, theology, and patristics. In June 1540 the colloquy that had been decided upon in Frankfurt met in Hagenau. It produced nothing more than a date and an agenda for the next meeting, which was held in Worms. Bucer saw to it that Calvin was present "as someone well read in the fathers."[33] This was taking place at the time that attempts were already being made to entice Calvin to return to Geneva. He wrote to the council of Geneva that he had been called to Strasbourg under their authority and by others.

In Worms, too, no substantial discussions took place. In Regensburg (1541), however, it seemed that there would be a breakthrough. Calvin wrote to Farel that a certain unity was emerging on the doctrine of justification:

> A formulation was drawn up that was accepted by both parties after a few corrections. You will be surprised, I think, by how much our opponents conceded. We held firmly to the main points of true doctrine, so that there is nothing in the agreement that cannot also be found in our writings. I know that you will want a clearer explanation, and I agree. But if you remember who it is that we are dealing with, you will admit that we have come a long way.[34]

The discussion ran aground on the question of the church and her authority, and especially the idea of transubstantiation. Calvin spoke about it without reserve: "Believe me, in these kinds of activities strong spirits are required!" By nature apprehensive and anxious, Calvin managed at the time to overcome his weaknesses. But when he looked back at the colloquies years later, he indicated that he had been forced to go to these large-scale meetings against his will.[35] He did not even wait until their end; despite protests from Bucer and Melanchthon, he left Regensburg and returned to Strasbourg, arriving there on August 8. Concern for his congregation weighed heavily on him.[36] The flow of refugees from France remained large, and the departure of his temporary replacement in the pastorate made his return necessary. Moreover, Capito's illness had slowed down work at the academy. And finally, he was concerned about his family.

---

33. Hans Wirck et al., eds., *Politische Correspondenz der Stadt Strassburg im Zeitalter der Reformation*, vol. 3, *1540–1545*, ed. Otto Winckelmann (Strasbourg: Trübner, 1898), 108–10.
34. CO 11:215.
35. CO 31:25ff.
36. CO 11:251.

MARRIAGE

At the beginning of August 1540, Calvin married Idelette de Bure, the widow of Anabaptist Jean Stordeur, who had come back to the congregation. Calvin had seriously considered marriage before, but his desire for such a relationship was tempered by rather rational considerations:

> I am not one of those foolish lovers who, once they are attracted by the figure of a woman, indulge even their faults. The only beauty attractive to me is if she is modest, cooperative, not haughty, but frugal and patient, and if I may hope that she would look after my health.

Various plans, some also contrived by friends, came to naught. Calvin got to know Idelette when he provided pastoral care for her husband, who died of the plague in 1540. He had also baptized one of her children. His relationship with her seems to have given him another view of the significance of marriage. When she died in 1549, Calvin lamented the deep loss of his dearest life companion. He was convinced that she would have willingly shared with him poverty, exile, and even death. The children they had together died very shortly after birth. When Calvin was taunted about that, he was able to write that he had children by the thousands all over the Christian world.[37] In his letters from Regensburg in 1541, Calvin sounded very concerned about his wife and her children, which hastened his return to Strasbourg.

CONNECTION WITH GENEVA

Meanwhile other things were also unsettling him. From the beginning of his sojourn in Strasbourg, he had followed the situation in Geneva with great interest. He certainly never intended to return. Already on July 30, 1539, he had purchased citizenship in Strasbourg and was registered with the tailors' guild. In his mind, his future lay in Strasbourg. This is not to say, however, that he did not closely follow events in Geneva. He still felt a bond with the congregation there. In a tense situation there, in which things seemed to be heading toward a schism in the church, he wrote a couple of pastoral letters.[38] He writes of the need for trying to preserve the unity of the church, as he himself and Farel had done when they were still in Geneva. In submission to God's leading and in true humility and repentance, the congregation could

37. CO 9:576.
38. CO 10:250–55, 350–55.

truly be comforted by the confidence that God would not withhold his help from them.

In the first letter, Calvin emphasizes an attitude of submission to God's will, and in the second, he shows the parties that had formed in the meantime the need to recognize the legitimacy of the office-bearers as brothers. Quarreling and discord could only hinder any improvement of the situation. He underscores the objective dignity of the office. The calling of the ministers in Geneva did not happen apart from the will of God, and the evaluation of the office-bearers ought to be done by answering the question whether the Word of God is being rightly proclaimed. Calvin did not wish to raise doubts about whether the ministers currently preaching in Geneva in fact did that. He had no doubt that they faithfully preached the main elements of the Christian religion and what was necessary for salvation. Schisms and sects would only tear the body of Christ apart; while this had the appearance of resisting fellow church members, it was actually waging war against God himself.[39] The pastoral tone of the letter shows something of the greatness of Calvin, who at this moment was in no way thinking about himself. He saw his future in Strasbourg, but he could not refrain from completely and unselfishly seeking what was good for the peace of the church in Geneva.

In Geneva, tensions between the parties were gradually increasing. The "Guillermins," supporters of Farel and Calvin, had more or less coalesced around Antoine Saunier and Mathurin Cordier, both with ties to the gymnasium. When they refused to participate in the service of the Lord's Supper on Christmas Day 1538, they were banished from the city, and the Lord's Supper that was to be celebrated on Easter 1539 was anticipated with some fear. A conciliation was achieved between Farel and the ministers in Geneva, however, and Farel and Calvin were eventually rehabilitated as faithful ministers—a first step toward full reconciliation.

RETURN TO GENEVA

Two important things played a major role in Geneva during this time. The first was the letter by Jacopo Sadoleto (1477–1547), bishop of Carpentras, written on behalf of a conference of bishops in Lyon to the council and people of Geneva (March 18, 1539). The letter appealed to the senate and church of Geneva to preserve and return to the unity of the church in its historical lineage. Sadoleto was known for his learning and integrity. He had taken part in the meeting of

---

39. CO 10:353, 354.

cardinals who had developed proposals for improving the church.[40] He had also corresponded with Johannes Sturm in Strasbourg and had won respect for his commentary on the Letter to the Romans, which did not get past the censors in Rome without some difficulty.

The accusation in the letter that Calvin and Farel had acted out of self-interest, however, was something that Calvin could easily refute. After it became clear that none of the preachers in Geneva was in a position to write a response, Calvin himself did so within a very short time, and on September 1, 1539, one of the most powerful defenses of the Reformation ever written appeared. There Calvin explained how *he* understood the unity of the church: it is based on doctrine, discipline, and the administration of the sacraments.[41] The church consists of the society of all the saints who, though spread throughout the whole world and across all times, nevertheless are bound together by the one doctrine of Christ and by one Spirit, and hold to the unity of the faith and brotherly concord.

This letter by Calvin was a testimony to the basic truth of the Reformation: justification through faith. It stated unequivocally that both Rome and the Anabaptists had abandoned the confession of the Spirit. Both had used an appeal to the Spirit as a weapon, but this appeal was actually nothing other than the erection of their own edifice of lies on the grave of the suppressed Word of God. The letter was also a very personal testimony by Calvin himself, who saw himself placed before the judgment of God and there, in the freedom of faith itself, declared the great importance that the church, the Spirit, and justification had for him. One cannot say that the letter to Sadoleto marked the beginning of his return to Geneva, but it did become clear to everyone that he still felt a bond with the church there.

His return was tied in particularly with the political changes that had taken place in Geneva. These were brought about by the strained relationship with Bern, in which the question of the authority of Bern in the Vaud region played a role. Conflict over that issue led to a temporary defeat of the "Articulants" at the hands of the "Guillermins." The first party, named after the articles that regulated the relationship between Geneva and Bern, suffered a major loss in the elections of 1540 that saw the supporters of Farel gain seats.

On September 21, 1540, Ami Perrin was given the task of trying to win Calvin back to Geneva. From then on, requests for him to return came in from everywhere, some with great urgency and some even from the other Swiss churches. The religious colloquies to which Calvin had been delegated gave

---

40. See *Consilium delectorum cardinalium et aliorum Praelatorum, de emendanda Ecclesia*, and *Ioannes Sturmius cardinalibus caeterisque Praelatis delectis* (Strasbourg, 1538). See also *Epistulae Duae duorum amicorum, Bartolomaei Latomi, et Ioannis Sturmii* (Strasbourg, 1567).

41. CO 5:394.

him good reason to adopt a reserved attitude. Inside himself, he could not face the prospect of another stay in Geneva: "I would rather die a hundred deaths than on that cross, on which I would daily perish a thousand times over."[42]

The magistracy in Strasbourg was also of the opinion that he should continue to serve the church there. But when Farel used his powers of persuasion to urge him to go back, Calvin no longer dared refuse—although his plan was only to travel to Geneva with Bucer to sort things out and then return to Strasbourg. The council of Strasbourg, however, did not grant Bucer permission to carry out the mission, and thus Calvin left in early September 1541 without him. He traveled by way of Neuchâtel, where he met with Farel, and then arrived in Geneva on September 13. Supplied with letters from Strasbourg and Basel, he reported to the council, apologizing for the delay that had occurred. Then he requested the council to decide about the organization of the church. (Energetic as he was, already at this first meeting he was making a proposal about his view of the way things should proceed.) Councillors should be appointed to consider the matter. And as for himself, he declared that he was ready to be the servant of Geneva forever.

Strasbourg had communicated that he ought to return to their church, but now that Calvin had offered himself to Geneva, the Genevan council decided to report to the council of Strasbourg, with an expression of thanks, that he was firmly in place and would remain there. Without any delay, Calvin went back to work, a sign of what he had written to Farel: "If it were up to me, I would rather do anything else than oblige you. But because I know that I do not belong to myself, I offer my heart to the Lord."[43]

CHAPTER BIBLIOGRAPHY

Adam, Johann. *Evangelische Kirchengeschichte der Stadt Strassburg bis zur französischen Revolution*. Strasbourg: J. H. E. Heitz, 1922.

Anrich, Gustav. *Martin Bucer*. Strasbourg: K. J. Trubner, 1914.

———. *Strassburg und die Calvinische Kirchenverfassung: Reden bei der Rektoratsübergabe am 3. Mai 1928 im Festsaal der Universität*. Tübingen: J. C. B. Mohr, 1928.

Augustijn, Cornelis. "Calvin in Strasbourg." In *Calvinus Sacrae Scripturae Professor: International Congress on Calvin Research, August 20–23, 1990, in Grand Rapids*, edited by Wilhelm H. Neuser, 166–77. Grand Rapids: Eerdmans, 1994.

———. *De godsdienstgesprekken tussen rooms-katholieken en protestanten van 1538 tot 1541*. Haarlem: F. Bohn, 1967.

Beza, Theodore. *Psaumes mis en vers Français*. Edited by Pierre Pidoux. Geneva: Droz, 1986.

42. CO 11:30.
43. CO 11:100.

Brady, Thomas A. *Ruling Class, Regime and Reformation at Strasbourg, 1520–1555*. Leiden: Brill, 1978.

Bucer, Martin. *Martin Bucers Deutsche Schriften*. Vol. 1, *Frühschriften 1520–1524*. Edited by Robert Stupperich. Gütersloh: Gütersloher Verlagshaus, 1960.

Chrisman, Miriam U. *Strasbourg and the Reform: A Study in the Process of Change*. New Haven: Yale University Press, 1967.

Douglas, Richard M. *Jacopo Sadoleto, 1477–1547: Humanist and Reformer*. Cambridge: Harvard University Press, 1959.

Eells, Hastings. *Martin Bucer*. New York: Russell & Russell, 1971.

Église réformée d'Alsace et de Lorraine, Commission Synodale. *Calvin à Strasbourg, 1538–1541: Quatre études publiées à l'occasion du 400e anniversaire de l'arrivée de Calvin à Strasbourg*. Edited by C. Bartholomé. Strasbourg: Éditions Fides, 1938.

Erasmus, Desiderius. *Opus epistolarum Desiderii Erasmi Roterdomi*. Vol. 2, *1514–1517*. Edited by P. S. Allen. Oxford: Clarendon, 1910.

Erichson, Alfred. *Die calvinische und die altstrassburgische Gottesdienstordnung: Ein Beitrag zur Geschichte der Liturgie in der evangelischen Kirche*. Strasbourg: J. H. E. Heitz, 1894.

Gérold, Théodore. *Les plus anciennes mélodies de l'Église protestante de Strasbourg et leurs auteurs*. Paris: Alcan, 1928.

Greschat, Martin. *Martin Bucer: Ein Reformator und seine Zeit*. Munich: Beck, 1990.

———. *Martin Bucer: A Reformer and His Times*. Translated by Stephen E. Buckwalter. Louisville, KY: Westminster John Knox Press, 2004.

Herminjard, Aimé-Louis. *Correspondance des réformateurs dans les pays de langue français*. Geneva: Georg, 1866–97.

Hulshof, Abraham. *Geschiedenis van de Doopsgezinden te Straatsburg van 1525 tot 1557*. Amsterdam: J. Clausen, 1905.

Hurlbut, Stephen A. *The Liturgy of the Church of Scotland since the Reformation*. Part 1, *Calvin's Liturgy at Strasburg and Geneva*. Washington, DC: St. Albans Press, 1944.

Jenny, Markus. *Die Einheit des Abendmahlgottesdienstes bei den elsässischen und schweizerichen Reformatoren*. Zürich: Zwingli-Verlag, 1968.

———. *Luther, Zwingli, Calvin in ihren Liedern*. Zurich: Theologischer Verlag, 1983.

Köhler, Walther. *Zürcher Ehegericht und Genfer Konsistorium*. Vol. 2, *Das Ehe- und Sittengericht in den Süddeutschen Reichsstädten, den Herzogtum Württemberg und in Genf*. Leipzig: Heinsius, 1942.

Kuhr, Olaf. *Die Macht des Bannes und der Busse: Kirchenzucht und Erneuerung der Kirche bei Johannes Oekolampad (1482–1531)*. Bern: Lang, 1999.

Lexutt, Athina. *Rechtfertigung im Gespräch: Des Rechtfertigungsverständnis in den Religionsgesprächen von Hagenau, Worms und Regensburg 1540/41*. Göttingen: Vandenhoeck & Ruprecht, 1996.

Livet, Georges. *Strasbourg au coeur religieux du XVIe siècle: Hommage à Lucien Febvre; Actes du Colloque international de Strasbourg, 25–29 mai 1975*. Strasbourg: Librairie Istra, 1977.

Nauta, Doede. "Calvijn en zijn gemeente." In *Zicht op Calvijn*, edited by J. van Genderen et al., 103–41. Amsterdam: Buijten & Schipperheijn, 1978.

Neuser, Wilhelm H. "Calvins Urteil über den Rechtfertigungsartikel des Regensburger Buches." In *Reformation und Humanismus: Robert Stupperich zum 65. Geburtstag*, edited by Martin Greschat, 176–94. Witten: Luther Verlag, 1969.

Old, Hugh O. *The Shaping of the Reformed Baptismal Rite in the Sixteenth Century*. Grand Rapids: Eerdmans, 1992.

Pannier, Jacques. *Calvin à Strasbourg: Extrait de la Revue d'histoire et de philosophie religieuses.* Strasbourg: Alsacienne, 1925.

Pidoux, Pierre. *Le psautier huguenot du XVIe siècle: Melodies et documents.* 2 vols. Basel: Edition Baerenreiter, 1962.

Richter, Aemilius L., ed. *Die evangelischen Kirchenordnungen des sechszehnten Jahrhunderts.* Nieuwcoop: DeGraaf, 1967.

Rott, Jean. "Documents strasbourgeois concernant Calvin." In *Regards contemporains sur Jean Calvin: Actes du colloque Calvin, Strasbourg 1964,* edited by R. Mehl, 28–73. Paris: Presses universitaires de France, 1965.

Schindling, Anton. *Humanistische hochschule und freie Reichsstadt: Gymnasium und Akademie in Strassburg 1538–1621.* Wiesbaden: Steiner, 1977.

Spijker, Willem van 't. "Bucer und Calvin." In *Martin Bucer and Sixteenth Century Europe: Actes du colloque de Strasbourg (28–31 août 1991),* edited by Christian Krieger and Marc Lienhard, 1:460–70. Leiden: Brill, 1993.

Stricker, Eduard. *Johannes Calvin als erster Pfarrer der reformirten Gemeinde zu Strassburg, nach urkundlichen Quellen.* Strasbourg: J. H. E. Heitz, 1890.

Wendel, François. *L'église de Strasbourg, sa constitution et son organization 1532–1535.* Paris: Presses universitaires de France, 1942.

Wirck, Hans, Walter Friedensburg, Harry Gerber, Hans Virck, and Otto Winckelmann, eds. *Politische Correspondenz der Stadt Strassburg im Zeitalter der Reformation.* Vol. 3, *1540–1545.* Edited by Otto Winckelmann. Strasbourg: Trübner, 1898.

7

Geneva, 1541–1546

Organization

Calvin's return to Geneva happened without fanfare. In his first sermon, he refrained from any harsh judgment about the past. Although everyone expected something unusual, he limited himself to a few words about the value and meaning of congregational office and of doctrine. Then he turned to the biblical text that he had been treating before his departure and continued his *lectio continua* to indicate that he regarded what had happened as a temporary interruption and in no way a relinquishing of his official ministry.[1]

Meanwhile, he had already reported to the magistracy that he was ready to help with the organization of the church. Here, too, he was tying in with views that he and Farel had earlier developed for the council in the articles concerning the organization of the church.[2] Among the conditions that Calvin and Farel, at a synod in Zurich in early May 1538, had laid down for their eventual return to Geneva was the establishment and maintenance of church discipline. The city would have to be divided into parishes and the use of excommunication restored. And the congregation of Christ would have to be gathered around the Lord's Supper.[3]

At his first meeting with the magistracy on September 13, 1541, it became clear that Calvin had not changed his mind. He requested the appointment of a committee, chosen from the senate, with the mandate to draft a church order and regulations for a consistory. The council consented and within just fourteen days a draft had been prepared, which was discussed on September 29. The council proceedings report that some of the articles were accepted and

1. CO 11:349.
2. CO 10:5–14.
3. Herminjard, *Correspondance*, 5:5.

others rejected. These were passed by the Large and Small Councils, though not without some difficulty. Calvin wrote to Martin Bucer on October 15 that undoubtedly agreement on the draft would be reached. He wanted to see the whole thing presented to the German churches, by which he meant Strasbourg, Basel, and Constance.[4] In those congregations was a form of church discipline based on the idea that the church ought to be holy, and in his view of the church, Calvin followed Bucer and Oecolampadius completely.

A comparison with the articles of 1537 shows a view here of the offices, the necessity of discipline, the preservation of doctrine and unity, and the doctrinal and moral caliber of the ministers that can be distinguished from the earlier document. Bucer had not been able, as originally intended, to accompany Calvin to Geneva, but the church order that Calvin now presented was certainly in the spirit of Bucer.

THE FOUR OFFICES

"There are four kinds of offices that the Lord instituted for the ruling of his church"—so reads the opening of the church order.[5] The reference to the institution of the offices by Christ himself corresponded to Bucer's ideas about the foundation of the offices in the congregation.[6] Immediately upon his return, Calvin had already stated "that the church cannot exist unless a certain government is established that is prescribed in the Word of God and was observed in the early church."[7] That articulates a fundamental conviction that can be found again in a large number of Reformed confessions later on. Agreement with Scripture provides a reliable basis that should give shape to the structure of the church.

The four offices, which again are reminiscent of Bucer's ideas, are those of pastor, teacher, elder, and deacon. The particular calling of the pastoral office, which is also referred to in the Bible as elder or minister, is the proclamation of the Word of God publicly and privately, the administration of the sacraments, and brotherly admonition in cooperation with the elders. Admission to this office happens by means of an examination that is concerned primarily with purity of doctrine and the ability to teach in such a way that the congregation

---

4. Ibid., 7:292.
5. For the text of the *Ordonnances ecclésiastiques*, see CO 10:15–30 (OS 2:328–45); *Registres de la Compagnie des pasteurs de Genève*, vol. 1, *Registres de la Compagnie des Pasteurs de Genève au temps de Calvin* (Geneva: Droz, 1964), 1–13; Émile Rivoire and Victor van Berchem, eds., *Les sources du droit du canton de Genève*, vol. 2, *De 1461 à 1550* (Arau: Sauländer, 1930), 377–90.
6. Karl E. Rieker, *Grundsätze reformierter Kirchenverfassung* (Tübingen: Mohr, 1907), 97.
7. CO 11:181.

is built up. It must also be certain that the candidate's conduct is beyond reproach. The ministers select candidates whom they consider suitable for the office, and they are then presented to the council. If the council concurs, that is followed by the presentation to the congregation "so that he will be received with the general agreement of the assembly of believers." Calvin pleads in the *Institutes* for an ordination ceremony with the laying on of hands. To avoid superstition, it was decided that the ceremony would be limited to an explanation of the office by one of the ministers and a prayer for God's grace. After that, the new preacher was sworn in by the civil authority.

Because agreement in doctrine was necessary for the unity of the church, the church order prescribed that the ministers gather weekly to ensure purity and harmony in doctrine. When differences of viewpoint surfaced, agreement should be reached collectively, with the elders also playing a part. If that did not work because one of the parties would not budge, then the magistracy would straighten things out.

COMPAGNIE DES PASTEURS

The meetings of the preachers developed into an institution that had a strong influence on the course of events in Geneva. It reminds one of the Strasbourg *Kirchenkonvent* and the *Prophezei* in Zurich.[8] Every Friday morning at seven o'clock the Genevan *Congrégation* (Bible study) met together in the Auditoire. Portions of Scripture were discussed in systematic order—introduced by one of the preachers, expounded by one of those present, and nearly always including a contribution by Calvin that sounded very much like a full lecture. After these public meetings of the preachers and their assistants, a session was held of just the *Compagnie des pasteurs*, devoted to a discussion of current issues. The *Compagnie* was also meant to be an instrument for *censura morum* (mutual censure), which was held once a quarter. Any office-bearer could take this opportunity to speak in a brotherly way about the doctrine or conduct of another. This mutual supervision, too, served the cause of unity in doctrine and life.

So far as the latter was concerned, the church order contained a few articles detailing the sins that could not be tolerated in a minister: among them were heresy, fomenting schism, rebellion against the church order, blasphemy, and simony. In addition, the church order lists a series of faults that require correction: among them were a lack of zeal for study, a way of treating Scrip-

8. John Calvin, *Deux congrégations et Exposition du catéchisme*, ed. Rodophe Peter (Paris: Presses universitaires de France, 1964). Calvin's description of these is found in CO 13:435f.

ture that gives offense, the pursuit of idle questions, and an undisciplined life. The ministers of Geneva had to be examples for the congregation.

In these lists of sins and other regulations of the church order, we recognize some of the material that Bucer had written for the Diet of Regensburg in his *Notes on the Removal of Ecclesiastical Abuses*. Calvin had probably finished translating this work while still in Strasbourg, so that he was able to publish it yet in 1541.[9] For the ministers, the draft church order was already a sign of the humanistic educational ideal: high moral standards upheld by pure doctrine.

The second office that the church order discusses is that of the *doctores* (teachers). Their task is instruction in sound doctrine "so that the purity of the gospel not be corrupted by wrong opinions." Calvin portrays them as instruments for maintaining the doctrine of God, who have responsibility above all for the training of future pastors and ministers. He conceives of formal education in the schools in the broadest sense: theological lectures, for which the knowledge of languages is essential. The future of the church and of civil government depends on such education. Like the ministers, the *doctores* are subject to church discipline.

THE ELDER

The third office is that of elder. Elders must oversee the life of everyone and, when necessary, must admonish amicably those who are living a disorderly life. They are to report to the *Compagnie des pasteurs*, representatives of which carry out fraternal admonition. In the makeup of the body of elders, Calvin took the situation in Geneva into account:

> In the present condition of the church, it would be good to elect two of the Little Council, four of the Council of Sixty, and six of the Council of Two Hundred, men of good and honest life, without reproach and beyond suspicion, and above all fearing God and possessing spiritual prudence. These should be so elected that there be some in every quarter of the city, to keep an eye on everybody.[10]

Their election took place in consultation between the preachers and the Small Council, after which they were presented to the Council of Two Hundred. Following their approval by this body, they like the preachers were sworn in by the civil authority, promising to fight against any form of idolatry, blasphemy, and whatever else contradicted the honor of God and reformation

9. *Les Actes de la Iournée imperiale tenue en la cité de Regespourg*, in CO 5:627–48.
10. CO 10:22. English translation in J. K. S. Reid, ed., *Calvin: Theological Treatises* (Philadelphia: Westminster Press, 1954), 63–64.

according to the gospel. Whatever had to be reported to the consistory should be brought forward in good faith, without prejudice and only so that the city would be run in good order and with the fear of God. They also promised that they would honor the ordinances of the various bodies of the magistracy. Finally, the elders were to meet with the preachers every Thursday to deal with anything related to order.

Calvin thus created an administrative body that, in his view, was essential to giving the church its own jurisdiction. In this respect, he operated according to the model that Bucer, too, had envisioned in Strasbourg. The figure of the elder was not unknown in Lutheran circles. Already in the *Hallische Kirchenordnung* (1526), Johannes Brenz had argued for the appointment of "elderly, mature, stalwart, and honest men who were assigned to diligently watch over the church."[11] However, for Brenz and others, the office of elder functioned in the sphere of civil government, whereas Oecolampadius, Bucer, and Calvin emphasized its ecclesiastical character. Calvin placed special emphasis on the difference between spiritual power and civil law.[12]

With that in mind, a regulation was included in the definitive text of the church order that the ministers would have no control whatsoever over the civil jurisdiction. They would wield only the spiritual sword of God's Word. Nothing would be undertaken by the consistory that would detract from the authority of the magistracy. Civil authority would remain wholly intact. When it came to punishment or force, the ministers and the consistory should offer appropriate warnings and then report to the council, which would then make a decision as the matter required.[13] In this way, Calvin completely shielded the civil jurisdiction from that of the ecclesiastical community, thinking that in so doing, ecclesiastical power could be preserved in a sphere of its own. To the latter, there belonged, in his view, especially the right of excommunication.[14]

TENSION BETWEEN MAGISTRACY AND CONSISTORY

The question that continually arose in Geneva was how to interpret the article discussed above. The magistracy considered the consistory as an instru-

---

11. Aemilius L. Richter, ed., *Die evangelischen Kirchenordnungen des sechszehnten Jahrhunderts* (1846; reprint, Nieuwcoop: DeGraaf, 1967), 45; Martin Brecht, *Die frühe Theologie des Johannes Brenz* (Tübingen: Mohr Siebeck, 1966), 66ff.

12. "Volui enim, sicut aequum est, spiritualem potestatem a civili iudicio distingui"; CO 11:463.

13. CO 10:30.

14. Calvin's translation in CO 14:679 leaves no doubt about the fact that the power of the consistory is limited to the rule of the church. The spiritual sword takes nothing away from jurisdiction in civil affairs.

,ment of government, which was put together in cooperation with and with the help of ecclesiastical leaders.[15] They viewed the elders as those within the consistory who had been commissioned or deputized by the magistracy. As was also the case in Strasbourg, the government refused, for the most part, to view these functionaries as representatives of ecclesiastical authority, fearing that that would mean giving up some of its own authority.

The three preachers who with Calvin and Viret made up the committee that drafted the church order supported it during their meetings but then advised some council members to oppose its implementation. This led to long and sometimes heated discussions. Calvin had difficulty respecting these colleagues, who thwarted his plans, were rude and arrogant, and lacked zeal and understanding in doctrine.[16] For the sake of unity, however, he tolerated them, convinced that quarreling among the ministers of the church would only destroy it. And Calvin was not entirely unhappy with the result: "All the same, we now have a consistory (*presbyterorum iudicium*) and a form of discipline (*disciplina*), such as the weakness of our day can bear." One hears something of the arguments that were employed in the debate when, in a letter to Myconius in Basel, Calvin makes clear that he does not consider a reference to Moses and David to be valid. Both of them, along with the pious kings, preserved the established order with their authority, as was appropriate. "But they left to the church a capacity for exercising its own rights, such as the tasks entrusted by the Lord to the priests."[17]

For Calvin, the heart of the problems surrounding church order lay in the view of the relationship between the church and civil government. His wish certainly was not entirely fulfilled, but he was able to interpret the proposed order in such a way that for him the freedom of the church was guaranteed. A major battle would still have to be waged when on Sunday, November 20, 1541, the *Ordonnances ecclésiastiques* was adopted by the General Council and the people with the blast of trumpets and ringing of bells, as was the old custom. It would not be until January 24, 1555, that the controversy over the disciplinary authority of the consistory would finally end. Only then did the magistracy state in no uncertain terms that people should adhere to these decisions, and only then was the church order understood in the way that Calvin had intended in 1541. What Calvin wrote to Myconius already in 1542 would be true for many years: "Do not think that we got this without the greatest effort."

Although the fourth category of office, the deacons, was not considered part of the consistory, it did, according to Calvin, constitute a part of church

15. CO 10:21 n. 4.
16. CO 11:378f.
17. CO 11:379.

government. With an appeal to the practice of the early church, he distinguished between two kinds of deacons. The first was engaged primarily in collecting and managing money and goods and in distributing them to the needy, strangers, widows, and orphans. Living in society called for social concern, promoted in part from within the church. The second kind of deacon had as its task the responsibility and direct care for the hospital, where lodging was also provided for the elderly and children of the poor. For the latter especially, it was thought necessary to have a teacher in the hospital (or hospice), to teach them good habits and to assist with their intellectual and spiritual development, particularly through catechesis.

The church order also contained regulations for the administration of baptism and the Lord's Supper, consecration of marriage, and visitation of the sick and imprisoned. At the end, the church order is declared valid also for those areas around Geneva for which the magistracy bore responsibility.[18] The preachers of those churches were expected at the weekly meetings of the *Compagnie des pasteurs*, and if anyone was absent for more than a month, he was reproached for gross negligence. From Geneva itself, regular church visitation was conducted in the surrounding villages as a way of monitoring the evangelical character of the whole area. Geneva, therefore, functioned as a model for miles around.

A day after the public adoption of the *Ordonnances ecclésiastiques*, Calvin and a few representatives of the government were assigned the task of updating Geneva's civil code.[19] To be able to devote all his time to the drafting process, Calvin received permission to reduce his share of the preaching to one service a Sunday, and he was also freed from his weekly church services.

In the revised code, the powers of the different councils were balanced off against each other, while the democratic character of the government as a whole in relation to the people was regularized. Revolutionary activity by a mob of people, as had happened in the past on more than one occasion, was prohibited. Legal procedures were simplified. Calvin followed the old Genevan law and tried to harmonize Roman law with it. According to the church order, his objective in church and theology now also became that of the civil law: to create a *modus vivendi* for the *regime du peuple* through the involvement of councils.[20]

18. CO 10:30.

19. CO 21:287; 10:126–46. See also Robert M. Kingdon, "Calvin et la constitution Genèvoise," in *Actualité de la réform*, ed. Jean-Marc Chappuis (Geneva: Labor & Fides, 1987), 207–19, and Josef Bohatec, *Calvin und das Recht* (1934; repr., Aalen: Scientia Verlag, 1971), 209–79. The texts are found in Rivoire and van Berchem, eds., *Les sources du droit*, 2:394–408 ("Édit du lieutenant"), 409–34 ("Ordonnances sur les offices et officiers").

20. CO 21:287: "Az este ordonne que il soyent fayct ordonnances sus le regime du peuple. . . ."

Behind that lay the idea that the magistracy had its own, well-defined author-ity, clearly distinguished from that of the church.

Calvin's earlier study of law had now borne fruit, and on November 17, 1542, it was decided to give him a vat of aged wine as a token of appreciation for his labor on behalf of the city.[21] On January 28, 1543, the constitution was adopted by the General Council of citizens.

CATECHESIS AND LITURGICS

The church now had its laws, and the society had been organized, something to which Calvin had made a substantial contribution. In the meantime, he had also been involved in various publications in the areas of catechesis, liturgy, and congregational singing. At the farewell to his colleagues on April 28, 1564, Calvin reported that upon his return, he had prepared the catechism in great haste. Among the terms that he had laid down for his return was that both the catechism and the church discipline be observed.[22] In the *Ordonnances* it was now prescribed that on Sunday afternoon in the three churches, catechetical instruction must be given to the small children. This had as its goal the public profession of faith, by which one was admitted to the Lord's Supper.[23] As a gen-eral rule, children would profess their faith between their tenth and fifteenth year, in accordance with what they had been taught in their catechism classes.

For that purpose, Calvin prepared a brief children's catechism reminiscent of the one that Capito had published in 1527.[24] It is also possible that this cat-echism was influenced by Bucer's *Kurtze schrifftliche erklärung für die Kinder und angohnden* (1534), which was certainly true in the case of the larger cate-chism that Calvin composed to replace the *Instruction et confession de foy* of 1537. The *Instruction* was, for the most part, a summary of the 1536 *Institutes*, but Calvin now changed his method by working with questions and answers, thus making the material more accessible. He also departed from the earlier orga-nization of the material, replacing the Lutheran order of law-faith-prayer with his own sequence of faith-law-prayer. In so doing, he gave his theology a dis-tinctive stamp, something seen already in the *Institutes* of 1539. This larger cat-echism was published in 1545, complete with a dedication to the ministers in Oost-Friesland—a sign of the ecumenical character of his efforts. In the ded-ication, he stresses the need to pass on the gospel in a reliable way to the next

21. CO 10:125.
22. CO 9:892.
23. M. B. van 't Veer, *Catechese en catechetische stof bij Calvijn* (Kampen: Kok, 1942).
24. *De pueris instituendis Ecclesiae Argentinensis Isagoge.*

generation. He also states that the unity of the church is to be found above all in agreement in pious doctrine.[25] The multitude of churches leads inevitably to a variety of catechisms, and differences in method of instruction may exist so long as each is united in orientation to the one Christ: "By his truth, if we are united to it, we may grow together into one Spirit."

The view of the Lord's Supper that Calvin expresses in this catechism appears to agree with that of Bucer. The Supper is not just a *significatio* but also an *exhibitio* (presentation) of the benefits of Christ, understood in the sense of making us real participants in the substance of the sacrament, by which we grow together with Christ into one body.[26] With this publication, therefore, Calvin also contributed to the revived controversy over the Lord's Supper and tried to support the preachers of Emden and its vicinity in the battle they had to wage with the Lutheran preachers.

In 1542 Calvin also drafted a liturgical handbook for the church of Geneva: *La Forme des Prieres et Chantz ecclesiastiques.* He borrowed the prayers for the Sunday worship service, in large part, from the liturgy of Strasbourg. The rest, the forms for baptism and the Lord's Supper, he composed on his own. The marriage form he took from Farel's liturgy. Parts of the baptismal form harkened back, as we have seen, to the text he had prepared in Strasbourg. At his farewell to the Genevan preachers, he recalled, "What I made then was a rough draft, but I would not recommend that you change it."[27]

Calvin could more easily abandon the psalms that he himself had set to verse in Strasbourg. The arrival of Clémont Marot in Geneva opened up the prospects for a collection of versifications of high quality. Calvin recommended to the magistracy that Marot be appointed to complete the Psalter. In the long run, however, Marot did not feel at home in the city, and the collection that appeared in 1545 still contained nine versifications from Calvin's own hand. The fact that he contributed less, however, does not mean that the songbooks no longer bore his stamp. Calvin appealed to Augustine for his principle that one cannot sing any better songs than the psalms of David, for then we can be certain that God himself puts the words in our mouths. The criterion for determining a spiritual song is insight, along with a sensitive heart. And Calvin had two requirements for the melody, *poids* (weightiness) and *majesté*, as befits the subject matter of the songs of the church.[28]

---

25. CO 6:5.

26. CO 6:128.

27. CO 9:894. See also Alfred Erichson, *Die calvinische und die altstrassburgische Gottesdienst-ordnung: Ein Beitrag zur Geschichte der Liturgie in der evangelischen Kirche* (Strasbourg: J. H. E. Heitz, 1894), 16ff.

28. Pierre Pidoux, *Le psautier huguenot du XVIe siecle: Melodies et documents* (Basel: Baerenrei-ter, 1962), 2:15–17, 20f.

THE CORRELATION BETWEEN
DOCTRINA AND *DISCIPLINA*

With the composition of the church order, the catechism, the liturgy, and the psalmbook, Calvin had realized the program whose principles he and Farel had developed in 1537 and whose most important points were included in the conditions that they both had laid down for their return.[29] The ideal that lay behind this, however, was clear. Purity of doctrine must be matched with purity of life. *Doctrina* and *disciplina* were correlate ideas. The preaching must be powerful and the ministers competent, radiating a strong unity. Along with the elders, they were to keep watch over the moral life of the city and state. In a certain sense, since Calvin's return, the civil authorities and the consistory continued the moral legislation, customs, and punishments that had been in effect in Geneva for years,[30] but now all social life fell under the supervision of the consistory, which was represented in every district of the city. It was expected of the civil authorities that they would support the leadership of the consistory and, if necessary, take a spiritual penalty and in a judicial decision turn it into a *civilis poena* (civil penalty).

Starting in early 1541, the church leaders began to clamp down on all sorts of moral and religious abuses, and from 1546 onward, there was a certain homogeneity within the *Compagnie des pasteurs* that enabled them to administer discipline more confidently. Only after 1555, however, when the civil authority no longer denied the consistory the right of excommunication, did church discipline grow in frequency: the approximately eighty cases per year around 1555 doubled in 1556 and grew to three times that number in each of the years from 1557 to 1561. In the area of religion, it was especially reversions to Roman Catholicism that they had to contend with, as well as heretical views, inadequate knowledge of the faith, or suspicious ideas. Numerous times people were called before the consistory for their negligence in church attendance or laxity in participation in the Lord's Supper. Insulting the preachers, especially Calvin, being insubordinate to the consistory, and later also engaging in insulting behavior toward French immigrants—all led to serious admonishment.

---

29. Herminjard, *Correspondance*, 5:3–6. Cf. the *Articles concernant l'organisation de l'église*, CO 10:5–14.

30. Walther Köhler, *Zürcher Ehegericht und Genfer Konsistorium*, vol. 2, *Das Ehe- und Sittengericht in den Süddeutschen Reichsstädten, den Herzogtum Württemberg und in Genf* (Leipzig: Heinsius, 1942), 545–55; William G. Naphy, *Calvin and the Consolidation of the Genevan Reformation* (New York: St. Martin's Press, 1994), 30ff., 108ff.; Johannes Plomp, *De kerkelijke tucht bij Calvijn* (Kampen: Kok, 1969), 213–49, 291–310.

Moral behavior was also carefully scrutinized. Adultery, prostitution, fornication, and homosexuality were severely punished, as was the immorality associated with dancing, the singing of indecent songs, magical practices, brawling, drunkenness, and manslaughter. Calvin and his consistory repeatedly addressed meetings of the council, where they sought to preserve the rights of the church. An ongoing source of tension was the question of who had ultimate jurisdiction over church discipline. In 1543 the council wrestled with the question of whether the consistory had the power to deny someone access to the Lord's Supper. They decided that the consistory had no such jurisdiction or power whatsoever. The consistory was authorized to admonish wrongdoers but then to leave the judgment to the civil authorities. Ten years later, it was proposed in the council that the friction between church and civil government be eased by stipulating that the civil authorities decide the question of who should be barred from the Lord's Supper, and that they alone decide on the grounds for such a prohibition.

The enormous tensions that surfaced over this jurisdiction, however, cannot be attributed solely to a difference in viewpoint between Calvin and the consistory, on the one hand, and the magistracy, on the other. Calvin looked upon Geneva as a city in which the seeds of dissension seemed particularly ready to sprout.[31] The old, established families, which already had enough tensions of their own, sometimes collectively turned against the reformers. There was something of a resurgence of classic nationalism, in which the "Enfants de Genève" confronted "the Frenchmen."[32] The preachers managed to strengthen their position in this situation by appealing to the anticipated arrival of Viret and Farel. Many of the conflicts were defused from the pulpit and in parallel negotiations in the council.

The makeup of the parties also sometimes changed when Genevan society came under pressure from the lust for power in Bern, which had a significant influence in the Vaud region. The threat still posed by Savoy and later by France influenced the pattern of power relationships within the city. The outbreak of the Schmalkald War (1546–47) heightened tensions in Geneva, and the outcome gave Charles V the opportunity to put pressure on the city,[33] which also led to a change in scenes. Financial obligations and repayments to Bern and Basel also had their impact.

Within the complex of all these problems, Calvin was allotted the role of legal counsel and adviser, and he acted as the advocate for Geneva in Bern.[34]

---

31. "In urbe, ut iam dixi, habemus intestinum semen dissidii." Letter from Calvin to Myconius, March 14, 1542, in CO 11:378.
32. On the "Enfants de Genève," see the index entry in Naphy, *Calvin and the Consolidation*.
33. Ibid., 100–104.
34. Carl A. Cornelius, *Die ersten Jahre der Kirche Calvins* (Munich: Franz, 1895), 14–30.

He drafted regulations for social life,[35] was active in attracting a textile industry, and was even involved in plans to thwart a possible military incursion by France or the emperor. Perhaps it was precisely this form of active presence in so many areas of life, in which he was able to make decisions and give advice with authority, that kept alive the resistance to his fundamental concept of discipline as primarily an ecclesiastical matter. People saw him as someone grabbing for as much power as he could. What is more, it is precisely on this point that the reformation movement in Switzerland and south Germany was not of the same mind. Conceptions of the relationship between church and state differed almost from city to city. This diversity did not change Calvin's outlook, and he continued to appeal to Scripture and the tradition of the early church. But this variety of opinion in the surrounding churches may well have contributed to the creation of a climate favorable to the magistracy, one that made it easier for the magistracy to reject the implications of Calvin's point of view.

During this period, Calvin succeeded in surrounding himself with colleagues who, in many respects, shared his positions. They formed a unity that was made possible by the removal of incompetent and, for Calvin, unacceptable characters. Some of them were transferred to the surrounding countryside, which was also under the control of Geneva and which could be monitored by means of regular church visitation. The rest were suspended or dismissed because of ministerial incompetence or serious moral lapses. The deficiency of the team of preachers in their pastoral work is evident from their failure to act during an outbreak of the plague. In the spring of 1543, the magistracy declared that those suffering from the illness must be "helped and comforted." The director of the hospital had to report that the preachers had been negligent in the exercise of their office. After calling the preachers together, the magistracy announced what was expected of them, which in Calvin's case was that he might not engage in this work because he was needed to advise the church as a whole. The preacher who had volunteered for the task died, and the other pastors informed the council that although visiting the sick did indeed belong to their office, "God had not yet granted them the grace of strength and perseverance to go to the hospital."[36] They asked for understanding, and the council consented for the time being, since someone else had made himself available. It is clear, however, that this behavior was not only regarded as a lack of perseverance but also served to alienate the Genevan citizens from the preachers, many of whom had come from France. It is also distressing that in 1545 the belief in witches led to

35. W. Fred Graham, *The Constructive Revolutionary: John Calvin and His Socio-Economic Impact* (Atlanta: John Knox, 1978); Ronald S. Wallace, *Calvin, Geneva and the Reformation: A Study of Calvin as Social Reformer, Churchman, Pastor and Theologian* (Grand Rapids: Baker, 1988).
36. CO 21:314; Naphy, *Calvin and the Consolidation*, 90.

thirty-five death sentences for those who were considered causes of the plague. Already in 1543 there was talk in the council about poisoners who were spreading the plague throughout the city at night.[37] In 1545, severe torture was used, according to the prevailing law, to procure their confession.[38]

SEBASTIAN CASTELLIO

The council and the preachers did not entirely agree in the way they thought about pastoral care in times of great need.[39] When it came to unity of doctrine, however, they closed ranks. In 1543 Sebastian Castellio announced his interest in the office of pastor in Geneva. During his stay in Strasbourg, Calvin had gotten to know him as a specialist in classical languages and had procured a position for him in the gymnasium in Geneva. Castellio, however, wanted to exchange the rectorship at the gymnasium for the pastorate. In the examination that was conducted according to the requirements established in 1541 for admission to the office, Castellio let it be known that he had difficulty with the canonicity of the Song of Solomon. For him, it was an immodest love poem that Solomon had written in his youth. He also indicated that he could not agree with Calvin's view of Christ's descent into hell, and he asked for a public debate with Calvin on the topic. The council denied that request but did support a discussion of the matter within the circle of preachers. No agreement was reached, and Castellio was refused admission to the office.

Castellio left the city with an affidavit in hand from Calvin and the ministers of Geneva, in which they recommended him as someone fit for the office of schoolmaster. No mention was made of deficiency in doctrine or life. Calvin did not want someone who thought differently than he did about the descent into hell to be considered a heretic: "We do not condemn churches that have a different interpretation. Our only concern is that a difference of interpretation not lead to great harm." The question of the interpretation of the Apostles' Creed, however, was not the most important point. Far more weighty was the question whether the Song of Solomon could be considered a part of the canon of Scripture. On this Calvin was clear. All churches have considered the Song of Solomon, which is a wedding song in the sense of Psalm 45, as part of the text of the Old Testament. On that score, there could

---

37. CO 21:314.

38. Oskar Pfister, *Calvins Eingreifen in die Hexer- and Hexenprozesse von Peney, 1545, nach seiner Bedeutung für Geschichte & Gegenwart* (Zurich: Artemis, 1947); Ernst Pfisterer, *Calvins Wirken in Genf: Neu gepruft und in Einzelbildern dargestellt* (Neukirchen: Verlag der Buchhandlung des Erziehungsvereins, 1957), 46–53.

39. CO 21:312–14.

be no allowance in the church of Geneva for different points of view. It would only lead to confusion.

When Castellio left the city, he found a position at the University of Basel and engaged in Bible translation. He had experienced a lack of toleration in Geneva and from then on pleaded for a broader conception of the catholicity of the church. Ten years later, Calvin would have to deal with him again in connection with the case against Servetus.[40]

Calvin's position over against Castellio was rooted in the conviction that unity in doctrine was necessary within the cadre of preachers. The organization of the church of Geneva rested on the belief that Scripture must have the first and the last word, because that is how Christ himself exercised his kingship. The reformation of Geneva ought to encompass not only the church but also the whole of society by means of the church. Calvin considered it his calling to bring about a "christocracy." His personal influence in ecclesiastical and political instruments of government served a great religious-pedagogical ideal. Liberation from Roman Catholicism was not the ultimate goal but only the beginning of a building process (*aedificatio*) in which the lordship of Christ could be realized. In their respective roles, both state and church were subject to the norm of Scripture, of which Calvin considered himself, along with his colleagues, to be the interpreter. It was in that context that the tensions between the church as the *corpus Christi* (body of Christ) and society as the *corpus christianum* (Christendom) came to light. Luther's doctrine of the two kingdoms did not function the same way in Geneva as it did in Saxony. Calvin's view came down to the distinction of a twofold kingdom under one Lord. He was convinced that his own interpretation of the voice of this Lord was the right one, a feeling not shared by everyone in Geneva.

CHAPTER BIBLIOGRAPHY

Anrich, Gustav. "Strassburg und die calvinische Kirchenverfassung." In *Reden bei der Rektoratsübergabe am 3. Mai 1928 im Festsaal der Universität*, edited by Universität Tübingen, 13–31. Tübingen: J. C. B. Mohr (P. Siebeck), 1928.

Bohatec, Josef. *Calvin und das Recht*. 1934. Reprint, Aalen: Scientia Verlag, 1971.

Brecht, Martin. *Die frühe Theologie des Johannes Brenz*. Tübingen: Mohr Siebeck, 1966.

Calvin, John. *Deux congrégations et Exposition du catéchisme*. Edited by Rodophe Peter. Paris: Presses universitaires de France, 1964.

Choisy, Eugène. *L'état chrétien calviniste: Genève au XVIme siècle*. Geneva: Georg, 1909.

———. *La théocratie à Genève au temps de Calvin*. Geneva: C. Eggimann, [1898].

Cornelius, Carl A. *Die ersten Jahre der Kirche Calvins 1541–1546*. Munich: Franz, 1895.

---

40. Hans R. Guggisberg, *Sebastian Castellio, 1515–1563: Humanist und Verteidiger der religiösen Toleranz im konfessionellen Zeitalter* (Göttingen: Vandenhoeck & Ruprecht, 1997).

————. *Die Gründung der Calvinischen Kirchenverfassug in Genf 1541*. Munich: G. Franz, 1892.

Erichson, Alfred. *Die calvinische und die altstrassburgische Gottesdienstordnung: Ein Beitrag zur Geschichte der Liturgie in der evangelischen Kirch*. Strasbourg: J. H. E. Heitz, 1894.

Graham, W. Fred. *The Constructive Revolutionary: John Calvin and His Socio-Economic Impact*. Atlanta: John Knox, 1978.

Guggisberg, Hans R. *Sebastian Castellio, 1515–1563: Humanist und Verteidiger der religiösen Toleranz im konfessionellen Zeitalter*. Göttingen: Vandenhoeck & Ruprecht, 1997. ET, *Sebastian Costellio, 1515–1563: Humanist and Defender of Religious Toleration in a Confessional Age*. Translated and edited by Bruce Gordon. Aldershot: Ashgate, 2003.

Herminjard, Aimé-Louis. *Correspondance des réformateurs dans les pays de langue français*. Geneva: Georg, 1866–97.

Hurlbut, Stephen A. *The Liturgy of the Church of Scotland since the Reformation*. Part 1, *Calvin's Liturgy at Strasbourg and Geneva*. Washington, DC: St. Albans Press, 1944.

Kingdon, Robert M. *Adultery and Divorce in Calvin's Geneva*. Cambridge: Harvard University Press, 1995.

————. "Calvin and the Establishment of Consistory Discipline in Geneva: The Institution and the Men Who Directed It." *Nederlands archief voor kerkgeschiedenis* 70 (1990): 158–72.

————. "Calvin et la constitution Genèvoise." In *Actualité de la réform*, edited by Jean-Marc Chappuis, 209–19. Geneva: Labor & Fides, 1987.

————. "The First Calvinistic Divorce." In *Sin and the Calvinists: Moral Control and the Consistory in the Reformed Tradition*, edited by Raymond Mentzer, 1–13. Kirksville, MO: Sixteenth Century Journal Publishers, 1994.

————, ed. *Registres de la Compagnie des pasteurs de Genéve*. Vol. 1, *Registres de la Compagnie des Pasteurs de Genève au temps de Calvin*. Geneva: Droz, 1964.

Köhler, Walther. *Zürcher Ehegericht und Genfer Konsistorium*. Vol. 2, *Das Ehe- und Sittengericht in den Süddeutschen Reichsstädten, dem Herzogtum Württemberg und Genf*. Leipzig: M. Heinsius Nachfolger, 1942.

Lang, August. "Die Entstehung und der ursprüngliche Sinn der reformierten Gemeindeordnung." In *Reformation und Gegenwart: Gesammelte Aufsätze vornehmlich zur Geschichte und zum Verständnis Calvins und der reformierten Kirche*, 174–91. Detmold: Meyers, 1918.

Monter, E. William. "The Consistory of Geneva." *Bibliotheque d'humanisme et renaissance: Travaux et documents* 38 (1976): 467–84.

Naphy, William G. *Calvin and the Consolidation of the Genevan Reformation*. New York: St. Martin's Press, 1994.

Pfister, Oskar. *Calvins Eingreifen in die Hexer- und Hexenprozesse von Peney, 1545, nach seiner Bedeutung für Geschichte und Gegenwart*. Zurich: Artemis, 1947.

Pfisterer, Ernst. *Calvins Wirken in Genf: Neu gepruft und in Einzelbildern dargestellt*. Neukirchen: Verlag der Buchhandlung des Erziehungsvereins, 1957.

Pidoux, Pierre. *Le psautier huguenot du XVIe siecle: Melodies et documents*. Basel: Baerenreiter, 1962.

Plomp, Johannes. *De kerkelijke tucht bij Calvijn*. Kampen: Kok, 1969.

Reid, J. K. S., ed. *Calvin: Theological Treatises*. Philadelphia: Westminster Press, 1954.

Richter, Aemilius L., ed. *Die evangelischen Kirchenordnungen des sechszehnten Jahrhunderts*. 1846. Reprint, Nieuwcoop: DeGraaf, 1967.

Rieker, Karl. *Grundsätze reformierter Kirchenverfassung.* Tübingen: J. C. B. Mohr, 1907.

Rivoire, Émile, and Victor van Berchem, eds. *Les sources du droit du canton de Genève.* Vol. 2, *De 1461 à 1550.* Arau: Sauländer, 1930.

Veer, M. B. van 't. *Catechese en catechetische stof bij Calvijn.* Kampen: Kok, 1942.

Wallace, Ronald S. *Calvin, Geneva and the Reformation: A Study of Calvin as Social Reformer, Churchman, Pastor, and Theologian.* Grand Rapids: Baker, 1988.

8

Geneva, 1546–1555

Crisis

PIERRE AMEAUX

Already in 1546, it became clear that Calvin's return to Geneva did not mark the end of tensions in the republic. Rather, they came to light in a whole new way. In 1545 in response to the council elections, Calvin wrote to Viret, "I don't know what I should hope for, since under the pretext of Christ they wish to rule without Christ."[1] And at the beginning of 1546, he wrote Viret, "I am a stranger in this city," a complaint that he would repeat many times.[2]

In the same year, a conflict arose with a distinguished citizen, Pierre Ameaux, in which patterns emerged that were typical of the first decade. Ameaux belonged to the Small Council and was the owner of a business that manufactured playing cards, a livelihood that he had to give up in the new situation in Geneva. He had also been involved in a divorce suit because of the scandalous behavior of his wife, caused by a pathological fanaticism: she viewed all children of God as potential husbands. Calvin wanted to allow the divorce after he became aware that she desired him, too, as a potential mate, even though he was married. For a long time, however, the council pressed for a reconciliation between the two spouses. Ameaux could not bring himself to do so, and the divorce was finally settled.

In the meantime, it came to light that in the circle around Ameaux, the magistrates, and especially the consistory under Calvin's leadership, were being strongly criticized (for details, see below). At a meal at which the wine flowed

---

1. CO 12:32.
2. CO 12:251: "Hospes enim sum in hac urbe." Again in 1556: "peregrinus in hac urbe"; CO 16:43.

freely, Ameaux expressed such criticism in a private circle. Even according to Calvin, Ameaux, on this occasion, was not entirely responsible for his actions.[3] Calvin wanted to take a conciliatory posture, so that the judges would not think that he was being spiteful. He made clear his insistence, however, that nothing of the reproaches against him should survive and that the honor of Christ should be preserved. Ameaux had called Calvin a bad man, a mere Picard, and claimed that he preached false doctrine. The first statement especially galled Calvin, but also the charge that his preaching was not sound. Dissension in the council rapidly increased, with some wanting to settle the matter with a simple confession, and others wanting to follow Calvin, who felt supported by the preachers in the orthodoxy of his doctrine. Surrounded by the entire consistory, he pleaded before the council for a form of discipline by which this offense could be removed from the church. Ameaux was sentenced to make a circuit of the city, clad only in his shirt, with a burning torch in hand, and to beseech God, the council, and even Calvin for grace. This deep humiliation led to severe unrest in the part of the city where Ameaux was held in high regard. In the presence of the council, surrounded by a well-armed force, a gallows was erected in front of the church of St. Gervais as a warning. Quiet was restored, but the peace was gone.

Ameaux had voiced his complaints to a private group, but he spoke for many who might have put up with Calvin's teaching if it had been presented less stringently, and especially with fewer consequences for everyday life. Ameaux was advancing an argument that would become steadily louder in the years to come: Calvin was a Picardian who proclaimed a false doctrine. Resonating with this is an undertone of growing resistance to the French nationality of the preachers.

CHALLENGE TO CHURCH AUTHORITY

In 1546 resistance also arose spontaneously from a large group belonging to the old Genevan families. Bound together by blood ties, they formed a coalition against Calvin and the preachers. They refused to bow before the outside authority of the consistory, which they charged with abuse of power. These *enfants de Genève* were also called "patriots." For them, Calvin especially was a foreign intruder, who posed a threat to the freedom of the city. Under the leadership of the Favre family, who worked together with other distinguished representatives of the upper class, they functioned as actual rulers. They disregarded any summons to appear before the consistory, and if they were constrained to appear, they made no attempt to hide their arrogance. They would

3. CO 12:284: ". . . inter coenandum adversum me debacchatus est, ut constet non fuisse tunc mentis compotem."

disturb church services if the preacher did not suit them. They did not observe the official prohibition on dancing, refused to comply with ecclesiastical admonitions about dice and other forbidden games, and adopted a haughty attitude, particularly toward the French preachers.

These people came to be called "Libertines," because they took special liberties with the church's discipline, especially in the loose way in which many of them lived their lives. Their religiosity had little to do with that of the quietist mysticism of the sectarian movement that Calvin attacked in a treatise in 1545, *Contre la secte phantastique des libertins*.[4] Their combined expressions of personal displeasure with the preachers pointed the way to the formation of new party relationships. They called to mind the behavior of the "Epicureans" in Strasbourg, who had declared themselves free from any form of ecclesiastical authority.[5] The boundary lines between the groups were no longer the same as between the earlier "Guillermins" and "Articulants." This is evident from the participation of Ami Perrin in the activities of the Libertines. The last time we heard about Perrin was in September 1540, when he was designated by the Council of Geneva to take steps to secure Calvin's return. Now he belonged to the party that took a disparaging attitude toward the consistory and was not prepared to recognize its authority. Calvin labeled him the "little Caesar" yet tried to remain at peace with him and to maintain a good relationship; but the Favre family, to which Perrin was related through his marriage to Françoise Favre, managed to keep Calvin outside their sphere of influence.

The various problems that arose in 1546 did nothing to help Geneva become a pure Christian city. First, there was the controversy over the staging of a drama based on the Acts of the Apostles. Calvin had taken a look at it, and the play met with his approval.[6] The city council also endorsed it, but some of the preachers objected. Calvin reported this to the council: there was certainly nothing in the play to find fault with, but the production could have some undesirable results. Even Calvin now advised against the performance. The council, however, decided that it could go forward and even granted a subsidy. Michael Cop, an old friend of Calvin's, condemned the actors from the pulpit in the sharpest of terms—so sharply that after the sermon a mob was actually waiting for him with less-than-friendly intentions. He was given protection by the magistracy, which also gave him a warning. Calvin, too, sternly

4. Wulfert de Greef, *The Writings of John Calvin: An Introductory Guide*, trans. Lyle D. Bierma (Grand Rapids: Baker, 1993), 169–71.

5. Marc Lienhard, ed., *Croyants et sceptiques au XVIe siecle: Le dossier des "Epicuriens"* (Strasbourg: Librairie Istra, 1981).

6. William G. Naphy, *Calvin and the Consolidation of the Genevan Reformation* (New York: St. Martin's Press, 1994), 98; Ernst Pfisterer, *Calvins Wirken in Genf: Neu gepruft und in Einzelbildern dargestellt* (Neukirchen: Verlag der Buchhandlung des Erziehungsvereins, 1957), 70f.

reprimanded him. In the afternoon sermon, Calvin tried to set things straight, and on Sunday, July 4, the production was held. Calvin did not attend but did receive a report afterward from Viret, who had been there.[7]

It was clear, however, that the whole affair had not been good for mutual relationships. In the area of drama and art, apparently, the right way was not easy to find. A short while later, the council decided to defer the staging of similar plays to a more suitable time. Some of Calvin's colleagues felt that the interpretation of the gospel should be left to the preachers, but the actors responded that what they were doing was not meant to be an attack against the preachers. In any case, the whole event left a bitter aftertaste.

During this same time period, the Small Council and the Council of Two Hundred decided to close all the taverns, while in each sector of the city an "abbey" was opened under the personal supervision of a member of the high magistracy. This measure was connected with the political situation and provided for the security of the city against spies.[8] The keepers of these eating establishments had to see to it that grace was said at meals. Bibles were also made available, a decision that must be viewed against the background of the cost of books at that time. As it turned out, however, this experiment did not catch on with the people and met with protests by the owners of the taverns. The "abbeys" were closed in June, having existed for only a short time. Obviously, other measures were necessary to strengthen ties between the church and the young people.

BAPTISMAL NAMES

A matter that occupied people's minds for a long time and caused considerable damage to the gospel was the naming of children at baptism.[9] On August 30, Calvin urged the magistracy to decide about names that were ineligible at the administration of baptism. The occasion for this was an incident where a father had presented his child for baptism and wished to give him the name Claude, but the presiding minister had forbidden that name and, on his own authority, chose to name him Abraham instead. The man protested to the council after registering his complaint with the consistory.

Calvin asked for a list of forbidden names. His opponents managed to keep the matter off the table for three months, but a decision was finally reached on November 22. Any names that evoked the saints of Geneva's past were vetoed.

7. CO 12:356.
8. Pfisterer, *Calvins Wirken*, 78f.
9. Naphy, *Calvin and the Consolidation*, 144–53; CO 10:49f.; *Registres de la compagnie des pasteurs de Genève*, ed. Olivier Fatio, vol. 1, *1546–1553*, ed. Jean-François Bergier (Geneva: Droz, 1962), 29.

The name Claude, which was commonly given to both boys and girls, was particularly suspect, because there was a (Catholic) shrine to this saint in the vicinity of Geneva. The preachers wanted to stick closely to Scripture, and they did not hesitate to inform parents at baptism that a name was not suitable.

A nasty spectacle ensued, which provoked fierce reactions. The preachers were of the opinion that a violation on this issue was just as significant as a violation of civil law. Here especially the fact that the ministers of the church were, for the most part, originally from France played a role. This only exacerbated tensions that already existed on other points. Leading members of Genevan society resisted, and as a result the problem of baptismal names now became a matter of family pride, mixed with national consciousness. It contributed substantially to a widening of the gap between church and society. When Michael Cop on May 31 refused to baptize a child by using the name Balthasar, the father in turn took the child back and would not recognize the legitimacy of the baptism. People were no longer going to tolerate this state of affairs: "The foreigners rule everything here!"[10] When the preachers began giving names on their own authority, it led to disturbances that could hardly be controlled. Here, too, an anti-French sentiment became intertwined with the actual question, leading to frequent outbursts in the coming years.

At the same time, the old question of the authority of the consistory and the preachers surfaced again. In March 1547, a conflict arose between Favre and his supporters on the one hand, and the consistory on the other. Favre refused to recognize the authority of the consistory. He was deeply angry for being summoned to appear before them for, among other things, irregularities in baptismal names. The preachers complained that they were being accused by the council of violating the decrees concerning the authority of the consistory.[11] They sent wrongdoers who showed no signs of repentance to the magistracy, and if such individuals persisted in their sin, the consistory expected the magistracy once again to place them at the disposal of the consistory, so that they could finally treat them according to the provisions of church discipline. This, according to the consistory, was in accordance with the order of the church and the will of God. The preachers insisted that in the presence of the consistory, Favre be admonished by the magistracy to reconcile with them. Calvin appeared before the council and urged them to act against Favre and his family. But on March 31 the council announced that peace had to be sought in an amicable way. Favre was indeed sent back to the consistory, but the latter was ordered to say nothing more than "good admonitions, in agreement with the Word of God."[12]

10. Naphy, *Calvin and the Consolidation*, 148.
11. CO 22:399.
12. CO 22:402; Naphy, *Calvin and the Consolidation*, 147.

TENSIONS AND THREATS

The early summer of 1547 was filled with tension. In June, Calvin wrote to Viret that a fierce battle was being waged against the consistory. They had summoned Françoise Perrin, daughter of Favre and wife of the "comical Caesar," in connection with her attendance at a dance party, while her husband was in France on a private diplomatic mission. In her appearance before the consistory, she called one of the preachers a lying swine. She was ousted from the consistory by force and later withdrew to her country estate outside Geneva. On the journey there, she once again grossly misbehaved toward the same preacher. This whole incident only aggravated further Calvin's relationship with the Libertines.

During this time, a document was found on the pulpit threatening the pastors with death if they did not make adjustments in their preaching. The council ordered a thorough investigation and discovered that Jacques Gruet, a former monk, was the author. Letters and notes were found in his house with Calvin's name in them. In the interrogation that followed, Gruet at first denied any involvement with the pamphlet in the pulpit. However, when he was threatened with torture and it was actually carried out, he revealed that in the circle around Favre a bitter aversion to the French foreigners was developing, which could lead to revolt. Favre allegedly said that the children of Geneva were letting themselves be ruled by the preachers. If they were allowed to do as they pleased, they would become exactly like the bishops that preceded them. And if the bishops had done this in their day, they would not have been tolerated. The day would come when the preachers would no longer rule the roost. People should watch out that the foreigners not usurp complete control over the citizens.[13]

Gruet was condemned to death and was executed on July 26, 1547. In 1550 documents were found in his residence that led to a new trial, but the verdict was no different: blasphemy against God and his holy Word, and threats against the magistracy and the ministers—in short, defamation of the government deserving of capital punishment. As later with Bolsec and Servetus, this trial was one of those cases with which Calvin's name was associated. It is clear, however, that Calvin was not directly involved until the discovery of a certain book in Gruet's former house in 1550. The book was burned. Calvin's assessment of the case indicates that Gruet was viewed not only as a danger to the republic but above all as a threat to the Christian religion itself. It is clear from Calvin's letters that he had followed the case from a distance. For him, it was

---

13. CO 12:563–68; Naphy, *Calvin and the Consolidation*, 103f.; Émile Doumergue, *Jean Calvin: Les hommes et les choses de son temps*, vol. 6, *La lutte* (Lausanne: G. Bridel, 1926), 120–30.

an indication that a substantial number of the citizens of Geneva perceived his actions and those of the consistory with very mixed feelings.

The opposition organized itself under the leadership of Ami Perrin, who had returned from France in 1547. At the French court, as part of an anti-Hapsburg policy but on his own authority, Perrin had had himself appointed the commander of a contingent of soldiers that would be quartered in Geneva at France's expense. When this came to light, it also emerged that a wealthy French refugee, Laurens Maigret, who had been living in Geneva since the 1530s and enjoyed the trust of the senate and the preachers alike, had been secretly communicating with the French court. He, too, was seeking a coalition with France against the emperor, who had recently gained a victory over the evangelical princes in Germany. In Geneva, this led to a struggle, which was exacerbated especially by suspicion on the part of Bern, which saw an alliance with France as a threat to its confederation with Geneva. In December 1547, it produced a bloody altercation in the Council of Two Hundred, which Calvin managed to quell by stepping between the warring parties.

Compared with the real antagonism between the parties, this was only a minor incident. The main issue was still the authority of the church in the punishment of moral offenses.[14] It is worth noting that the magistracy, even during the years that the group around Perrin held a majority, stood behind Calvin when it came to doctrinal views—even to the point of sanctioning his particular views as the official position of the city. It thus became clear that the confrontation between the parties primarily involved not *doctrina* but *disciplina*. For Calvin, the two were inextricably bound together. For the "children of Geneva," however, that was not the case.

HIERONYMUS BOLSEC

In October 1551, Hieronymus (Jerome) Bolsec was imprisoned for publicly attacking Calvin's doctrine of predestination. Originally from France, Bolsec had set up a medical practice in the area around Geneva. His great interest in theology could be seen from the fact that he regularly attended the public meetings of the *Compagnie des pasteurs*. Calvin's teaching captivated him, with the exception of his view of double predestination. Bolsec had already discussed this doctrine with Calvin earlier but had not been satisfied. On October 16, he challenged Calvin's views at a meeting of the preachers. Farel tried to respond to him since Calvin himself had not yet arrived. Bolsec then also

14. August Lang, *Johannes Calvin: Ein Lebensbild zu seinem 400. Geburtstag am 10. Juli 1909* (Leipzig: Verein für Reformationsgeschichte, 1909), 128; Doumergue, *Jean Calvin*, 6:114ff.

attacked the preachers, who held the same view as Calvin. Calvin slipped into the meeting unnoticed and witnessed a vehement public protest against a concept close to his heart. When Bolsec was finished, Calvin rose to his feet and, with references to Scripture and Augustine, refuted the accusations by Bolsec, who had concluded that Calvin made God out to be the author of sin. Calvin charged Bolsec with reversing the order of election by placing it after faith and thereby putting faith itself under human control.[15]

Bolsec was imprisoned by a representative of the magistracy, who interrogated him with the help of a number of questions prepared by the preachers. Bolsec disputed the legality of an investigation that was not instigated by the civil authority. The latter judged that the question was a difficult one and wanted advice from the churches in Zurich, Basel, and Bern. The answers from these Reformed churches were not wholly favorable to Calvin. Zurich encouraged moderation, and Basel characterized Bolsec as a heretical sophist, something that, in Calvin's view, did not go far enough. Bern could not imagine that Geneva would tolerate different doctrinal viewpoints, but it also stated that the doctrine of predestination was not milk for children but solid food for adults. Hence the Genevans should curb their belligerency.[16]

In letters to his friends, Calvin complained about what seemed to him like a lax position that the neighboring churches were taking. In the advice that arrived, however, the magistracy found sufficient grounds to sentence Bolsec to banishment for life. He left the city and stayed for some time in the territory of Bern, until he was also driven away from there. Returning to France, he rejoined the Roman Catholic Church. In his biographies of Calvin and Beza, he offered ample material from which people could draw to place the reformers of Geneva under suspicion of lying and deceit.[17]

In a subsequent *congrégation* (Bible study meeting), Calvin once again gave a detailed explanation of his views, to which his colleagues completely assented.[18] Bolsec was then found guilty by the magistracy, which declared that the question was not an easy one and that they certainly had little understanding of the arguments advanced by Bolsec. Nevertheless, they deferred to the preachers as theological experts. The case, however, was not adjudicated before the consistory. Bolsec was apparently viewed as a violator of the laws of

15. "Car renversant l'ordre de la Predestination ou election de Dieu, et la mettant apres la foy, il faisoit que la foy estoit en la puissance d'un chacun, et par ce moyen chacun se baillant la foy à soymesme, ne devoit faire difficulté d'estimer qu'il obtiendroit salut, encore que sa vie fust remplie d'impietez et toutes ordures"; CO 8:90.

16. Doumergue, *Jean Calvin*, 6:152ff.

17. *Histoire de la vie, moeurs, actes, doctrine, constance et mort de Jean Calvin* (1577); *Histoire de la vie, moeurs, doctrine et deportemonts de Théodore de Bèze* (1582).

18. *Congrégation faite en l'église de Genève* (1551), in CO 8:85–138.

Geneva, and on that basis he was convicted and banished on the authority of the civil government.

JEAN TROLLIET

A second case in which the magistracy supported the preachers on a matter of doctrine was that of Jean Trolliet.[19] He had been a monk in Burgundy, where he joined the Reformation. Returning to Geneva, he expressed a desire to serve as a preacher. Calvin prevented this, and an estrangement developed that became even greater when Trolliet, appointed as a notary for the magistracy, made public a letter that Calvin had written to Viret. When called to account, Calvin had trouble explaining the expressions he had used for the Genevan magistracy in this letter, and ever since then he numbered Trolliet among his avowed opponents.

Trolliet had played a questionable role in the case of Ameaux against Calvin, and in June 1552, less than a year after the banishment of Bolsec, he registered a complaint with the magistracy about Calvin's preaching.[20] In the discussions that followed, what came up most often was Calvin's doctrine of predestination. Trolliet declared that this doctrine, as found in the *Institutes*, made God out to be the author of sin. Calvin defended himself in a note to the council.[21] As had often happened earlier, he asked Farel and Viret to come to Geneva to assist him. Farel called upon the council to give Calvin the opportunity to carry out his ministry in the congregation in good faith and with a pure heart. Calvin himself objected to administering the Lord's Supper under these circumstances and declared that he would rather be released from his office than to continually have to suffer this way.

The case dragged along until in August it was decided to read the relevant passages from the *Institutes* in a meeting of the council itself. In November, Farel and Viret urged the council to bring the matter to an end, and on November 9 the council officially declared that Calvin's *Institutes* had been written in a good and holy manner and that its doctrine was the holy doctrine of God. The council also stated that Calvin was a good and true minister of the city and that from that moment on, no one should dare to say anything against the book or its intended doctrine. Everyone should adhere to it. Trolliet backed off, indicating that he was satisfied and recognized his mistake. He confessed that he had not understood the matter well and was ready to shake Calvin's hand.

---

19. Doumergue, *Jean Calvin*, 6:162–69.
20. CO 14:371–77, 383.
21. CO 14:378–83, 384f.

This decision of the council had far-reaching significance, for Calvin's doctrine had now become the official doctrine of Geneva, to which people in the future also had to adhere. This pronouncement also guaranteed a unified understanding of doctrine within the Genevan church. This did not mean, however, that Calvin overlooked the variety that had emerged within the broader Reformation movement. In his defense before the council, Trolliet had also appealed to Melanchthon's *Loci communes*, which Calvin had translated into French in 1546. Calvin looked upon Melanchthon as a man of great learning but as one who did not like to involve himself in hairsplitting debates because the primary focus ought to be on the edification of the church.[22] Perhaps he could have said more about free will and predestination and done so more definitively. But Melanchthon taught clearly enough that the spiritual benefit that we need for salvation must be ascribed entirely to the grace of God. So far as predestination was concerned, Calvin asked that people try to understand Melanchthon's point of view. Because there were too many unstable spirits who knew no moderation on this issue and let themselves be driven by curiosity, Melanchthon, afraid of pointless disputes, had limited himself to what was necessary to know. Calvin went further: "I confess that of everything that it pleased God to reveal to us in Scripture, nothing may ignored, whatever the consequences might be." At the same time, he defended Melanchthon: "Since his goal is education for the profit of his readers, he deserves to be excused if he sticks to that which he deems most appropriate, while easily passing over or leaving alone that from which he does not expect much gain."[23]

When Trolliet tried to drive a wedge between Calvin and Melanchthon, Calvin reminded the magistracy of the long-standing friendship that the two had kept up. Trolliet, therefore, was doing an injustice to them both and even more generally to the church of God as a whole. "I value Melanchthon as much for the outstanding knowledge he possesses as for his good qualities, and above all because he labors faithfully to preserve the gospel. Whenever I find fault with him, I do not hide it from him, since he has given me the freedom to do so."[24]

Calvin assured the magistracy that he was convinced in his conscience that what he had taught and written had not sprouted out of his own brain but had been received from God. "I must insist on that if I do not want the truth to be denied." Thus Calvin tried to combine the unity of the preaching in Geneva, which rested on his firm conviction that it was in agreement with Scripture and therefore also according to the will of God, with an unmistakable openness to less rigid formulations when the unity of the Reformation movement

22. CO 9:848.
23. CO 9:849.
24. CO 14:382.

itself, in all its rich variety, was not at stake. That is why Calvin's friendship with Melanchthon did not come under pressure.

MICHAEL SERVETUS

A doctrinal case of a wholly different sort revolved around Michael Servetus (1553). From the very beginning, this case had hanging over it a sentence that Calvin had pronounced on Servetus in a letter to Farel. "He would like to come here if I would agree. But I cannot at all guarantee his safety. For if he should come, I will never allow him to depart alive, if my authority means anything."[25] The reasons for this harsh statement were, first, Calvin's conviction that there was no way to carry on a rational discussion with Servetus, but more important was Calvin's sense that at issue here was the very essence of the Christian faith. Calvin had carried on some correspondence with Servetus,[26] in which he encountered an inflexibility that he could only explain as an arrogance in Servetus. In this exchange, Servetus spoke of the Trinity of Father, Son, and Holy Spirit as a "three-headed Cerberus."

Oecolampadius and Bucer had similar feelings about Servetus. Oecolampadius had been able to form a judgment about him when for ten months in 1530–31 Servetus had stayed at his home. There Servetus was able to acquaint himself with the editions of the church fathers that were being published in Basel. Oecolampadius regarded Servetus as a man of violent and stubborn temperament, who disseminated outrageous opinions.[27] Servetus no longer felt safe in Basel when, after the union with the Reformation in 1529, strict provisions were adopted against Anabaptists, scorners of the sacraments, and those who denied the deity of Christ. He thought he would find a better reception in Strasbourg. However, his book *De trinitatis erroribus* (1531) encountered stiff opposition, and he had to leave Strasbourg after Bucer refuted him in a public lecture.[28]

In 1534 Servetus had an appointment to meet with Calvin, but he never showed up, something that Calvin would not soon forget. Servetus later devoted himself to medical studies, published astrological treatises, and also did research on the pre-Nicene fathers. He became thoroughly versed in rabbinic and cabalistic literature and arrived at an overall conception of the Christian faith, which met with considerable opposition in the correspondence with Calvin. He reproduced a summary of his views in the *Christianismi restitutio*,

---

25. Letter from Calvin to Farel, February 13, 1546, in CO 12:283.
26. For Servetus's letters to Calvin, thirty in all, see CO 8:649–714.
27. Ernst Staehelin, *Das theologische Lebenswerk Johannes Oekolampads* (1939; repr., New York: Johnson, 1971), 535–39.
28. Hastings Eells, *Martin Bucer* (New Haven: Yale University Press, 1931), 132f.

which appeared in 1553 from a publisher in Vienne whose name (Balthasar Arnoullet), like that of the author, was carefully kept hidden.

Of the one thousand copies that were printed, a few turned up in Geneva, one in the hands of a friend of Calvin's. This friend, Guillaume de Trie, was called to account by a cousin in Lyon about the low moral state of the Reformed city, so he replied that people must not be aware of the kind of great heretic that could live in Vienne with impunity. When de Trie was asked how he could prove this, he inquired of Calvin whether he might use the letters as evidence, along with a copy of Calvin's *Institutes* containing opprobrious marginal notations by Servetus. Since Servetus had received the book from Calvin and then sent it back, his identity could be established from both the book and the letters. De Trie wrote to his cousin, "I can assure you that it was not easy getting from Calvin what I am sending you—not because he wants such execrable blasphemies to go unreproved, but because he regards it as his duty to convict heretics by doctrine rather than by other means, for he does not bear the sword of justice." That Calvin agreed to have the letters sent to Lyon can be explained by the fact that, for him, the reputation of the reformation in Geneva was at stake. Calvin later denied that it was by his doing that Servetus was imprisoned in Vienne.[29] Servetus was interrogated by the (Roman Catholic) Inquisition in Vienne, and on June 17, 1553, on the basis of material made available by Calvin, among others, he was sentenced to death. He managed to save himself by escaping, however, and was executed in effigy.

CALVIN'S ROLE IN THE CONVICTION OF SERVETUS

Servetus showed up in Geneva on August 13, 1553, and was recognized during a worship service by a few brothers from Lyon, who informed Calvin. He in turn reported it to the magistracy, and Servetus was imprisoned. According to the *Carolina*,[30] the penal code established by Charles V, Calvin as the accuser was supposed to be confined with the accused. His secretary, Nicolas de la Fontaine, however, was put under lock and key in Calvin's place until the public prosecutor took over the case on August 24. Calvin now functioned as a theological expert: as in the Bolsec case, he formulated questions and gave advice and theological assistance to the council.

---

29. Roland H. Bainton, *Hunted Heretic: The Life and Death of Michael Servetus, 1511–1553* (Boston: Beacon, 1953), 157: "Calvin's words have been construed as strictly true in the sense that he had exchanged no letters of his own with the inquisitors, but this is only to save him from a lie by making him guilty of a subterfuge."

30. The *Constitutio criminalis Carolina* (1532).

This case was not explicitly about specific Reformation doctrines. Even the council was convinced that at issue here was the essence of the Christian faith. For as long as the civil code of Justinian had been in effect, confession of the Trinity had been an essential point of the Christian faith. Whoever deviated from that was considered to be an enemy of society itself. Servetus's denial of the Trinity went so far that he branded Trinitarians as atheists.

The council decided to conduct an investigation in Vienne into the grounds for his arrest, and also to seek the advice of the Swiss churches once the records of the interrogation had been sent to them. In a letter to Bullinger, Calvin explained this measure by the fact that the magistracy did not trust him: "Our council members have gone so far in their folly and rage that everything that we say to them seems suspicious. If I were to say, for example, that it is light in the afternoon, they would begin to doubt even that."[31] There was indeed a deep distrust of Calvin, but there is no evidence that the Libertines, who at this time held a solid majority in the council, wished to conspire against Calvin in the case of Servetus.[32]

Nor can it be asserted that Calvin alone was responsible for Servetus's death. It was the magistracy on its own authority, in accordance with the advice obtained from the evangelical churches in Switzerland, that pronounced sentence on Servetus.[33] The magistracy of Bern declared that Servetus was an archheretic, a plague upon the churches. The ministers of Bern communicated that without a doubt Servetus would have been burned in their city if the trial had been held there.[34] Zurich indicated that Servetus should be dealt with firmly, since the Swiss churches already had the reputation of being heretics and favoring heretics. According to Basel, Servetus was worse than every heretic who had ever lived. In their eyes, blasphemy was more deplorable than any other offense. One should try to restore Servetus, but if that did not work, by the authority that God had bestowed upon the magistracy of Geneva, he would have to be punished in such a way that he could no longer damage the church of Christ.

On the advice of these reports from the neighboring cities, the magistracy reached its verdict on October 26, 1553, and Servetus died the following day at the stake. Farel accompanied him on the way there. Through a combina-

---

31. Letter from Calvin to Bullinger, in CO 14:611.
32. However, see the letter from Musculus to Bullinger, in CO 14:628: "Servetus . . . nuper Genevam venit, abusurus invidia, qua magnates illic Calvinum prosequuntur. Speravit se illic sedem invenire posse, unde et reliquis ecclesiis negotium favere posset." See also Doumergue, *Jean Calvin*, 6:320; and Bainton, *Hunted Heretic*, 168–81.
33. For the responses of the magistracy and church in Zurich, Schaffhausen, Bern, and Basel, see CO 8:808–24.
34. Letter from Haller to Bullinger, in CO 14:647.

tion of circumstances, it was a particularly painful death. Calvin had pleaded in vain for an execution by beheading, but the council stayed with its sentence, which made reference especially to the blasphemy of the Trinity and the denial of infant baptism. It was conscious of its authority to preserve true Christians and believing young people in the untainted Christian religion.[35]

Servetus, therefore, was not condemned on Calvin's authority; the government bore full legal responsibility. As already mentioned, Calvin did write Farel in early 1546 that if it were up to him, Servetus would not leave the city alive, at least if he had any authority at his disposal.[36] But Servetus's burning at the stake cannot be attributed to Calvin's authority. It was the result of the magistracy's view that the fundamentals of the Christian faith, and Christian society itself, were under attack.

Nevertheless, there is still much that betrays uncertainty in Calvin's position. His friend de Trie, who had sent Servetus's letters to Vienne, reported that it was only with difficulty that he had been able to obtain them from Calvin because Calvin thought that heretics should be convicted with arguments and that he himself did not bear the power of the sword. But once Servetus made the inexplicable decision to show up in Geneva, Calvin seized the opportunity to accuse him before the authorities, even though he must have known that Servetus was only passing through. Their personal relationship had already been ruined years before. Servetus's arrogant behavior, first in the correspondence and then during the interrogation in Geneva, irritated Calvin to no end. Servetus regarded him as a Simon Magus, whereas Calvin had to struggle hard to defend himself on many sides as a prophet who was merely obediently fulfilling his calling and neither would nor could depart from it. Servetus was a man who, in exaggerated apocalyptic expectations, probably anticipated the end of all things in his lifetime, whereas Calvin was hard at work establishing the kingdom of God in this city. The confrontation between these two men could lead only to a clash, a clash between two worlds.

The sentence won the approval of practically all the leading figures of the day. Bullinger in Zurich, Haller in Bern, and Melanchthon in Wittenberg all concurred with the execution of Servetus.[37] Calvin provided an account of his involvement in the Servetus case in his *Defensio orthodoxae fidei de sacra trinitate*

35. Bainton, *Hunted Heretic*, 207–9.
36. CO 12:283.
37. Bullinger (CO 14:621): "Haereticos, qui vere sunt pertinaces haeretici, gladio iustitiae persequi"; Haller (CO 14:627): "Haereticissimus est homo, et dignus quo exoneretur ecclesia"; Melanchthon (CO 15:268): "Affirmo etiam vestros magistratus iuste fecisse, quod hominem blasphemum re ordine iudicata interfecerunt."

(1554).[38] There he argues that heretics must be suppressed with the sword. He defends the conviction and execution of Servetus and champions the confession that, he is deeply convinced, lies at the heart of the Christian religion, thereby giving expression only to what all of Christendom confesses as truth. This view, however, was not shared by everyone, and certainly the religious persecution that began to grip France and the southern Netherlands was opposed by many.

On May 16, 1553, five evangelical theologians were executed in Lyon, at the very time that religious persecution was raging in France and Flanders. In response to the events in Geneva, Castellio published a treatise that would earn him a reputation as an advocate of toleration: *De haereticis an sint persequendi* (1554), a work that was quickly translated into German and French.[39] Castellio sharply attacked the killing of heretics. He did indicate later on, however, that he had not read Servetus's writings. According to him, Calvin had portrayed Servetus as a monster and a godless man or atheist, and he, too, would not wish to defend such a person. He also was of the opinion that anyone who would abandon God ought to disappear.[40]

In 1566 the anti-Trinitarian Valentin Gentilis was executed with the sword in Bern. It would still be centuries before the notion prevailed that it is not the government's role to make judgments about religious expressions. Calvin had entrusted this task to the government in the case of Servetus, and the government accepted it, more than it wanted to. The consistory was kept out of the process, thereby enabling the magistracy to operate on its own authority and to reduce Calvin's control. The conviction of Servetus was not in the least a victory for Calvin. Rather, it signified a confirmation of the authority of the government. Indeed, at this very time Calvin was contemplating leaving Geneva; the prospect led Bullinger, whom friends had informed of Calvin's thoughts, to write an encouraging letter, urging him to stay in Geneva. His argument is striking: Calvin's departure would play into the hands of the despisers of Christ in France, and he would be exposing the French exiles in Geneva to great dangers. "Stay, therefore. Stay, and suffer all the scoffing, contempt, danger, and evil that the Lord allows to come upon you. The Lord will not forsake you!"[41]

---

38. CO 8:453–644.

39. Hans R. Guggisberg, *Sebastian Castellio, 1515–1563: Humanist und Verteidiger der religiösen Toleranz im konfessionellen Zeitalter* (Göttingen: Vandenhoeck & Ruprecht, 1997), 80–106; Étienne Giran, *Sébastien Castellion et la Réforme calviniste: Les deux réformes* (1914; repr., Geneva: Slatkine, 1970); Uwe Plath, *Calvin und Basel im den Jahren 1552–1556* (Zurich: Theologischer Verlag, 1974); Joseph Leclerc, *Geschichte der Religionsfreiheit in Zeitalter der Reformation* (Stuttgart: Schwabenverlag, 1965), 1:447–95. Beza wrote a defense of Calvin entitled *De haereticis a civili Magistratru puniendis Libellus, adversus Martini Bellii farraginem, et novorum Academicorum sectam* (1554).

40. Pfisterer, *Calvins Wirken*, 45; *TRE*, s.v. "Calvin."

41. CO 14:621.

CONTROVERSY OVER THE INDEPENDENT
AUTHORITY OF THE CHURCH

Actually, the suit against Servetus was playing out at the same time that tensions between church and state were reaching a critical point. Calvin's toying with the idea of leaving Geneva was related to his conviction that his work of Christianizing the city was not bearing any fruit. In 1549, at Calvin's urging, the council had issued a proclamation in the churches, calling upon everyone to abide by the regulations of God's law. Even the preachers were admonished to remain faithful in their teaching and exposing of faults.[42]

On the matter of church discipline as an effective means of combating sins and shortcomings, however, tension between the magistracy and the consistory continued to exist. On more than one occasion, Calvin was called upon to be more moderate in his preaching,[43] a means that he was using to propagate his belief about church discipline. Philibert Berthelier had been excommunicated by the consistory, but he refused to recognize that authority and appealed to the Small Council to be freed of the ecclesiastical ban.[44] When the council granted him permission to attend the Lord's Supper, Calvin let them know that he would resist this. On Sunday, September 3, 1553, he declared from the pulpit that he would administer the sacrament according to the prescription of his Master. This meant that he would refuse to serve the elements to those to whom this had been forbidden by the consistory. The council had, in the meantime, already decided to secretly urge Berthelier not to participate in the Lord's Supper. That afternoon Calvin preached from Acts 20:18ff., with the idea in mind that this would be his last sermon in Geneva. He quoted the words of farewell by the apostle Paul, "Now I commit you to God and to the word of his grace" (Acts 20:32 NIV).[45] The following day Calvin appeared before the council, and a debate arose about the interpretation of the provisions of the *Ordonnances*, the copies of which did not have identical texts. On September 7, the preachers attended the meeting of the council without Calvin and insisted that they would choose death or banishment over the desecration of the sacrament. The Berthelier matter continued to drag on for another year, even though it sometimes appeared that peace had been restored. In a meeting of the consistory on March 20, 1554, however, Berthelier declared that there were no other lords in the city than those of the magistracy.[46]

<hr>

42. CO 13:158–60; *Registres de la compagnie des pasteurs*, 1:45f.
43. Richard Stauffer, "Les discours à la première personne dans les sermons de Calvin," in *Regards contemporains sur Jean Calvin: Actes du Colloque Calvin, Strasbourg 1964* (Paris: Presses universitaire de France, 1965), 216f.
44. CO 21:512ff.
45. Stauffer, "Les discours," 218; CO 21:551f.
46. CO 21:571.

As had happened in the case of Servetus, the council finally asked the advice of the other Swiss churches about how discipline should work.[47] Calvin informed Bullinger of the problem in a personal letter, summarizing his ideas once again to make it perfectly clear.[48] On October 25, the letters from Bern, Basel, and Zurich were read.[49] Zurich encouraged Geneva to stay with the established order, because a change would require a lot of time and would create more turmoil than peace. Zurich also sent a copy of the order being used there, with the observation that in each area the government had its own authority.[50] Bern wrote that excommunication there was practiced in a way wholly different than in Geneva.[51] From this terse response, it is clear that Bern and Geneva at that time were not on the best of terms. Basel sent its own documents related to church discipline, without choosing sides.[52]

On December 31, Calvin urged the council to make a decision on the basis of the advice it had received. A small committee made preparations for the discussion of the matter in the Council of Two Hundred. Things seemed to have taken a turn already on October 25, 1554, when Berthelier was instructed to reconcile with the consistory and thus create a climate in which he could live with them in peace.[53] Three months later, on January 24, 1555, a large majority of the Councils of Sixty and Two Hundred decided that the decisions made in the past by the General Council should remain in place.

In this meeting, Calvin managed, on behalf of the consistory, to demonstrate his authority "with passages from Holy Scripture and from the practice that had always been followed in the church, regardless of its purity." He explained the proper use of excommunication and who had the right to excommunicate individuals and receive them back into the community of the church. According to the *Registres*, in this meeting the first syndic (*le premier Sindicque*) declared to the pastors that God had won the victory.[54] This was a strong statement for a member of the magistracy: the position of the consistory remained as originally intended. This was the beginning of a turnaround in the relationship between the magistracy and the consistory. The latter would now be able to exercise its "normal" authority "in accordance with the Word of God and as the church orders established earlier had required."[55]

47. CO 14:685f.

48. CO 14:678–82.

49. Walther Köhler, *Zürcher Ehegericht und Genfer Konsistorium*, vol. 2, *Das Ehe- und Sittengericht in den Süddeutschen Reichsstädten, den Herzogtum Württemberg und in Genf* (Leipzig: Heinsius, 1942), 2:610.

50. CO 14:699f.

51. CO 14:691.

52. Plath, *Calvin und Basel*, 94–111; CO 14:722.

53. CO 21:588.

54. *Registres de la compagnie des pasteurs*, 2:59.

55. Ibid.

The decision was taken with a large majority.[56] Calvin wrote to Bullinger, "Recently, after a long struggle, the right of excommunication was finally confirmed for us."[57] Calvin's interpretation of the *Ordonnances* was thereby legitimated, and this interpretation would hold sway in Geneva from now on. The city would soon learn that the climate had changed. In the very next elections, Calvin's supporters gained a majority in the council, and one of the first decisions made by this council stipulated that, in the future, men and women should sit separately in the church services.[58]

OUSTER OF THE LIBERTINES

When it became clear that the Libertines had lost their majority, it was not long before conflicts between the "children of Geneva" and the refugees from France intensified. Refugees received the opportunity to purchase citizenship, and the supporters of Perrin, who had a very powerful position as captain-general, tried with all their might to change this course of events.[59] Within a few months, the number of citizens had been augmented with persons of rank and station, educated and financially well-to-do asylum seekers, whom the original inhabitants looked upon as foreigners. Perrin resisted when refugees took the place of his followers, who were kept out of influential positions.

During these months, the rumor circulated that the recent arrivals were operating as a kind of fifth column, working with Savoy on behalf of France to take over power. In the background was Bern, playing a role that was not always even clear. Rumors of an imminent coup by the French sympathizers were used by Perrin and his friends, among them Berthelier, to make a grab for power at the beginning of a riot on May 16, 1555. In all the jostling, Perrin tried to snatch the baton of office from one of the syndics, who acted to prevent any bloodshed. The magistracy viewed this move as high treason, and Perrin and a few of his friends managed to escape and settle in the territory of Bern, outside the reach of Geneva. He and the others were sentenced to death *in absentia*. Four participants were put to death in the city after their confessions had been obtained under torture. On the scaffold, however, they recanted and died as faithful citizens of the city.

Perrin had brought Calvin back to Geneva in 1541. With Perrin and his followers gone, the city would finally become an example of what Calvin had

56. CO 14:594.
57. CO 15:449.
58. CO 14:595.
59. Abraham Ruchat, *Histoire de la réformation de la Suisse* (Nyon: Giral-Prelaz, 1835–38), 6:133–41; Doumergue, *Jean Calvin*, 7:26–49.

long envisioned, for he now had the opportunity to focus completely on the rule of Christ and his Word.

CHAPTER BIBLIOGRAPHY

Bainton, Roland H. *Hunted Heretic.* Boston: Beacon Press, 1953; GT, *Michael Servet: 1511–1553.* Gütersloh: G. Mohn, 1960.

Collins, Ross W. *Calvin and the Libertines of Geneva.* Edited by F. D. Blackly. Toronto: Clarke, Irwin & Company, 1968.

Cornelius, Carl A. *Die ersten Jahre der Kirche Calvins: 1541–46.* Munich: G. Franz, 1896.

Doumergue, Émile. *Jean Calvin: Les hommes et les choses de son temps.* Vol. 6, *La lutte.* Lausanne: G. Bridel, 1926.

Eells, Hastings. *Martin Bucer.* New Haven: Yale University Press, 1931.

Giran, Étienne. *Sébastien Castellion et la réforme calviniste: Les deux réformes.* 1914. Reprint, Geneva: Slatkine, 1970.

Greef, Wulfert de. *The Writings of John Calvin: An Introductory Guide.* Translated by Lyle D. Bierma. Grand Rapids: Baker, 1993.

Guggisberg, Hans R. *Sebastian Castellio, 1515–1563: Humanist und Verteidiger der religiösen Toleranz im konfessionellen Zeitalter.* Göttingen: Vandenhoeck & Ruprecht, 1997. ET, *Sebastian Castellio, 1515–1563: Humanist and Defender of Religious Toleration in a Confessional Age.* Translated and edited by Bruce Gordon. Aldershot: Ashgate, 2003.

Holtrop, Philip C. *The Bolsec Controversy on Predestination, from 1551 to 1555: The Statements of Jerome Bolsec, and the Responses of John Calvin, Theodore Beza, and Other Reformed Theologians.* Lewiston: E. Mellen, 1993.

Kingdon, Robert M. *Adultery and Divorce in Calvin's Geneva.* Cambridge: Harvard University Press, 1995.

Kingdon, Robert M., and Jean-François Bergier, eds. *Registres de la Compagnie des Pasteurs de Genève au temps de Calvin.* Vol. 1, *1546–1553.* Geneva: Droz, 1964.

———. *Registres de la Compagnie des Pasteurs de Genève au temps de Calvin.* Vol. 2, *1553–1564.* Geneva: Droz, 1962.

Köhler, Walther. *Zürcher Ehegericht und Genfer Konsistorium.* Vol. 2, *Das Ehe- und Sittengericht in den Süddeutschen Reichsstädten, den Herzogtum Württemberg und in Genf.* Leipzig: Heinsius, 1942.

Lang, August. *Johannes Calvin: Ein Lebensbild zu seinem 400. Geburtstag am 10. Juli 1909.* Leipzig: Verein für Reformationsgeschichte, 1909.

———. "Melanchthon und Calvin." In *Reformation und Gegenwart: Gesammelte Aufsätze vornehmlich zur Geschichte und zum Verständnis Calvins und der reformierten Kirche,* 88–135. Detmold: Meyers, 1918.

Leclerc, Joseph. *Geschichte der Religionsfreiheit im Zeitalter der Reformation.* Stuttgart: Schwabenverlag, 1965.

Lienhard, Marc, ed. *Croyants et sceptiques au XVIe siecle: Le dossier des "Epicuriens."* Strasbourg: Librairie Istra, 1981.

Naphy, William G. "Baptisms, Church Riots and Social Unrest in Calvin's Geneva." *Sixteenth Century Journal* 26, no. 1 (1995): 86–97.

———. *Calvin and the Consolidation of the Genevan Reformation.* New York: St. Martin's Press, 1994.

————. "The Renovation of the Ministry in Calvin's Geneva." In *The Reformation of the Parishes: The Ministry and the Reformation in Town and Country*, edited by Andrew Pettegree, 112–32. New York: St. Martin's Press, 1993.

Pfeilschifter, Frank. *Das Calvinbild bei Bolsec und sein Fortwirken im französischen Katholizismus bis ins 20. Jahrhundert.* Augsburg: FDL-Verlag, 1983.

Pfisterer, Ernst. *Calvins Wirken in Genf: Neu geprüft und in Einzelbildern dargestellt.* Neukirchen: Verlag der Buchhandlung des Erziehungsvereins, 1957.

Plath, Uwe. *Calvin und Basel im den Jahren 1552–1556.* Zurich: Theologischer Verlag, 1974.

Ruchat, Abraham. *Histoire de la réformation de la Suisse.* 7 vols. Nyon: Giral-Prelaz, 1835–38.

Seeger, Cornelia. *Nullité de marriage, divorce et separation de corps à Genève, au temps de Calvin: Fondements doctrinaux, loi et jurisprudence.* Lausanne: Société d'histoire de la Suisse romande, 1989.

Staehelin, Ernst. *Das theologische Lebenswerk Johannes Oekolampads.* New York: Johnson, 1971.

Stauffer, Richard. "Les discours à la première personne dans les sermons de Calvin." In *Regards contemporains sur Jean Calvin: Actes du Colloque Calvin, Strasbourg 1964*, 206–38. Paris: Presses universitaire de France, 1965.

9

Geneva, 1555–1564

Consolidation

RELATIONSHIP WITH BERN

The victory over Perrin and his followers represented a break in the alliance between Geneva and Bern that had existed since 1526. The treaty in which the relationship had been established came to an end in March of 1556. Bern, which took on the role of protector of the Libertines who had fled, stalled by rejecting new proposals from Geneva.[1] Bern also demanded restoration of the refugees who were now located in Bernese territory and were seizing every opportunity to provoke the Genevans. The Council of Geneva decided in January to inform Bern that they could not agree to the demands that Bern had made, and Calvin was assigned to formulate this response. It passed all the bodies of the magistracy, including the General Council.[2] Geneva referred to the freedom that it won and to the help of God that it had earlier experienced. Calvin left the door open for a new alliance with Bern by thanking them for the friendship they had enjoyed. This was certainly not true for him personally, but he was able to distinguish between his own feelings and the interests of Geneva, which, for the sake of the Reformation in general, had to rely on the continuation of the existing relationship with Bern because of the interests that both cities had in the Vaud region.

Geneva, meanwhile, asked Zurich, Basel, and Schaffhausen to serve as mediators, and Bullinger personally devoted himself to the restoration of rela-

---

1. Eugène Choisy, *La théocratie à Genève au temps de Calvin* (Geneva: Eggimann, 1897), 191ff.; Abraham Ruchat, *Histoire de la réformation de la Suisse* (Nyon: Giral-Prelaz, 1835–38), 6:228–33.
2. CO 21:625.

tions.[3] Calvin, too, had this as his only goal, since he feared the political and military power of France. Finally, Geneva and Bern were compelled to seek a rapprochement when in October 1557 a threat arose from the side of the Duke of Savoy. Bern indicated that it was willing to separate the question of an alliance from the problems with the refugees from Geneva. On the second Sunday of January 1558, the alliance was proclaimed as an "eternal covenant" in both Bern and Geneva.[4] With that, the defeat of the Perrinists was finally sealed. Within the alliance, the freedom that Geneva had still to chart its own course meant that Calvin's contribution to the Swiss reformation would essentially no longer be in jeopardy.

This alliance, however, in no way assured Bern's agreement with Calvin's theological views, nor even with Geneva's form of church organization, both of which Bern strongly repudiated. Along with this, different views of the Lord's Supper had been playing a role in the background since 1536, the year of the Wittenberg Concord.[5] Bern was becoming increasingly less appreciative of what Bucer's ecumenical activities had produced, and Calvin's conception of the Lord's Supper was seen in the light of Bucer's. But it was not on this point that the theological and ecclesiastical conflict between Bern and Geneva would explicitly emerge; it was especially on the doctrine of predestination that difficulties arose. After his expulsion from Geneva, Bolsec had sought refuge in the jurisdiction of Bern, where he found both supporters and detractors. The debates that ensued were stirred up by a number of decrees from the magistracy of Bern. Before the council, Calvin himself protested about the slurs to which his doctrine was being subjected in Bern.[6]

On November 17, Bern tried through its ministers to urge moderation on both sides.[7] Two months later, the Council of Bern forbade all innovations in liturgy and doctrine—especially "certain erroneous and subtle doctrines, opinions, and human traditions, particularly concerning the lofty subject of divine predestination, a matter that seems nonessential to us and more suited to bringing about factions, foolish polarities, and licentiousness than edification and comfort."[8] The Academy of Lausanne protested through Viret and

---

3. André Bouvier, *Henri Bullinger, réformateur et conseiller oecuménique: D'après sa correspondance avec les réformés et les humanistes de langue française* (Zurich: Imprimerie Delachaux et Niestle, 1940), 164–72.

4. Émile Rivoire and Victor van Berchem, eds., *Les sources du droit du canton de Genève*, vol. 3, *De 1551 à 1620* (Arau: Sauländer, 1933), 55–73.

5. Ernst Bizer, *Studien zur Geschichte des Abendmahlsstreits im 16. Jahrhundert* (Gütersloh: Bertelsmann, 1940; repr., Darmstadt: Wissenschaftliche Buchgesellschaft, 1962), 155f., 204.

6. CO 21:585.

7. Ruchat, *Histoire de la réformation*, 7:299ff.

8. Ibid., 7:301f.

Beza, but Bern was not deterred, not even when Calvin himself and a delegation from Geneva demanded in person the approval of the official doctrine of predestination.[9] The preachers supporting Geneva were sharply warned, and the use of Calvin's *Institutes* at the Lausanne Academy was prohibited.[10] The oppostion to "Calvinism" and "Bucerianism," which the preachers of Bern mention in the same breath,[11] was related not only to the view of the Lord's Supper but especially to the doctrine of election. On this point, Beza was in total agreement with Calvin, as can be seen from his *Summa totius christianismi*, the famous schematic representation of election and reprobation that was anonymously published during this time.[12]

The conflict came to a head over the meaning of the church order. Viret's view of the independence of church discipline corresponded with that of Calvin.[13] In 1558 this led to a sharpening of differences between Bern and the ministers who took Calvin's point of view. When Viret was dismissed in early 1559, he left for Geneva, where Beza had already moved. That same year the chasm between Bern and Geneva grew even wider when Calvin's academy was established. Shortly before he died, Calvin commented on the relationship with Bern, which had continually frustrated him: "They more feared me than loved me."[14]

CALVIN'S INFLUENCE ON THE CITY

The theological and ecclesiastical rupture with Bern boosted Calvin's influential position in Geneva, and he used it to implement his theocratic ideal on a larger scale. The chilly relationship with Bern was inversely proportional to the growing interest in developments in France. In opposition to the Perrin party, which found its power predominantly in family ties, there emerged a group of Calvinists sympathetic to France, and over the years its number grew. An unusually large number of refugees were granted citizenship in 1555 and 1556. Their power lay, for the most part, in their financial capabilities, as well

9. Henri Vuilleumier, *Histoire de l'Église réformée du Pays de Vaud sous le regime bernois* (Lausanne: Editions La Concorde, 1927–1933), 651.

10. CO 15:600–604: letter from Calvin to the senate of Bern.

11. CO 12:730.

12. Paul F. Geisendorf, *Théodore de Bèze* (Geneva: Labor & Fides, 1949), 74f.; Cornelis van Sliedregt, *Calvijns opvolger Theodorus Beza: Zijn verkiezingsleer en zijn belijdenis van de drieënige God* (Leiden: Groen, 1996), 75–109.

13. Doeda Nauta, *Pierre Viret, 1511–1571: Medestander van Calvijn in leven en werken geschetst* (Kampen: De Groot Goudriaan, 1988), 69–83; Robert D. Linder, *The Political Ideas of Pierre Viret* (Geneva: Droz, 1964), 65–81.

14. CO 9:894.

as in their talent and intellect. Within a short time, they occupied important positions in the social, political, and ecclesiastical life of the city.[15] Their acquisition of citizenship represented a considerable financial advantage to the city, which could now pay off its debts to Basel.

The growing authority of the consistory can be seen from the revision of the *Ordonnances ecclésiastiques*, which was completed on November 13, 1561. Already on November 12, 1557, the General Council had stipulated in a statute that contempt for ecclesiastical discipline should be treated like rebellion and punished with banishment for one year.[16] In a meeting of the council on January 30, 1560, Calvin and Viret argued for a clearer separation between ecclesiastical administration and the jurisdiction of the magistracy.[17] On February 9, 1560, four measures were adopted that secured the independence of ecclesiastical rule. First, the presiding syndic would no longer wield his official baton in meetings of the consistory, because he served there as a spiritual functionary and not as a member of the magistracy. Second, in the future the ministers would be given an active role in the council in the election of elders. Third, in the spiritual sphere of the church, the distinction between *citoyens* and *bourgeois* would no longer apply; people should simply elect the most qualified brothers. Finally, the public exercise of the ban and restoration to the congregation should take place before the entire congregation, so that it would be aware of its involvement in the exercise of church discipline. For Calvin, this was an essential part of the reformation of the city. The completely revised church order, including the marriage legislation, was promulgated on November 13, 1561. The articles were solemnly announced, with all the additions, along with the regulations concerning church discipline. Every three years the people would have to swear to them again in church.[18]

In addition to a revision of the ecclesiastical legislation, adjustments were also made to some of the civil laws, something in which Calvin had a hand as well. Ordinances and regulations from the time before the Reformation were tightened. From the increase in the number of excommunications, one can conclude that Geneva also managed to see to it that the law was obeyed. As mentioned earlier, from 1550 to 1554, we know of about eighty excommunications per year. In the year 1556 alone, there were 140 serious discipline cases, whereas in 1559 around 300 persons were excommunicated.[19] The consistory, supported by a large number of assistants, kept a watchful eye on the entire

15. William G. Naphy, *Calvin and the Consolidation of the Genevan Reformation* (Manchester: Manchester University Press, 1994), 121–43.

16. CO 10:118–20; Rivoire and van Berchem, eds., *Les sources du droit*, 3:50f.

17. CO 10:120.

18. Rivoire and van Berchem, eds., *Les sources du droit*, 3:127.

19. Naphy, *Calvin and the Consolidation*, 178ff.

population—every inhabitant in practically every area of life, without respect of persons. The morality legislation was repeatedly revised and strictly enforced. Marriage was promoted as a great good; fornication and prostitution were strongly punished. Restrictions were placed on luxurious clothing and meals, and festive occasions could be celebrated only with sobriety.[20]

In many respects, societal life was able to develop freely. With the help of the civil government, a weaving mill was established, which was able to compete with enterprises in France. Calvin was opposed to usury, but he defended reasonable interest rates, which would promote trade and industry. Especially famous were the Genevan printers, who were ready to promote the Reformation with their contributions.

A city under the dominion of the gospel—that is what Calvin had in mind. In meetings of the consistory, *censura morum* (mutual censure) was applied, in which members' actions as office-bearers were reviewed in their presence. In 1557 the Small Council decided to institute a similar *censura* among themselves before the Lord's Supper, "so that each person would do his duty toward the republic, to the glory of God."[21] That the council was serious about ruling the city with the help of God is apparent from the decision taken on November 7, 1558, to call in one pastor each time elections to the government were held, to present what God's Word required for the administration of the city—"so that we might be wholly ruled by the Spirit of God."[22] This decision was made "because in everything we depend on God and have no other help, power, support, and hope than from him alone."

The impression that the city of Geneva made on John Knox during this time produced the following description from his pen: "I can affirm without hesitation that in this place is found the most perfect school of Christ that ever was in the earth since the days of the apostles. In other places I confess Christ to be truly preached; but manners and religion to be so seriously reformed, I have not yet seen in any other place besides."[23]

THE ACADEMY

John Knox's picture of Geneva was related especially to the academy that had been founded there in 1559. Surprisingly enough, one of the contributing fac-

---

20. Ford L. Battles, "Against Luxury and License in Geneva," in *Interpreting John Calvin—Ford Lewis Battles*, ed. Robert Benedetto (Grand Rapids: Baker, 1996), 319–41; W. Fred Graham, *The Constructive Revolutionary: John Calvin and His Socio-Economic Impact* (Atlanta: John Knox, 1978), 97–115.

21. Rivoire and van Berchem, eds., *Les sources du droit*, 3:54.

22. Choisy, *La théocratie à Genève*, 199.

23. CO 16:333.

tors to this was the breakdown of relations with Bern, which resulted in Viret's and Beza's availability for teaching posts in Geneva. Already in 1541, the church order had mentioned the office of teacher, which would contribute to society in the service of church and state. In Strasbourg, Calvin had come to know firsthand the institution led by Johannes Sturm, and since his return to Geneva, he had kept in front of him the ideal of a university patterned after the one in Strasbourg. In addition, the buildings in which the *Collège de Rive* was housed were in serious need of renovation.

The renewal of the alliance with Bern created a situation in which attention could now be given to the development of education. On January 17, 1558, the magistracy decided to look for a location suitable for the *schola privata*, as the gymnasium was called, and a *schola publica*, or academy. Initially, it was difficult to find competent professors, but that changed with the departure of Beza and Viret from Lausanne.

In Bern it was thought that the new institution had little viability: "It is unlikely that with the high cost and the uncertainty of the situation, the academy will be able to attract many students."[24] Haller, who wrote this to Bullinger, was mistaken, for 162 students enrolled in 1559.

At the formal opening of the school and the academy on June 5, 1559, Beza, as rector, delivered the inaugural address. He realized that this was an undertaking by the whole city for the benefit of those who, as the council believed, "were eager to learn." In the early years, France would produce the most students, but students did come from all over Europe, giving the academy an international character. In 1564, Beza counted 1,200 pupils in the *schola privata* and 300 in the *schola publica*.

With Beza's assistance, Calvin drew up an *Ordre du Collège*, which, together with Beza's opening address, was published and distributed by Robert Estienne, to give the academy more publicity.[25] It was clear that the overall emphasis in this education was on theology. Highly significant was the library; its catalog gives a picture of the extant theological literature.[26] Calvin's conviction fit closely with the ideas that Melanchthon had in mind when he reformed university education and that Calvin had seen as the aim of the education in Strasbourg under the leadership of Johannes Sturm and Bucer. One should also remember the ideal of Erasmus, which emphasized the value of classical texts. All of this represented a model whose features were reminiscent of the piety and efforts of the *devotio moderna* movement of the Middle Ages, together

24. CO 17:659.
25. Charles Borgeaud, *1559, pages d'histoire universitaire réunies à l'occasion du jubilé de 1909* (Geneva: Georg, 1908), 26.
26. Alexandre Ganoczy, *La bibliothèque de l'Academie de Calvin: Le catalogue de 1572 et ses enseignements* (Geneva: Droz, 1969), 138f.

with the classical education found also in Strasbourg under Sturm. The regulations for the academy reflected the striving after *pia eloquentia* (pious eloquence) and *sapiens et eloquens pietas* (wise and eloquent piety).[27]

The structure of the education in the *schola privata* focused on the acquisition of such knowledge as would qualify one to serve church and society with the use of logic and rhetoric. The core education at the academy, however, was primarily of an exegetical nature. Here is where Calvin's perspective came to clearest expression. The Bible lay at the foundation of everything that was taught. At the same time, upon their enrollment, students had to subscribe to the confession of Geneva as articulated in a short dogmatic summary of the whole of theology.[28] There reference was made to the creeds of the early church, and heresies, including that of Servetus, were rejected. With only a few exceptions, all students signed the confession, a practice that continued until later, under Beza, it was thought sufficient for the rector to admonish students "to conduct themselves modestly and virtuously and to do their duty in the fear of God, according to the regulations of the church."[29]

In his role as professor of Holy Scripture, Calvin had been giving lectures on the books of the Bible ever since his arrival in Geneva in 1536. The founding of the university did not change that, although he now focused especially on the books of the Old Testament. It was out of this activity that his commentaries developed.[30] According to Jean Budé, who wrote a foreword to Calvin's commentary on the Minor Prophets, Calvin had barely a half hour each time to prepare for a lecture. Usually, he would read the text in Hebrew, translate it into Latin, and then begin his explanation. According to the publisher of this series of commentaries, Jean Crespin, Calvin spoke without the use of notes, "extemporaneously and fluently."[31] He gave three lectures a week, each a full hour, keeping time in the *Auditoire* by the striking of the clock of St. Peter's Church next door.

Hence in almost all of his activities, Calvin operated in the sphere of Holy Scripture. The academy was there for the church and thus, at first, offered lectures only in theology. After Calvin's death, Beza succeeded in adding faculties in medicine and law to the one already existing in theology. For the time being, however, the institution bore the character of a theological seminary.

27. Lewis W. Spitz and Barbara S. Tinsley, *Johann Sturm on Education: The Reformation and Humanist Learning* (St. Louis: Concordia, 1995).

28. "Subscripsimus praecedentibus Genevensis Academiae legibus ac nominatim Genevensis Ecclesiae confessioni"; Borgeaud, *Jubilé de 1909*, 31. For the "Confession des escholiers," see CO 9:721–30.

29. Borgeaud, *Jubilé de 1909*, 46.

30. T. H. L. Parker, *Calvin's Old Testament Commentaries* (Edinburgh: T&T Clark, 1986; repr., Louisville, KY: Westminster John Knox Press, 1993), 13–29.

31. CO 42:183–88.

In that form, it exercised a powerful influence in spreading the Reformed branch of the Reformation throughout Europe, and it served as a model of university education for France, Germany, the Netherlands, and Scotland—in short, in every land where Calvinism gained a firm foothold.[32] The founding of the academy was the pinnacle of Calvin's work, and it marked the beginning of a movement that could no longer be stopped. Behind all of this was a strong conviction that Calvin himself laid out in a very carefully thought-out way in the last edition of the *Institutes*, which also appeared in 1559.

THE 1559 *INSTITUTES*

For Calvin himself, the 1559 *Institutes* was more than an updated reprint of an earlier Latin edition. It was considerably larger in size, partly because of an expansion of the exegetical material, and partly because of the greater role that apologetics now played. This was due chiefly to Calvin's ongoing study of the church fathers.

Calvin had his Latin editions of the *Institutes* also published in French translation.[33] In the "Argument" that he placed at the front of the French edition of 1560, he explains the purpose of the work by pointing to the perfect doctrine of Scripture, to which, of course, one does not have to add anything, but which does require some clarification for those not practiced in interpreting Scripture. For what should we look for in the Bible? Someone who has received more light is duty-bound to take others by the hand and to treat the weightiest matters of "Christian philosophy." With this kind of help, someone can learn more in one day in the school of God than someone else can in three months.

It was with this goal in mind that Calvin composed the *Institutes*. From this French preface, it becomes clear that for Calvin the emphasis falls on the doctrine of salvation. The book is not intended for intellectual enjoyment but for the strengthening of piety; it is an aid to spiritual growth. This pastoral intent becomes clear when Calvin characterizes his work as a key that opens the way for all the children of God to a right understanding of Scripture. He expresses the firm conviction that true and sound doctrine proceeds from God himself: "I shall in all simplicity declare that I think this work to be more from God than from me."

This would be sheer pride if Calvin were not absolutely convinced that his doctrine perfectly conformed to the truth of God's Word itself. He had no

---

32. Aart A. van Schelven, *Het calvinisme gedurende zijn bloeitijd*, vol. 1, *Geneve-Frankrijk* (Amsterdam: Ten Have, 1943), 58.

33. The 1539 *Institutes* appeared in French translation in 1541, the 1543 edition in 1545, and the 1550 edition in 1551. The 1559 edition was translated in 1560.

doubts about his interpretation of that Word. Whoever has no reverence for the Word of the Lord, and whoever is not really concerned about piety, he asserts, will not attach much value to the book. Whoever reads his work, however, to get a summary of Christian doctrine and to gain access to the Bible will "realize by experience that I have not at all meant to misuse words."[34]

The last edition of the *Institutes* comes off as a kind of last will and testament. Calvin informs us that it took special effort to get this work ready for the church of God. For a long time, his health was such that he could not do any work, and a debilitating, four-day fever seemed to him a portent of his impending death. This illness forced him to muster all his strength to be able to leave behind at least this book. His efforts were rewarded, however, in that the work was now also in a form with which he himself was satisfied.[35]

In his *Reply to Pighius*, who had plagiarized the famous first sentence of the *Institutes*, Calvin relates what the secret of his approach in the *Institutes* was. The *cognitio Dei et hominis* (the knowledge of God and ourselves) seemed to him particularly suitable for instruction.[36] For him, this was more than just an approach; it also involved his whole theological method. Here he was in agreement with Luther, who saw in the encounter between God and humanity the essence of true theology. In his determination of the object and subject of theology, Calvin was very close to Luther. For Calvin, theology was never a matter of *nuda speculatio* (empty speculation), pointless intellectual reflection on God and humanity; rather, it was a matter of "mutuality," a correlation between the knowledge of God and knowledge of self.

What is specific about the *Institutes* is the fact that the actual object of theology also functions as the formative structural principle. That is why the word "system," in the strict sense of the term, does not really apply to Calvin's thought as a whole. His book is not an unified construct, a *Summa* of religious truths. At every significant point, every "locus," it is a living out of the truth itself, that is, out of Christ, who is the way, the truth, and the life. The *ordo docendi* (method of teaching), the *modus loquendi* (way of speaking), is derived from the object. That is why it is understandable that up to the present day no one has been able to give a satisfactory answer to the question of what philosophical method Calvin used. There is no outside organizing principle that, as it were, rests atop the material. The material itself, Scripture itself, Calvin is convinced, determines the content and the method. His intent was to be a disciple of Scripture.

34. "Ilz congnoistront, par experience, que ie ne les ay point voulu abuser de parolles"; CO 3:23.

35. "Nunquam tamen mihi satisfeci, donec in hunc ordinem qui nunc proponitur digestum fuit"; CO 2:1.

36. "At ego excipiam illo me usum esse, quia optimus, et ad docendum aptissimus videretur"; CO 6:246.

If we keep this mind, we will not be asking Calvin improper questions. His distinction between the *cognitio Dei et hominis* does not lead to freestanding anthropology. Nor does his distinction between the knowledge of God as Creator and as Redeemer lead to an independent theology of creation. It arises out of the structural principle, which cannot for one moment be dissociated from its real object. This means that questions and problems connected with developments in theology after Calvin cannot right away be directed at him, as has happened, for example, with the question of the "natural knowledge of God." Calvin's theology in the *Institutes* is not a closed, well-rounded whole, subordinated to one central idea. His religious thought is open toward God and toward humanity and the world, without the bigger picture becoming lost in the diversity of the "parts," the loci. There is an existential unity here, located in the fact that faith is always nourished by the simplicity belonging to *docilitas* (teachableness), an openness to the fear of the Lord that belongs to an obedient heart.

Calvin's conversion account in 1557,[37] two years before the last edition of the *Institutes*, illustrates the "manner of speaking" (*modus loquendi*) by which he determined the content and structure of his doctrine book on the Christian religion. It reflects the growth of his own existence on the basis of Scripture. For that reason, he could be certain that the *Institutes* would serve as a good introduction to the understanding of Scripture itself. Whatever part of "doctrine" is being examined always functions within and on the basis of this existential framework.[38] The *Institutes* is therefore a "devotional" book, characteristic of Calvin's spirituality. It has not only provided thousands of readers with doctrinal insight but also helped them to be good disciples of Scripture.

Part of the reason for this is the arrangement of the material, which follows the order of the Apostles' Creed. Book 1 of the *Institutes*, which covers the first article of the creed ("I believe in God the Father almighty, creator of heaven and earth"), is entitled "The Knowledge of God the Creator." Book 2 treats Christology ("I believe in Jesus Christ, his only Son . . .") under the title "The Knowledge of God the Redeemer in Christ, First Disclosed to the Fathers under the Law, and Then to Us in the Gospel." The third article of the creed has to do with the Holy Spirit ("I believe in the Holy Spirit"), and in Book 3 Calvin treats "The Way in Which We Receive the Grace of Christ: What Benefits Come to Us from It, and What Effects Follow." Book 4 talks about "The External Means or Aids by Which God Invites Us into the Society of Christ and Holds Us Therein," and deals with the significance of the church, the sacraments, and the civil government.

37. CO 31:21.
38. Parker, *Calvin's Old Testament Commentaries*, 131.

These four books, divided into chapters and subdivided into paragraphs, present the material in a well-organized manner. The 1559 *Institutes*, compared with the earlier editions, was really a new work.[39] It was a testimony not only to an incredible intelligence, an orderly mind, and a capacity to absorb and assimilate; it was also a permanent testimony to a man who knew what it meant to be called by grace to freedom because he felt bound to the Word of the caller, God himself. "We are not our own," the adage that typifies the Christian life as a whole, was characteristic of Calvin personally.[40] In this sense, he considered the publication of the *Institutes* to be his life's calling, a calling from God himself that was reflected in his work.[41]

THE CHURCH AT THE CENTER

In all of Calvin's work, the church was central. Its doctrine was described in the *Institutes* and its structure laid out in the *Ordonnances*, completed in 1561. But when it came to his *doctrina* and *disciplina*, Calvin had more than Geneva in mind. For him, the church of Christ was universal, a community of all believers throughout the world. It was out of this consciousness that his ecumenical calling originated, something of which he was very aware and which he fulfilled in all sorts of ways.[42] Right from the beginning, this was a matter for Calvin, as it was for Augustine, of the confluence of grace and church. In the doctrine of grace, he followed the church father deep into the *abyssus*, where grace is hidden from our view. At the same time, he wanted to hold firmly to the visibility of the church, where especially the unity of the church of Christ in this world receives full emphasis. On the basis of this principle, Geneva became the city from which Reformed ecumenicity was promoted in full force.

Calvin's principle entailed that he keep clearly in mind the need for unity of doctrine within the church of Geneva. At the same time, however, he made a distinction between fundamental and nonfundamental articles of faith. This explains his attitude to those both inside and outside of Geneva. By "fundamental" he meant the confession of something absolutely essential to the

---

39. François Wendel, *Calvin: Origins and Development of His Religious Thought*, trans. Philip Mairet (New York: Harper & Row, 1963; repr., Grand Rapids: Baker, 1997), 133–34, 137–38.

40. Battles, "The Theologian as Poet: Some Remarks about the 'Found' Poetry of John Calvin," in *Interpreting John Calvin—Ford Lewis Battles*, ed. Benedetto, 270–71.

41. CO 2:505f.

42. Gottfried Locher, *Calvin: Anwalt der Ökumene* (Zollikon: Evangelischer Verlag, 1960), 16.

Christian faith and thus distinguishable from what churches could disagree about without doing damage to the unity of the faith.[43]

Maintaining this distinction enabled Calvin to operate with full latitude within the boundaries of ecumenicity. To him, these boundaries were perfectly clear. Both inside and outside of Geneva, he took strong action against the anti-Trinitarians who for some time had been a part of an Italian refugee congregation that since 1542 had been meeting first in a chapel of St. Peter's church, and then in the Madeleine church. In 1554, shortly after the Servetus case, Matteo Gribaldi (d. 1564) came into contact with this congregation. Later, Valentino Gentile (d. 1566), Gian Paolo Alciati (d. 1565), and Giorgio Biandrata (1516–1588) also joined this assembly.

Gribaldi's intention was to establish religious freedom and toleration in the congregation. A meeting with Calvin did not produce agreement. Gribaldi was suspected of the same sentiments as Servetus and banished from Geneva in 1555. On May 18, 1558, when the Italian congregation imposed a Trinitarian confession drafted by Calvin,[44] Gentile refused to subscribe to it and landed in prison, where he repented and renounced his views. He burned his writings with his own hand, but was banished from the city.[45] In 1566 he was imprisoned in Bern and beheaded. Alciati, who also belonged to this group, left Geneva after Calvin had put things in order. Biandrata joined this congregation in 1557, where he touched off a debate with the preacher Celso Martinengo and later with Calvin. In May 1558, he had been brought back to the point where he could subscribe to Calvin's views on the divinity of Christ. Shortly thereafter, he settled in Zurich, which he then had to leave for ignoring a request by Bullinger to reconcile with Calvin.[46] Biandrata finally settled in Poland, where he stirred up some unrest in which Calvin became involved.

For Calvin, the anti-Trinitarians, or Unitarians, had left the borders of the Christian faith far behind. He would claim something similar about the Anabaptists, but not so dogmatically, since he had managed to bring several of them back to the church and viewed the rest more or less as simple folk who were easily led astray. One of his first writings possibly had such Anabaptists in mind. For some time, Capito succeeded in holding off its publication, but

---

43. CO 2:755f.: "Non enim unius sunt formae omnia verae doctrinae capita. Sunt quaedam ita necessaria cognitu, ut fixa esse et indubitata omnibus oporteat. . . . Sunt alia quae inter Ecclesias controversa, fidei unitatem non dirimant."

44. The confession is found in CO 9:385–88.

45. In 1561, Calvin reproduced both the views of Gentile and the official documents of the magistracy in *Impietas Valentini Gentilis detecta et palam traducta*, in CO 9:361–420.

46. *Ad quaestiones Georgii Blandratae responsum*, in CO 9:321–32.

in 1542 his treatise on soul sleep, Calvin's *Psychopannychia*, appeared.[47] This was followed by a little book in 1544 in which Calvin warned believers about the errors of the Anabaptists.[48] He adopts the same tone as the people whose ideas he is refuting, which gives his polemical language a sharp edge.[49]

RELATIONSHIP WITH ROME

In the writings in which he carries on the debate with Rome, Calvin adopts a wholly different tone. The letter to Sadoleto is an example of the high level at which such discussions could be conducted. There two humanistically trained scholars encounter each other, and with respect. For Calvin, however, the flowing eloquence of this letter is placed in the service of a deep respect for the one church of God and for God himself.[50] The tone is totally different, however, when he attacks abuses, as in the treatise on relics,[51] or when he enters into debate with the Sorbonne.[52] Here something of the humanist's ridicule can be seen.

In 1543, at Bucer's request, Calvin pressed Emperor Charles V for a radical implementation of the reform begun by Luther: *A Petition to Charles V*.[53] In drafting this appeal to the emperor, he enlisted the help of Farel. Calvin knew the atmosphere of the parliamentary diets and did not expect much to come of his effort. Nevertheless, it becomes clear from his appeal in this statement that he has not given up all hope. When the Council of Trent actually convened, however, and its first decrees became known, Calvin's assessment made clear that, in his judgment, the breach could no longer be healed.[54] In fact, the matter was now closed.

The coming of the Augsburg Interim (1548) produced another reaction from Calvin, in which he explained once again how the church could truly be reformed. There he enumerates those doctrines that are nonnegotiable, such

47. *Psychopannychia: Vivere apud Christum, non dormire animis sanctos, qui in fide Christi decedent,* in CO 5:165–232. Willem Balke, *Calvin and the Anabaptist Radicals*, trans. William J. Heynen (Grand Rapids: Eerdmans, 1981), 25–34.

48. *Briefve instruction pour armer tous bons fideles contre les erreurs de la secte commune des Anabaptistes,* in CO 7:45–142. Balke, *Calvin and the Anabaptist Radicals*, 171–83.

49. Francis M. Higman, *The Style of John Calvin in His French Polemical Treatises* (London: Oxford University Press, 1967), 6.

50. CO 5:385–416.

51. CO 6:405–52: *Advertissement tresutile du grand proffit qui reveindroit à la Chrestienté, s'il se faisoit inventoire de tous les corps sainctz, et reliques qui sont tant en Italie, qu'en France, Allemaigne, Hespaigne, et autres Royaumes et pays.*

52. CO 7:1–44: *Articuli a facultate sacrae theologiae parisiensi determinati suer materiis fidei nostrae hodie controversis. Cum antidoto.*

53. CO 6:453–534: *Supplex adhortatio ad Caesarem Carolum Quintum.*

54. CO 7:341–64: *Acta Synodi Tridentini cum Antidoto.*

as justification through faith, repentance and confession, the service of God, the church, and the sacraments.[55]

By the end of the 1540s, Calvin had become convinced that the conflict with Rome could no longer be resolved. According to him, the deepest cause of the breach was the primacy of the papacy. In his view, the structure of the hierarchically organized church did not allow for any more real reformation, and thus a common basis for reform was out of the question. A serious appeal to Scripture would not do any good.

Gradually the relationship with Rome became dominated by this controversy. A meeting of theologians who on a personal level are on good terms does not certainly lead to a breakdown of the barriers that exist between their churches. Protestants would always be viewed as defendants. That is how Calvin expressed himself about the efforts in which Beza, at the behest of a few Protestant leaders in France, was participating. And the religious colloquy in Poissy (1561) did indeed produce nothing. It never got down to a real discussion because the bishops judged that the heretics must be instructed and condemned.[56]

The structure of the Roman hierarchy could not be pried open even in France. Therefore, in his ecumenical efforts, Calvin turned away from this church, which did not correspond to the marks by which the true church may be identified. This was also the reason why he urged the "Nicodemites" to make a definite choice. They should be open about their standpoint, even though it may require sacrifices. God must be served as much by external action as by internal conviction. Idolatry is sin, and the mass is an open idolatry. The decisive tone that Calvin adopts here was intended to help the Protestants, particularly those in France, in their crisis of conscience. If one knows the truth of the gospel, one ought to live in accordance with that truth—not sitting with one's faith in the dark but coming out into the open with it.[57]

Calvin tried to support his viewpoint, which did draw some criticism, in a reprint of his first treatise on the subject, along with letters by Melanchthon, Bucer, and Peter Martyr Vermigli. The choice, according to Calvin, was simply and clearly one of either exile or enduring persecution and, if need be, martyrdom. He himself had chosen the former. Partly because of his writings against the Nicodemites, many followed his example and, as the pressure increased,

55. CO 7:545–674: *Interim adultero-germanum, cui adiecta est: Vera christianae pacificationis et Ecclesiae reformandae ratio.*

56. Donald Nugent, *Ecumenism in the Age of the Reformation: The Colloquy of Poissy* (Cambridge: Harvard University Press, 1974), 89.

57. CO 6:537–88: *Petit traicte, monstrant que c'est que doit faire un homme fidele congnoissant la verité de l'evangile: quand il est entre les papistes, Avec une Epistre du mesme argument.* In 1544 Calvin wrote *Excuse de Iehan Calvin, a Messieurs les Nicodemites, sur la complaincte qu'ilz font de sa trop grand' rigueur;* in CO 6:589–614.

sought a safe haven in Geneva. In the period from 1549 to 1559, they numbered approximately five thousand. Calvin's appeal to the Nicodemites was a direct result of his rejection of the church of Rome as a reasonable option for anyone who had come to know the gospel. Calvin was stopped here at the boundaries of ecumenism, whose aim it was to pursue the unity of the church.

RELATIONSHIP WITH THE ZWINGLIANS
AND LUTHERANS: THE LORD'S SUPPER

When it came to relations with the Zwinglians and Lutherans, Calvin's ideal of church unity looked very different. In the 1550s he did everything he could to bring about the unity of the Reformation movement, viewing the differences between the followers of Zwingli and those of Luther as secondary in nature and definitely surmountable. In his *Short Treatise on the Lord's Supper*, he had offered a summary of the viewpoints that he wished to overcome.[58] For him, the possibility of rapprochement lay in the reality of communion with Christ, which was signified and sealed in the sacrament. He had already composed a *Confessio* about that in 1537, which became the occasion for Bucer and Capito to seek further contact with him.[59] Here Calvin was following fully in Bucer's footsteps, and he further worked out his ideas in an intensive correspondence with Bullinger, in the hope that it would lead to agreement.[60]

In Zurich there was little understanding of the Wittenberg Concord (1536), and not much demand either to resolve the dispute with the Lutherans over the Lord's Supper. Still in 1539 Luther regarded Zwingli as a Nestorian, and in 1541 he classified him with the Anabaptists. In 1544 Luther published a short confession on the Lord's Supper, in which he placed Zwingli and Oecolampadius in the same category as Andreas Karlstadt and Caspar Schwenckfeld: among the *Schwärmer* (enthusiasts) and enemies of the sacraments. Zurich responded with the *Wahrhaftes Bekenntnis der Diener der Kirche zu Zürich* (1545), and Bullinger explained his view in great detail in the *Absoluta de Christi Domini et catholicae eius ecclesiae sacramenti ratio* (1546).[61]

Calvin saw it as his task to prevent a new controversy over the Lord's Supper. He thought he could do that because, with his emphasis on the work of the

58. CO 5:429–60: *Petit Traicte de la saincte Cene de nostre Seigneur Iesus Christ* (1541).
59. CO 9:711f.: *Confessio fidei de eucharistia* (1537).
60. Wilhelm Kolfhaus, "Der Verkehr Calvins mit Bullinger," in *Calvinstudien: Festschrift zum 400. Geburtstage Johann Calvins, 1909*, ed. Josef Bohatec (Leipzig: Haupt, 1909), 27–125; Bouvier, *Henri Bullinger*, 110–49; Paul E. Rorem, "The *Consensus Tigurinus* (1549): Did Calvin Compromise?" in *Calvinus Sacrae Scripturae Professor: Calvin as Confessor of Holy Scripture*, ed. Wilhelm H. Neuser (Grand Rapids: Eerdmans, 1994), 72–90.
61. Bizer, *Studien zur Geschichte des Abendmahlsstreits*, 229–33.

Holy Spirit, he could do justice to the reality of Christ's presence without diminishing the necessity of faith. In their correspondence, Bullinger and Calvin narrowed the gap between their positions. Bullinger, however, was reticent to affirm the rapprochement publicly. In May 1549, Calvin showed up in Zurich by surprise, accompanied by Farel. He had requested permission from the council of Geneva to pursue the matter of an alliance with the French king in Zurich.[62] This effort formed part of the background for his attempts to reach an agreement on the Lord's Supper: a broad alliance against the emperor, who was also receptive to the German princes. At the same time, Calvin's intent was, together with Bullinger, to improve relations with Bern, which had always been tense, with the aid of a common confession on the Lord's Supper.

In Zurich an agreement was reached through personal conversation during a meeting of less than two hours. Calvin adopted some of Bullinger's ideas; for him it was not a question of who could be considered the winner.[63] In any case, the *Consensus Tigurinus* (*Zurich Consensus*) served to align Geneva and Zurich in their confession of the Lord's Supper. They still had a difference of opinion about predestination and church discipline, but that did not endanger the unity between the two churches.[64]

The text of the *Consensus* was officially released for publication in 1551 and approved by most Swiss cities. Bern, however, refused to go along with it both because the city still had a different understanding of the sacraments and because it had not been consulted during the negotiations, as the ministers there, Haller and Musculus, had urged. Bullinger recounts in a letter to Beza in 1571 that he had had to move Calvin away from the "Buzerizantia" (Bucerization) that he had picked up during his stay in Strasbourg.[65] Calvin himself was able to recognize his own theological position in the formulations, even though at Bullinger's insistence he had to let go of the word *substantia*, which he had been using since 1537. Even Bucer, who by then was in England, expressed his approval. Central to the consensus was the idea of a communion with Christ that is effected by the Holy Spirit and received through faith, a view that Calvin had held from the very beginning. It is clear that in the search for substantial unity, for Calvin, as for Bucer, the final decision about this doctrine lay not in a particular way of phrasing it but in the experience of the mystery

---

62. CO 21:452.

63. Wilhelm Neuser, "Dogma und Bekenntnis in der Reformation: Von Zwingli und Calvin bis zur Synode von Westminster," in *Handbuch der Dogmen- und Theologiegeschichte*, ed. C. Andresen, vol. 2, *Die Lehrentwicklung im Rahmen der Konfessionalität* (Göttingen: Vandenhoeck & Ruprecht, 1980), 273: "Er übernimmt Bullingers Begrifflichkeit und Lehrweise; ohne Frage war sie für ihn tragbar."

64. Bizer, *Studien zur Geschichte des Abendmahlsstreits*, 234–74.

65. Bouvier, *Henri Bullinger*, 563; *Correspondance de Théodore de Bèze*, ed. Hippolyte Aubert, 28 vols. (Geneva: Droz, 1986), 12:246.

of the Lord's Supper.[66] For him, safeguarding this was a way of answering the call to church unity.

Calvin believed that, armed with the *Consensus*, he could now enter into discussion with the Lutherans and expect a positive result. What happened was just the opposite. Bullinger did not share this outlook, and with the challenge to the *Consensus Tigurinus* by the strict Lutherans, the Lord's Supper controversy flared up once again. In the wake of Luther's death, Melanchthon was entangled in the disputes that had broken out in Germany over a number of theological issues, partly in connection with the Interim. To Calvin's great disappointment, Melanchthon remained aloof because he was under suspicion of Crypto-calvinism. This did not change when Calvin had to face sharp attacks from Joachim Westphal, a Lutheran preacher in Hamburg.[67] Westphal wrote *Farrago confuseanarum et inter se dissidentium opiniorum* (1552), in which—with a long series of quotations from the writings of Karlstadt, Zwingli, Vermigli, Oecolampadius, Bucer, Bullinger, and Calvin himself—he tried to demonstrate that the *Schwärmer* (enthusiasts) contradicted themselves and twisted the words of institution in the Lord's Supper. In another work the following year, *Recta fides de Coena Domini*, Westphal once again deliberately attacked Zwingli's memory.

At the request of Johannes à Lasco, who with his congregation of refugees from England had not been able to gain asylum in Lutheran states or cities, Calvin took these refugees under his wing and defended the *Consensus* produced in Zurich. Bullinger did not endorse the first version of the defense because he felt that Calvin judged some of Luther's statements too positively. When his *Defensio sanae et orthodoxae doctrinae* did appear in 1555, it provoked a number of reactions. Westphal, later supported by Heshusius and others, produced a series of treatises in which he declared that on the issue of the Lord's Supper, the Swiss denied the truth of Scripture. In his responses, Calvin countered that the spokesmen for the Lutherans were conducting themselves like "apes" of the great master. "If only Luther were still living," Calvin sighed.[68]

The controversy seriously harmed Calvin's longing for unity, to which he had been ready to dedicate himself personally. When one of Westphal's works was

---

66. CO 2:1007: "Quamquam autem cogitando animus plus valet, quam lingua exprimendo, rei tamen magnitudine ille quoque vincitur et obruitur." Cf. CO 15:723: "Itaque hoc mysterium magis suspicio, quam comprohendere laborem . . ."; CO 2:1032: "Porro de modo si quis me interroget, fateri non putebit, sublimius esse arcanum quam ut vel meo ingenio comprehendi, vel enarrari verbis queat; Atque, ut apertius dicam, experior magis quam intelligam."

67. Neuser, *Handbuch der Dogmen- und Theologiegeschichte*, 2:274–76.

68. Calvin's *Secunda defensio piae et orthodoxae de sacramentis fidei contra Ioachimi Westphali calumnias* appeared in 1556. Westphal replied with his *Adversus cuiusdam sacramentarii falsam criminationem iusta defensio* (1555), and in 1557 Calvin responded to three other pamphlets with his *Ultima admonitio ad Westphalum*.

published in Frankfurt am Main, Calvin began communicating with the magistracy of the city. He dedicated his commentary on the Gospels to them, making reference to the kindness they had shown to the refugees from England and other stricken areas. He also referred in passing to Bucer, who in 1542 had managed to broker a consensus between the factions found among the preachers there. Calvin expressed his willingness to travel to Frankfurt and explain the doctrine of the Lord's Supper contained in the *Consensus Tigurinus*. The Lutheran ministers saw to it, however, that Calvin was not invited for such an occasion. When he was in the city for two weeks in 1556 to settle a dispute in the expatriate congregations involving Valerandus Polanus, they ignored him.

All of this led to a cooling of Calvin's relationship with the disciples of Luther and to a similar adverse effect on his relationship with Bullinger. Bullinger was just too afraid that Calvin had not entirely succeeded in protecting himself from Bucer's ideas on the unity of the church, and he was not wrong. Calvin constantly had the situation in France in mind, hoping that a rapprochement with the German princes would create a climate in which they could come to the aid of the oppressed Protestants in France.

CALVIN'S VISION OF THE UNITY OF THE CHURCH

Calvin's ecumenical activity, which the Lutherans thwarted and Bullinger followed with suspicion, was not only motivated by arguments from high-level European politics, to which he managed to make his contribution; it was also determined by his vision of the unity of the church. The breach with Rome should not be permitted to lead to a divided Protestantism. This was what drove him to keep striving for the unity of the church despite all the opposition. It is why he fully supported actions to bring about a real meeting with the Lutherans, something for which Beza had been entrusted. While still in Lausanne, Beza undertook a mission to Germany on three occasions. In 1557 he set off with Farel for Göppingen, where they pleaded the cause of the persecuted Waldenses before the Duke of Württemberg, with a reference to the similarity between the Waldenses and the church of Geneva.[69] The second time, Beza traveled on orders from Calvin to enlist the aid of German princes for the Huguenots who had been arrested in Paris in September 1557. He encountered Melanchthon in Worms and had to explain to him and other Lutherans once again that the Swiss were neither Anabaptists nor Papists.[70]

---

69. Geisendorf, *Théodore de Bèze*, 81–96; Euan K. Cameron, *The Reformation of the Heretics: The Waldenses of the Alps, 1480–1580* (Oxford: Clarendon, 1984), 196ff.
70. CO 16:703ff. The *Confession* that was presented on that occasion is in CO 16:659ff.

The third journey, in the spring of 1558, brought him to Frankfurt for the same purpose: to urge German princes to intervene before the king of France. The attempts to reach an agreement with the Lutherans ended in failure. In Worms, the theologians from Saxony and Brandenburg refused to extend a hand to the delegates from Switzerland.

Calvin, however, did not abandon his ideal. In 1554 he dedicated his commentary on Genesis to the princes in Saxony, with whom he expressed the hope that more and more a "holy and fraternal harmony" would grow.[71] They refused to interpret this gesture in a positive way and clearly distanced themselves from his plan because he deviated from Luther's doctrine of the Lord's Supper.[72] This, however, did not prevent Calvin in January 1556 from dedicating his *Secunda defensio* against Westphal to the ministers of Christ who proclaim the pure doctrine of the gospel in Saxony and other parts of Lower Germany. Calvin appealed to Christ himself, who is our peace. Should not his reconciliation bring it about that "we are able mutually to maintain a brotherly peace on earth?" How far Calvin was willing to go to reach accord with the Lutherans is evident from the *Conciliatio calvinica*, a brief confessional statement, in which differences were reduced to "mutually misunderstood expressions," a difference in words, not in substance.[73] Christians must be able to find each other on the basis of a mutual forgiveness. Whoever is not satisfied with that indicates that he is a "logomachus" (a battler over words). It is as if we are listening to Bucer here!

Nevertheless, all of these attempts came to naught. Bullinger continued to view Calvin's efforts with suspicion, until Calvin himself saw little point in them anymore. In 1560 Calvin wrote that he would no longer bother Bullinger with his pleas for a religious colloquy with the Lutherans.[74]

This did not mean the end of his efforts on behalf of the unity of the church. He frequently traveled to Zurich and other cities in Switzerland to promote unity in personal meetings. His intensive correspondence testifies to the same aspiration to bring brothers in the faith closer together. The refugee congregations in Germany and England, for example, could always count on his encouragement and advice. Especially in his last years, Calvin employed this means of communication, since his health seriously suffered under the weight of the work that he performed with great self-denial. Various illnesses limited what he could do, but he continued to stay busy almost to the end. The magistracy tried to encourage him and to express their thanks with gifts.

---

71. CO 15:199.
72. CO 15:260ff.: a letter from Burckhardt to Calvin about the negative reception of his commentary.
73. Bouvier, *Henri Bullinger*, 150–63; Willem Nijenhuis, *Calvinus oecumenicus: Calvijn en de eenheid der kerk in het licht van zijn briefwisseling* (The Hague: M. Nijhoff, 1959, 189–94.
74. CO 18:84: "Ad alea transeo."

THE END OF CALVIN'S LIFE

On December 25, 1559, Calvin was invited to become a citizen of the city of Geneva.[75] He let it be known that he had not asked for this himself in order to avoid suspicion of ulterior motives that people could easily associate with such a request. The realization that he could speak in prophetic freedom, bound only to what he saw as the message of the Bible, had made it possible for him to stay above all party factions. Now that citizenship in the city was being offered to him, however, he expressed his great thankfulness for the honor being shown him.

Upon his return to Geneva in 1541, Calvin had exhibited a deeply felt self-denial. He was convinced that God had called him and that behind this calling lay also his election. He confirmed both of these by connecting them closely to his own activity in the service of the church of Christ. This involved struggle, including the struggle against his own weaknesses. In the most difficult years, this consciousness of being called never left him. It did not lessen the anxiety and the tension, but it did make them bearable. On more than one occasion, Calvin showed a decisiveness and boldness of action that can only be explained by a strong sense of duty, since time after time he wrote that he was born with an anxious and timid nature.[76]

When on April 27, 1564, Calvin said his final farewell to the members of the Small Council, and a day later to the Venerable Company of Pastors, this sense of calling came clearly to the fore once again. He would not deny that God had made use of him, even though his service had been afflicted with many shortcomings. His task had been nothing other than the pure administration of the Word that had been entrusted to him. Before the ministers gathered around his bed, he confessed his lowliness:

> I have had many infirmities which you have been obliged to bear with, and what is more, all I have done has been worth nothing. The ungodly will greedily seize upon this word, but I say it again that all I have done has been worth nothing, and that I am a miserable creature. But certainly I can say this, that I have willed what is good, that my vices have always displeased me, and that the root of the fear of God has been in my heart; and you may say that the disposition was good, and I pray you, that the evil be forgiven me.[77]

Calvin knew all too well where his weaknesses and shortcomings lay. He sometimes had such a violent temper that he was completely powerless to

75. CO 21:725.
76. CO 31:25.
77. CO 9:893; ET from T. H. L. Parker, *John Calvin: A Biography* (Philadelphia: Westminster Press, 1975), 154.

control himself. He was impatient and occasionally very unreasonable. His attitude could be so satirical and cynical that bystanders could only conclude that this was an arrogant and haughty man. Bucer talked to him about it, and Calvin was accepting of his counsel: "Alas, it is true that with none of my great and numerous shortcomings have I wrestled harder than with such impatience. Yes, I am making some progress, but I have never reached the point yet of keeping this wild beast completely under control."[78]

It is possible that the frailty of his body played a role in all of this. A variety of illnesses gravely weakened him. According to Beza, Calvin's face in his older age looked so emaciated that it hardly resembled that of someone still alive: "In death he looked no different than when he was still living." Lack of sleep and food, nerve-racking stress, constant work—all of this took its toll on him to such an extent that his form dwindled away. Time and again, he had to remain in bed for weeks on end, from where he dictated his letters and treatises.

Toward the end of his life, Calvin's ailments grew worse. At the age of 54, his energies were spent, but he still had himself carried to the church to preach once more. After his farewell to the magistracy and his colleagues, he waited for death, completely lucid to the end. Farel visited him and brought greetings for the last time. On May 27, 1564, at eight o'clock in the evening, he died. He was buried the following day in the presence of the council, his colleagues, and a large crowd of people. No stone was placed on his grave. The person would lie hidden behind his work.

Calvin's own assessment of all the work he had done was equivocal. On the one hand, it was slight, insignificant, and small because it was the work of a miserable creature. On the other hand, it was a great work, for "I have not falsified a single passage of Scripture, to the best of my knowledge. I aimed at simplicity. I have written nothing out of hatred to anyone, but I have always faithfully produced what I esteemed to be for the glory of God."[79] That last statement applied not just to the many writings he produced, but also to his whole life's work. It all was directed at nothing other than the glorification of God's name.

CHAPTER BIBLIOGRAPHY

Balke, Willem. *Calvin and the Anabaptist Radicals*. Translated by William J. Heynen. Grand Rapids: Eerdmans, 1981.

Bauer, Karl. *Die Beziehungen Calvins zu Frankfurt a. M.* Leipzig: Verein für Reformationsgeschichte, 1920.

78. Cf. CO 9:859ff.
79. CO 9:893; ET from Parker, *John Calvin*, 154.

Benedetto, Robert, ed. *Interpreting John Calvin—Ford Lewis Battles*. Grand Rapids: Baker, 1996.

Beza, Theodore. *Correspondance de Théodore de Bèze*. 28 vols. Edited by Hippolyte Aubert. Geneva: Droz, 1986.

Bizer, Ernst. *Studien zur Geschichte des Abendmahlsstreits im 16. Jahrhundert*. Gütersloh: Bertelsmann, 1940. Reprint, Darmstadt: Wissenschaftliche Buchgesellschaft, 1962.

Borgeaud, Charles. *1559, pages d'histoire universitaire reunites à l'occasion du jubilee de 1909*. Geneva: Georg, 1908.

———. *Histoire de l'université de Genève*. Vol. 1, *L'Académie de Calvin, 1559–1798*. Geneva: Georg, 1900.

Bouvier, André. *Henri Bullinger réformateur et conseiller oecuménique, le successeur de Zwingli: D'après sa correspondance avec les réformés et les humanistes de langue française*. Neuchâtel: Delachaux et Niestlé, 1940.

Cameron, Euan K. *The Reformation of the Heretics: The Waldenses of the Alps, 1480–1580*. Oxford: Clarendon, 1984.

Choisy, Eugéne. *L'état chrétien calviniste à Genève au XVIme siècle*. Geneva: Georg, 1909.

———. *La théocratie à Genève au temps de Calvin*. Geneva: C. Eggimann, 1898.

Dourmergue, Émile. *Jean Calvin: Les hommes et les choses de son temps*. Vol. 6, *La lutte*. Lausanne: Georges Bridel & Co., 1926.

———. *Jean Calvin: Les hommes et les choses de son temps*. Vol. 7, *Le triomphe*. Lausanne: Georges Bridel & Co., 1927.

Eire, Carlos M. N. "Calvin and Nicodemism: A Reappraisal." *Sixteenth Century Journal* 10, no. 1 (1979): 45–69.

Ganoczy, Alexandre. *La bibliothèque de l'Académie de Calvin*. Geneva: Droz, 1969.

Geisendorf, Paul F. *Théodore de Bèze*. Geneva: Labor & Fides, 1949.

Graham, W. Fred. *The Constructive Revolutionary: John Calvin, His Socio-Economic Impact*. Richmond: John Knox Press, 1971.

Guggisberg, Kurt. "Die Auseinanderesetzung mit dem Calvinismus." In *Bernische Kirchengeschichte*, 212–22. Bern: P. Haupt, 1958.

Higman, Francis M. "The Question of Nicodemism." In *Calvinus Ecclesiae Genevensis Custos*, edited by Wilhelm H. Neuser, 165–70. New York: Peter Lang, 1984.

———. *The Style of John Calvin in His French Polemical Treatises*. London: Oxford University Press, 1967.

Kolfhaus, Wilhelm. "Der Verkehr Calvins mit Bullinger." In *Calvinstudien: Festschrift zum 400. Geburtstage Johann Calvins, 1909*, edited by Josef Bohatec, 27–125. Leipzig: Haupt, 1909.

Lewis, Gillian. "The Geneva Academy." In *Calvinism in Europe, 1540–1620*, edited by Andrew Pettegree et al., 35–63. Cambridge: Cambridge University Press, 1994.

Linder, Robert D. *The Political Ideas of Pierre Viret*. Geneva: Droz, 1964.

Locher, Gottfried W. *Calvin, Anwalt der Ökumene*. Zollikon: Evangelischer Verlag, 1960.

Maag, Karin. *Seminary or University: The Genevan Academy and Reformed Higher Education, 1560–1620*. Brookfield, VT: Ashgate Publishing Co., 1995.

McNeill, John T., and James H. Nichols. *Ecumenical Testimony: The Concern for Christian Unity within the Reformed and Presbyterian Churches*. Philadelphia: Westminster Press, 1974.

———. *Unitive Protestantism: The Ecumenical Spirit and Its Persistent Expression*. Richmond: John Knox Press, 1964.

Naphy, William G. *Calvin and the Consolidation of the Genevan Reformation*. New York: St. Martin's Press, 1994.

Nauta, Doede, and H. Smitskamp. *Calvijn en zijn academie te Genève.* Kampen: J. H. Kok, 1959.

———. *Pierre Viret, 1511–1571: Medestander van Calvijn in leven en werken geschetst.* Kampen: De Groot Goudriaan, 1988.

Neuser, Wilhelm. "Dogma und Bekenntnis in der Reformation: Von Zwingli und Calvin bis zur Synode von Westminster." In *Handbuch der Dogmen- und Theologiegeschichte.* Vol. 2, *Die Lehrentwicklung im Rahmen der Konfessionalität,* edited by C. Andresen, 165–352. Göttingen: Vandenhoeck & Ruprecht, 1980.

Niesel, Wilhelm. *Calvins Lehre vom Abendmahl.* Münich: C. Kaiser, 1935.

Nijenjuis, W. *Calvinus oecumenicus: Calvijn en de eenheid der kerk in het licht van zijn briefwisseling.* The Hague: M. Nijhoff, 1959.

Nugent, Donald. *Ecumenism in the Age of the Reformation: The Colloquy of Poissy.* Cambridge: Harvard University Press, 1974.

Parker, T. H. L. *Calvin's Old Testament Commentaries.* Edinburgh: T&T Clark, 1986. Reprint, Louisville, KY: Westminster John Knox Press, 1993.

———. *John Calvin: A Biography.* Philadelphia: Westminster Press, 1975.

Pfister, Rudolf. "Die Westschweiz bis zum Tode Johannes Calvins im Jahre 1564, 1 & 2." In *Kirchengeschichte der Schweiz,* vol. 2, pages 201–47. Zurich: Theologischer Verlag Zurich, 1974.

Reichel, Gerhard. *Calvin als Unionsmann.* Tübingen: J. C. Mohr, 1909.

Rivoire, Émile. *Les sources du droit du canton de Genève: Tome troisième de 1551–1620.* Arau: H. R. Sauerländer, 1933.

Rorem, Paul E. "The *Consensus Tigurinus* (1549): Did Calvin Compromise?" In *Calvinus Sacrae Scripturae Professor: Calvin as Confessor of Holy Scripture,* edited by Wilhelm H. Neuser, 72–90. Grand Rapids: Eerdmans, 1994.

Ruchat, Abraham. *Histoire de la réformation de la Suisse.* Vols. 6 and 7. Lausanne: Chez Marc Ducloux, 1836–1838.

Schelven, Aart A. van. *Het calvinisme gedurende zijn bloeitijd.* Vol. 1, *Geneve-Frankrijk.* Amsterdam: Ten Have, 1943.

Sliedregt, Cornelis van. *Calvijns opvolger Theodorus Beza: Zijn verkiezingsleer en zijn belijdenis van de drieënige God.* Leiden: Groen, 1996.

Spitz, Lewis W., and Barbara S. Tinsley. *Johann Sturm on Education: The Reformation and Humanist Learning.* St. Louis: Concordia, 1995.

Vuilleumier, Henri. *Histoire de l'église réformée du pays de Vaud sous le régime Bernois.* 4 vols. Lausanne: Editions La concorde, 1927–33.

Wendel, F. *Calvin: Origins and Development of His Religious Thought.* Translated by Philip Mairet. New York: Harper & Row, 1963. Reprint, Grand Rapids: Baker, 1997.

———. *Calvin, Ursprung und Entwicklung seiner Theologie.* Neukirchen-Vluyn: Neukirchener Verlag des Erziehungsvereins, 1968.

10

Contours of Calvin's Theology

Calvin's theology developed gradually. Since 1543, he published his editions of the *Institutes* with a reference in the foreword to a saying from Augustine: "I count myself one of the number of those who write as they progress and progress as they write."[1] The progress that Calvin made can be seen especially in the successive editions of the *Institutes*, which show an expansion of the material each time, based on his ongoing exegesis. Along with that was a conscious orientation to the church fathers, by which Calvin identified himself with the broad stream of catholic theology. Finally, we see a growing emphasis on polemics and apologetics.

So far as the substance of his theology is concerned, however, from 1536 onward we find a constant and consistent fundamental design, which is actually defined by the three themes of Scripture, grace, and the church. All three are individually, but especially in their interconnection, characteristic of Calvin's theology. On these topics the development that one can see from a comparison between Calvin and Luther comes most clearly to light.

AVERSION TO SCHOLASTIC THEOLOGY

Calvin's distance from official Roman Catholic theology grew over time. His aversion to *scholastica theologia*, which he described as a diabolical art of disputing, dated from his first period in Paris.[2] For him, the theology at the Sorbonne was an example of this art. It consisted of a labyrinth of *quaestiones*,[3] by

1. CO 2:4.
2. CO 52:252: "Diabolica ista ars litigandi."
3. CO 52:434.

127

which idle curiosity was provoked. One moved from one maze into another.[4] In this theology, Calvin disapproved of how people wanted to explore things that God has not revealed to us. True wisdom chooses to be silent where God is silent. The theologians of the Sorbonne want to inquire into what God has decided to keep hidden. That is why they are lacking in assurance. They can get no further than conjectures because they touch on matters that God has chosen not to reveal to us.[5] Calvin reproaches these theologians for engaging in word battles that become competitions in using clever arguments.[6] Theology has become a discipline reserved for a very few. True theology, however, is something for all the children of God, great and small. We must all be educated by God himself.[7]

Because these theologians occupy themselves with pointless questions, they make no contribution at all to really building up the church. They are silent about the mercy of God, the gracious forgiveness of sins, and how we can be assured of forgiveness so that we learn all the more to extol the goodness of God. Their theology is out of touch with life, which is full of spiritual attacks, and such theology lacks real comfort.[8] Calvin is especially critical of its content because the papal theologians teach people to trust in their own abilities. At the center stands the doctrine of free will: people believe that they possess enough virtue to cooperate with the grace of God. If they exercise their own powers, God will not deny his grace. They can also merit the grace of God through their good works, which Calvin sees as the cause of a permanent lack of assurance.

Over against this, Calvin places the preaching of salvation in Christ. Roman Catholic theology is a massive chaos and horrible maze because Christ is not central.[9] In doing theology, the theologian should be concerned about truth, assurance, and usefulness.[10] In a certain sense, what we have here is a reduction of theology, which should not be thought of as an impoverishment but rather as a soteriological and christological focus. Connected with that, according to Calvin, is also the simplicity with which sound doctrine should be passed on. The truth is one; therefore, the way in which it is expressed should also be simple, so that the "majesty of the Spirit" can manifest itself.[11]

---

4. CO 52:252: "Inanis curiositas nullum habet modum, sed ex labyrintho subinde in labyrinthum revolvitur."
5. CO 33:705ff.
6. CO 52:366.
7. CO 53:20.
8. CO 33:709.
9. CO 48:388f.
10. CO 2:120.
11. CO 52:251: "Sicut enim una est Dei veritas, ita simplex eius tradendae ratio, minime fucata scilicet et quae spiritus maiestatem potius quam humanae eloquentiae pompam resipiat."

Calvin's aversion to the scholastic theology of his day was radical. He considered its method and content to be in conflict with the majesty of Scripture, with the power of the Spirit, and with the sublimity of the prophets and earnestness of the apostles—a wholesale defilement of true theology.[12] "What, I beseech you, does one find there of faith or conversion or calling upon God? Of the weakness of humanity, the aid of the Spirit, or the gracious forgiveness of sins? Of the treatment of the ministry of Christ, and of the value it has for the real formation of piety?"

ERASMUS, LUTHER, AND BUCER

Calvin's critique of scholastic theology appeared already in the oration that he drafted for Nicolas Cop in 1533 and that became part of the reason for his flight from France. There he worked with material taken from Erasmus and Luther, the latter in a translation by Bucer. These three were the key names in the construction of his theology: Erasmus, because of his devotion to going back to the sources of theology; Luther, because he was the teacher whose disciple Calvin wished to be; and Bucer, because of the personal influence he exerted on Calvin, the significance of which cannot easily be overestimated.

Erasmus's significance for Calvin's theology was threefold. Before Calvin's conversion, the man from Rotterdam inspired him to study the classics and especially to publish the commentary on Seneca's *De clementia*.[13] Calvin was learning how to handle texts and to treat them with respect. It is to this, in part, that his exegetical method can be traced. After 1533 he was studying especially the editions of the church fathers, most of which had been edited by Erasmus. This turn to the fathers happened together with a change in his view of the doctrine of grace, so that he made a break with religious humanism on the issue of free will.[14]

The influence of humanism registered an impact also on Calvin's view of the importance and value of rhetoric.[15] This provided an accent to his theology that can also be found in Bucer and that has entirely to do with the technique of communication by means of the spoken and written word. The rhetoric we find in Calvin was a way in which the authority of his personality could make itself felt. He put it to work for the power of the gospel.

12. CO 52:335.
13. François Wendel, *Calvin et l'humanisme* (Paris: Presses universitaires de France, 1976), 40ff.
14. Ibid., 63ff.
15. Olivier Millet, "*Docere/Movere:* Les catégories rhéthoriques et leurs sources humanistes dans la doctrine calvinienne de la foi," in *Calvinus Sincerioris Religionis Vindex: Calvin as Protector of the Purer Religion*, ed. Wihelm H. Neuser and Brian G. Armstrong (Kirksville, MO: Sixteenth Century Journal Publishers, 1997), 35–51.

Luther's influence, unmistakable and ever present, perhaps originally led Calvin to shy away from the theology of Zwingli and Oecolampadius.[16] Nevertheless, Calvin did not become slavishly bound to Luther. He recognized Luther's faults, which, so as to highlight his talents, he did not want to pass off as virtues. But he also vigorously defended Luther against Pighius,[17] and no less against Bullinger.[18]

Luther's influence was clearly present already in the 1536 *Institutes*. Large sections of this edition, in which one hears echoes of Luther even in the very wording, were incorporated verbatim by Calvin into later editions. At the same time, however, Calvin had moved further along the path to which Luther had pointed him.[19] For him, Luther was not also the "last Elijah."[20] Calvin did not mean to undervalue Luther, but he was convinced that after Luther, God might well raise up someone similar or better.

The progress that Calvin had in mind had to do especially with the systematization of exegesis. It also had to do with the *modus loquendi* (way of speaking) or the *loquendi ratio* (manner of speaking). What Luther and Calvin say concerning the doctrine of free will and predestination, for example, is not much different in content. Luther, however, shows little restraint in the way he discusses the issue, especially in his disagreement with Erasmus. In Calvin, on the other hand, the sharp and mysterious contrast between the hidden God and the revealed and preached God is missing. At this point he prefers a "learned ignorance" (*docta ignorantia*): "We need not be ashamed of *not* knowing some things about these matters."[21] Calvin came to Luther's defense against Pighius when the latter ascribed Luther's serious spiritual wrestling to the direct work of the devil.[22] In Calvin's theology, too, there is evidence of spiritual wrestling, but it is quieted earlier than in Luther and does not know the same depths. The progress in Calvin's theology, therefore, when compared with Luther's theology, involves a certain harmonization of opposites.[23] That

16. CO 9:51.

17. CO 6:239, 245.

18. Cf. Calvin's well-known line (CO 11:774): "Even if he would call me a devil, I would still deem him worthy of honor and still recognize him as an outstanding servant of God." Willem van 't Spijker, *Luther en Calvijn: De invloed van Luther op Calvijn blijkens de Institutie* (Kampen: Kok, 1985).

19. CO 9:104: Luther showed the way, and "we have been going further along this path."

20. CO 9:238, 438.

21. CO 2:680.

22. CO 6:245; cf. CO 9:454.

23. Herman Bauke, *Die Probleme der Theologie Calvins* (Leipzig: Hinrichs, 1922); Ford L. Battles, "The Origin and Structure of Calvin's Theology," in *Interpreting John Calvin—Ford Lewis Battles*, ed. Robert Benedetto (Grand Rapids: Baker, 1996), 47–246; Karl Reuter, *Das Grundverständnis der Theologie Calvins: Unter Einbeziehung ihrer geschichtlichen Abhängigkeiten* (Neukirchen-Vluyn: Neukirchener Verlag des Erziehungsvereins, 1963); idem, *Vom Scholaren bis zum jungen Reformator: Studien zum Werdegang Johannes Calvins* (Neukirchen-Vluyn: Neukirchener Verlag, 1981).

the later Lutherans were unable to adopt such harmonization led to a grow-ing apart of the two traditions—also in a theological respect.

Bucer's influence on Calvin was particularly profound. A distance between them that Calvin felt at first was essentially overcome when the two came to know each other through close personal contact. Their views of the nature, sources, and purpose of theology were in complete agreement. Calvin held Bucer in especially high esteem for his contribution to the interpretation of Scripture, his appeal to the church fathers, and particularly for his emphasis on the practical character of theology: "True theology is the science of pious and happy living. Without it, even the demons can still know a lot and explain all sorts of things."[24] Theology is the "art of leading a godly life" (*scientia vivendi deum*).[25]

Like Bucer, Calvin was intent on strengthening the unity of the Reforma-tion movement with his theology, but they differed greatly in their presenta-tion of the material. Whereas Calvin strove for brevity and clarity (*perspicua brevitas*), Bucer, with his comprehensive spirit, felt the freedom to try to put things in a broad, catholic, theological context. When moving from Bucer to Calvin, one encounters the ideas of the Strasbourg theologian (Bucer) again but in a more clear and concise manner. On the main points, there was strik-ing agreement. The differences had to do with theological method, which for Calvin was closely connected to the way in which he used Scripture.

DIFFERENT APPROACHES, SAME MESSAGE

One can only do true theology if one has first become a student of Scripture. The origin of true knowledge lies in our reverential acceptance of what God has chosen there to reveal of himself.[26] This happens in different ways, how-ever, depending on whether one is in the study, the pulpit, the lecture hall, or in an apologetic argument.[27] The *Institutes* offers theological material in a coherent manner. It was meant for those who had come to know the taste of piety, as it says in the 1536 edition, but more and more it became a book for those intending to do theology as biblical scholarship. In all its revisions, how-ever, the book lost nothing of its original devotional character, in which the building up of faith was the goal. It sought to promote practical piety, the

24. Bucer, *In sacra quatuor Euangelia, ennarationes perpetuae* (Basel: Herwagen, 1536), 549.
25. Bucer, *Martini Buceri Scripta Anglicana fere omnia* (Basel: Perna, 1577), 563.
26. CO 2:54.
27. T. H. L. Parker, *Calvin's Old Testament Commentaries* (Edinburgh: T&T Clark, 1986; repr., Louisville, KY: Westminster John Knox Press, 1993), 9–41.

strengthening of spirituality. With the publication of the *Institutes*, Calvin had in view truth, assurance, and spiritual benefit. In his exegesis it enabled him to bypass the discussion of various *loci communes* that Bucer, for example, had included in his commentaries. The *Institutes* was based on a thorough exegesis, illuminating the connections whose secret Calvin thought he had discovered in the mutual relationship between the knowledge of God and the knowledge of self.

This does not mean that in the commentaries and sermons Calvin no longer discussed dogmatic material. There is plenty of it there, but it functions now in a different way. The interpretation operates within the same systematic framework as in the *Institutes*—sometimes purely grammatical-historical, but more often with a practical focus—in which the message of Scripture about grace and forgiveness, justification and sanctification, is developed. Calvin often transforms the message into a polemic against Roman Catholic theology, in which especially free will, the necessity of grace, and the work of the Spirit are highlighted.

Calvin also applied this formula to the work he did for students. A number of his commentaries began as lectures, and in his many surviving sermons he actually followed the same process: his own translation of the text, a practical exegesis of the passage, followed by an exhortation in which the congregation in all its variety is addressed. From these sermons one gathers a picture of everyday life in Geneva.[28] Calvin was convinced that it was his duty to Christianize the entire city and to raise all sectors of life to a higher plane. A comparison between his sermons and his commentaries shows that the message is substantially the same as what we hear in the *Institutes* or the commentaries. The underlying pattern is the same, and the message does not vary. There is, to be sure, an understandable difference in method, which led to the removal of some of the sharp edges of the doctrine formulated in the *Institutes*. But the Calvin of this book of doctrine is no different from the Calvin who regularly mounted the pulpit. He only said things there in a different way. One will never really learn to know the reformer unless this role as preacher is taken into consideration. This is how he made Geneva into a paradigm that would be replicated in many countries.[29]

---

28. Rodolphe Peter, "Genève dans la prédication de Calvin," in *Calvinus Ecclesiae Genevensis Custos*, ed. Wilhelm H. Neuser (Frankfurt: Lang, 1984), 23–48.

29. Richard Stauffer, "'Quelques aspects insolites de la théologie du premier article dans la prédication de Calvin," in *Calvinus Ecclesiae Doctor*, ed. Wilhelm H. Neuser (Kampen: Kok, 1980), 47–68; Wilhelmus H. T. Moehn, *God roept ons tot zijn dienst: Een homiletisch onderzoek naar de verhouding tussen God en de hoorder in Calvijns preken over Handelingen 4:1–6:7* (Kampen: Kok, 1996); T. H. L. Parker, *Supplementa Calviniana: An Account of the Manuscripts of Calvin's Sermons Now in Course of Preparation* (London: Tyndale, 1962).

WORD AND SPIRIT

In all his work, Calvin proceeded from the conviction that God reveals himself in the Scriptures. In this he followed Luther entirely,[30] guided by the principle of *sola scriptura*. For Luther, this meant an intensive concentration on justification through faith. The maxim "was Christum treibet" (that which conveys Christ) functioned not only as a criterion for determining the canonicity of a biblical book but also as a hermeneutical principle. On this point, however, Calvin had his own view: his hermeneutic operates also on the principle of *tota scriptura*—although not in a formal, legalistic, or biblicistic way, since his understanding of the inseparable connection between Word and Spirit makes that impossible. Scripture is given by God, and the certainty of that rests not upon the authority of the church but upon the testimony of the Spirit. Calvin's view of the relationship between law and gospel makes clear that this is not a matter of legalism in the strict sense of the term. His use of Holy Scripture was supported by his conception of the *doctrina caelestis* (heavenly teaching), which rules out any kind of superficial biblicism. Besides, for Calvin, Scripture always functioned within the context of the congregation, which certainly ought to be reformed according to God's Word.

Word and Spirit are bound together with an inseparable link.[31] Scripture itself is the product of the Spirit; Calvin repeatedly refers to Scripture as "dictation by the Spirit."[32] This does not exclude the fact that there are text-critical observations pointing to errors, but these errors can ascribed to copiers of the text. In his idea of inspiration, Calvin takes into consideration the individuality of the human authors of Scripture. God used them, and it is significant that through their voices we hear God himself speaking. Belief in the teaching of Scripture can never be established until we are first persuaded beyond a doubt that God is its author. "And therefore the highest proof of the truth of Scripture derives in general from the fact that God in person speaks in it."[33] Without Scripture we are unable to come to God or to know him as creator. Our coming to God, however, is preceded by God's coming to us. Through the relation of Word and Spirit, Calvin is able to give real meaning to the inspiration of Scripture. In this respect Calvin is a disciple of Bucer: "God is the

---

30. Thomas F. Torrance, *The Hermeneutics of John Calvin* (Edinburgh: Scottish Academic Press, 1988), 155ff.

31. CO 2:71.

32. Wilhelm H. Neuser, "Calvins Verständnis der Heiligen Schrift," in *Calvinus Sacrae Scripturae Professor: Calvin as Confessor of Holy Scripture*, ed. W. H. Neuser (Grand Rapids: Eerdmans, 1994), 67–71.

33. CO 2:58.

principal speaker of his own Word." Whoever appeals to Scripture will reach certainty in no other way than through the testimony of the Spirit, which is a more excellent way than all reasoning. One can try to establish the authority of Scripture with all sorts of proofs, but the Holy Spirit, who spoke through the mouths of the prophets, must penetrate our hearts to convince us. His testimony grants Scripture its own authority. This *autopistis* (self-authentication), which becomes effective through the testimony of the Spirit in our hearts, makes rational argumentation unnecessary. Afterward, the authority can be confirmed through a number of arguments. But this a posteriori approach actually adds nothing essential to the certainty of the truth. In the debate with Roman Catholic theology, this became the deciding point, and it worked just as strongly against the fanatics, who appealed to their own revelations.[34] The certainty of faith rests upon the mutual connection between Word and Spirit.

Characteristic of Calvin's hermeneutics was that it made possible a fully theological exegesis of the Old Testament. Law and gospel function in principle in the same way in the order of salvation as they do for Luther. The role of the law is to make way for the gospel. More than Luther, however, Calvin also uses a salvation-historical framework with respect to law and gospel, which leads to a different accentuation. The real contrast has to do not with law and gospel but with an understanding of the law with or without the Spirit. And this is just as true of the understanding and acceptance of the gospel, which one also comes to understand only through the Spirit. The order-of-salvation aspect receives less emphasis in Calvin than the salvation-historical, and it also functions now in a much broader context, which Calvin develops by emphasizing the unity of the covenant of God.[35] Despite all its variety, this covenant is substantially one. The new covenant is related to the old in a way that is reflected in comparatives: more of the Spirit, more knowledge, more assurance. Only in the eschaton does the believer reach completion; in this life we daily grow and increase and more and more develop in the faith. In this way salvation history plays itself out in the life of the believer on a small scale.

The idea of unity also comes to expression in Calvin's conception of *doctrina* as the constitutive factor in understanding Scripture. *Docilitas*, indispensable for any disciple who wants to be instructed by the Scriptures, is the posture of faith in which the teaching is appropriated. Calvin's thinking in pedagogical categories here is connected with his humanistic training. He now puts it into the service of the gospel, which for him is a way of expressing the

---

34. CO 2:69ff.

35. CO 2:313ff. See also Hans H. Wolf, *Die Einheit des Bundes: Das Verhältnis von Altem und Neuem Testament bei Calvin* (Neukirchen: Verlag der Buchhandlung des Erziehungsvereins, 1958), 38–54.

"Christian philosophy." He thus develops a system of truths that in their con- nection form the one truth of God:

> It is striking how much Calvin uses almost the same terminology to speak of the testimony of the Spirit, who ultimately leads us to under- stand Scripture as the Word of God, of the nature of faith, of the seal- ing with the Holy Spirit, and of the indwelling of Christ in our hearts through the Holy Spirit. The concepts he employs usually center on the same reality, which he approaches sometimes on the basis of Chris- tology and at other times pneumatology.[36]

This unity of conception rests on the fundamental conviction that the mes- sage of the Bible is about the *doctrina salutis* (doctrine of salvation), which gov- erns its cohesion. With his heavy emphasis on the testimony of the specific text, Calvin is able to avoid a superficial biblicism, because in a certain way the entire *doctrina* resonates with it. Furthermore, doctrine for him is not yet that system of truths over which Protestant Orthodoxy would later stand guard. It is preaching in action, instruction as it takes place, and at the same time it is the content of the gospel itself.

This *teaching* of Scripture occurs in the church. The tension in the con- nection between Word and Spirit harks back to the relation of Spirit and preaching in the congregation. The Word is there, waiting to be interpreted. Diversity in the forms of biblical interpretation, from exegesis through expo- sition to application, serves the living proclamation of the Word. Regardless of which genre Calvin is using, whether it be a lecture to a class, the writing of a commentary, or even in preaching itself, the Word is always and every- where directed toward the congregation. In all of Calvin's interaction with the Bible, the church is always present. In all the forms that can embrace it, the Word presents the truth, and as the Word of promise, by the Spirit it leads to assurance. It also brings about new life by the Spirit. The Scriptures are use- ful because they contain a *perfecta regula* (complete rule) for *bene beateque vivendi* (living well and happily). As Calvin notes in a comment on 2 Timothy 3:16, a characterization reminiscent of Erasmus and Bucer, "Whoever wishes to make progress in Scripture ought first of all to determine for oneself that the law and the prophets contain a doctrine not produced by human wisdom but dictated by the Holy Spirit."[37] God is the author of Holy Scripture. He speaks by means of it today, just as he moved the writers themselves to speak in their day. Thus the self-testimony of Scripture operates through the Spirit, who is the Spirit of Christ, for this is the way Christ himself comes to us: "This

---

36. Willem van 't Spijker, *Gemeenschap met Christus: Centraal gegeven van de gereformeerde the- ologie* (Kampen: Kok, 1995), 62 n. 147.
    37. CO 52:383.

is the true knowledge of Christ: when we receive him as he is offered by the Father, namely, clothed with his gospel," or "clothed with his promises."[38] The testimony of the Spirit can never be disconnected from the Scriptures, and even less so from him who reveals himself in the Scriptures—Christ.

GRACE

When Calvin talks about the work of the Spirit, it is particularly in connection with how we receive the grace of Christ. He devotes the third book of the *Institutes* entirely to this theme, and there the unique character of his theology becomes apparent. More strongly and even differently than in Luther, it is a theology of the exalted Christ. Luther pulls Christ down deep into the flesh. His theology of the cross places all the emphasis on the suffering of Christ. For Calvin, however, the line points upward. Through his suffering and resurrection, Christ is glorified. It is he himself who administers the reconciliation. Calvin employs the expression (which is not easy to grasp) of "the vivifying flesh of Christ" (*caro vivifica*),[39] with which he tries to preserve the unity of both the obtaining and the application of salvation. The cross is one stage on the way to glorification. The efficacy of grace is based on the power exercised by the exalted Christ.

A second special feature of Calvin's doctrine of grace is that of the threefold office of Christ, an idea borrowed from Bucer, which functions as a framework not only for the obtaining of salvation but also for the *applicatio salutis* (application of salvation). The kingship of Christ has a twofold aspect: it operates in the world as providence and in the church as election. Christ's office, therefore, has an eschatological dimension to it, the outworking of which will be seen only on the last day. The benefits of the reconciliation on the cross are fully manifest only in glory. The threefold office is unique, but it also provides an analogy for the differentiation in the offices of the church.

Highly significant is a third characteristic of Calvin's Christology. It is not only interwoven with his pneumatology; it also shapes its very content. The work of the Spirit consists in the glorification of Christ, as he is given to us for wisdom, righteousness, sanctification, and full redemption. Whoever pulls this chain apart, tears Christ apart.[40]

---

38. CO 2:410; CO 2:311: "Nec vero aliter Christo fruimur, nisi quatenus eum amplectimur promissionibus suis vestitum."

39. Marvin P. Hoogland, *Calvin's Perspective on the Exaltation of Christ in Comparison with the Post-Reformation Doctrine of the Two States* (Kampen: Kok, 1966), 115–20.

40. CO 49:331.

Calvin speaks of the unity of the *officia* (offices) of Christ, which also becomes visible in the unity of the person and work of Christ. Melanchthon had already joined these two together: knowledge of Christ consists in knowing his benefits. Calvin combines both in a substantial way. Christ is the actual object of faith, and anyone who knows what the benefits of Christ are also knows what faith is.[41] We share in the benefits because they exist in unity with the person of Christ.

The grace of Christ is granted to us in communion with Christ himself. In his treatise on the freedom of a Christian (1520), Luther illustrated the doctrine of justification, that miraculous exchange, with the image of marriage, in which there is a community of goods: what Christ has becomes ours, and vice versa. Calvin expanded this idea of communion with Christ and applied it to the doctrine of the Lord's Supper, which can be viewed as a prism in which all the lines of his theology converge. This is clearly seen in the themes of the third book of the *Institutes*, which has as its heading, "The Way in Which the Grace of Christ Is Received, What Benefits Come from It, and What Effects Follow It." Calvin treats the subject matter from the angle of the hidden work of the Spirit, which joins us to Christ. "So long as Christ is outside of us, and we are separated from him, what he has suffered and done for the salvation of the human race is useless and of no significance for us."[42] The Spirit incorporates us into Christ and at the same time also Christ into us. That is how full salvation is given to us.

Because this is the central idea, Calvin does not need to bother with the chronology of the *ordo salutis* (order of salvation). The Spirit is the inner teacher who penetrates our inmost being with the promises of salvation, which otherwise would only sound in our ears. Calvin locates this communion with Christ in the middle of his discussion of the nature and assurance of faith.[43] At the same time, he states that the gracious promise is the foundation of faith.[44] The relation between objective promise and subjective experience is maintained: we consider the promises of God's mercy to be true not only outside of ourselves. Because we embrace them internally, we appropriate the promises for ourselves.[45] Thus we learn not only who God is *in se* (in himself) but also how he exists for us, *qualis est* (what he is like).[46] This knowledge of God provides, for the most part, the content for the notion of faith: a firm and certain knowledge of God's benevolence toward us, founded upon the truth of

41. CO 49:332.
42. CO 2:393.
43. CO 2:417.
44. CO 2:421.
45. CO 2:411.
46. CO 2:402.

the gracious promise in Christ, revealed by the Holy Spirit to our minds and sealed in our hearts.

The inner relationship with Christ is effectuated in regeneration, understood as conversion. Calvin describes the process without slipping into a system. The longer we are in communion with Christ, the more faith restores our lives to true piety toward God and love for neighbor. Calvin portrays the Christian life in all its breadth.[47] It occurs not only in a negative way in the mortification of the old self. It is a living in the expectation that we will gain the victory and, at the same time, an ongoing reflection on the future life. The life of the Christian is formed on the basis of being called, since we no longer belong to ourselves. Calvin's ethics declare that this is true of every person and for the whole of life in all its facets. All of life awaits reformation.[48] Self-denial constitutes the main task of a Christian life. It happens not only by way of taking up one's cross. The foundation of the Christian life lies in the fact that the believer is the possession of God. "Oh, how far one has come who knows that he is not his own and who has relinquished the control and rule of his own understanding in order to grant it to God."[49]

It is striking that justification through faith comes up for discussion only after the treatment of faith and the Christian life—introduced, once again, with the observation that through our participation in Christ, we receive above all a twofold grace: reconciliation and renewal.[50] Like Luther, Calvin places all the emphasis on the imputation of Christ's righteousness.[51] "They should be accounted righteous outside themselves."[52] "Those who prate that we are justified through faith because we are reborn and live spiritually have never tasted the sweetness of grace, by which to consider that God is reconciled with them." At the same time, Calvin always combined justification by grace with the internal and external renewal of all of life:

> Therefore, we must come to this remedy: that believers nourish their hope for the inheritance of eternal life on no other ground than that they are engrafted into the body of Christ and by grace are accounted righteous. For, as regards justification, faith is something merely passive. It brings nothing of our own by which to earn the grace of God but receives from Christ what is lacking in us.[53]

47. CO 2:501–32.
48. CO 2:501.
49. CO 2:506.
50. CO 2:533.
51. Ibid.
52. "Iusti extra se censeantur"; CO 2:543.
53. CO 2:564.

ELECTION

The relation between justification and communion with Christ guarantees the unmerited favor and efficacy of grace. Both components play a role in the doctrine of election; in the *Institutes* of 1536, Calvin placed election in the confession concerning the church. In contrast to the untrustworthy institution of the church in France, he went back to the invisible *corpus mysticum* (mystical body), the church as the sum total of the elect. Referring to Romans 8:30 as the order of God's mercy, Calvin states that eternal election becomes manifest in calling and justification.[54] When we are in communion with Christ, we receive a testimony thereby that we belong to the elect,[55] for election happens "in Christ." A living relationship with him is a reliable sign that election is effective through the work of the Spirit. By a judgment of love, we deem the members of the church to be elect. Their confession of faith, example of life, and participation in the sacraments constitute the marks and signs of their gracious election.[56]

In later editions, Calvin subsumed the doctrine of election under the explanation of the doctrine of providence. In the 1559 edition it serves as the conclusion to soteriology. Here he entirely follows in the footsteps of Augustine and, in addition to Scripture, repeatedly cites him. His representation of the doctrine also shows a clear relationship to the early Luther, and especially to Bucer. All of them start with the empirical fact that the preaching of the gospel produces different results. This leads to the a posteriori observation that God's will alone is decisive for participation in salvation. However, Calvin continually warns against attempts to penetrate the hidden depths of God's eternal decree. Christ is the mirror of election. Calvin emphasizes the freedom of God's grace, which is not based on *praescientia* (foreknowledge), by which God would know who would accept the gospel in faith. For Calvin, as for Bucer, the doctrine of election is situated in the context of pastoral care, which places heavy emphasis on the necessity of sanctification, while the assurance of salvation rests unshakably firm outside of ourselves. The work of the Holy Spirit does not thereby take anything away from the perfection of the work of Christ. Only in Christ, the mirror of God's eternal mercy, do we find the assurance of our election. Among asylum seekers in Geneva and martyrs in France and the Netherlands, this doctrine functioned as a firm foundation of comfort in life and in death.

54. CO 1:73.
55. CO 1:74.
56. CO 1:75.

The fact that in the last edition of the *Institutes*, Calvin placed the doctrine of election at the end of and as the conclusion to the doctrine of salvation does not mean that it no longer had any relation to ecclesiology. The similarity to the discussions in the first edition is remarkable. The main theme is the same. This is especially true when it comes to the polemic against Rome, which is expanded in some points but also borrows whole passages unaltered from the first edition. Two things are changed. First, greater attention is paid to the visibility of the church, which according to the title of book 4 comes under "The External Means or Aids by Which God Invites Us into the Community of Christ and Holds Us Therein."[57] The alternatives are not external-internal but external-secret. The real secret that is efficaciously present in the church is the secret work of the Spirit. The tension between Word and Spirit again comes to the fore in the doctrine of the church, but here, too, it is relieved by the confession of the communion of believers with Christ. That lays the groundwork for the unity of the church, the second point to which Calvin pays considerable attention. He points to election: all the elect are united in Christ. One could not find two or three churches without Christ being torn asunder.[58] Every member participates in the benefits of Christ and by this participation is also bound to all the others.

THE CHURCH AS COMMUNION WITH CHRIST

The marks of the church are all connected with the mediation of salvation. "For whenever we see the Word of God purely preached and heard, and the sacraments administered according to Christ's institution, there it ought in no way to be doubted that a church of God exists."[59] Both preaching and administration of the sacraments will bear fruit by the blessing of God. They constitute the signs of the presence of Christ himself, according to the promise that wherever two or three are gathered in his name, he is there in their midst. Whoever does not join this community is viewed as a traitor and apostate from religion.[60]

The invisible church coincides with the body of Christ. The visible church also contains unbelievers and hypocrites whom we are not able to recognize. The judgment of love is fallible, but it is also essential. Only God judges the heart. That is why church discipline does not come into play until there is public sin, by which the unity of Christ's body is damaged. In the struggle against the Anabaptists, Calvin rejected their way of practicing church discipline, but he

57. CO 2:744.
58. CO 2:747.
59. CO 2:753f.
60. CO 2:754.

never abandoned the ideal of a holy community. It flows directly out of the view of the church as communion with Christ. That is why church discipline is not, to be sure, directly counted among the marks of the church, but at the same time, according to Calvin, a church without such a means is hardly conceivable. Sound doctrine forms the soul of the church, and discipline functions as the sinews in the body, "by which the members of the body, each in its own place, are connected with each other."[61] Like Bucer, Calvin made a distinction between the discipline that is exercised among members of the congregation and that which is applied to servants of the church.[62] The latter is considerably more strict. The office-bearers—teachers, pastors, elders, and deacons—have to provide the congregation with an example of purity in doctrine and life. Their authority is based on the Word alone. Apostolic succession consists in the permanent connection of Word and Spirit in the preaching of the truth of God in Christ.

Communion with Christ is also central in Calvin's doctrine of the sacraments. What is crucial here is faith in Christ: "For what is a sacrament received apart from faith but the most certain ruin of the church?"[63] Assurance of salvation is not dependent on participation in the sacrament. Whoever thinks that the sacrament confers anything more than we receive through faith in the promise is mistaken. But that does not mean that baptism and the Lord's Supper are merely signs, devoid of real content. Along with Augustine, Calvin distinguishes between sacrament and *res sacramenti* (the thing [content] of the sacrament). This distinction (*distinctio*) has validity only when "thing and sign" (*res et signum*) are seen as united (*coniunctio*).[64] The benefit of the sacraments is found in one's advancing in communion with Christ. "If one is to have not merely a sign empty of truth but really receive the matter with the sign, it is necessary to apprehend in faith the Word that is included in the sacrament."[65]

Baptism is the sign "by which we are received into the fellowship of the church, so that, engrafted into Christ, we may be reckoned among the children of God."[66] The practice of infant baptism is based on the promise of the covenant of grace, which in the Old Testament was signified and sealed by circumcision. "And if the covenant remains firm and steadfast, it has to do no less with the children of Christians today than it did with the children of the Jews under the Old Testament. And if they participate in the thing signified, why shall they be debarred from the sign?"[67]

61. CO 2:905.
62. CO 2:919.
63. CO 2:951.
64. CO 2:952.
65. Ibid.
66. CO 2:962.
67. CO 2:979.

The sacrament of the Lord's Supper is also a sign and seal of communion with Christ. We have come to know Calvin's conception of the Lord's Supper as referring to the cross of Christ and at the same time as a sign and seal of the resurrection life that is communicated to us by the Spirit. Calvin intends thereby to steer a middle course between a diminishing of the signs, by which they are detached from the mystery to which they are bound, and an over-valuing of the signs, by which the mysteries of the Lord's Supper are obscured.[68] Here Calvin employs a concept that Bucer had also used and with which it was thought the break with the Lutherans could be bridged: *exhibitio*. Christ offers us the bread in order to nourish us, and he gives us a share of it through faith. He became the bread by giving his body on the cross as a reconciliation once for all. Now he gives it daily by offering himself to us in the gospel as the crucified one, by signifying and sealing this gift through the mystery of the Lord's Supper, and by fulfilling internally what he signifies and points to externally.[69] Christ himself fulfills his promise in believers by nourishing and refreshing us in his communion.

CORPUS CHRISTI **AND** *CORPUS CHRISTIANUM*

The way in which Calvin understands the relationship between the church as the body of Christ and the mystery of the Lord's Supper, which for him is also the real body of Christ, means that his concept of the church is completely filled with a spiritual content that can only be characterized as a mystery. What is true of the Lord's Supper is similarly true of the church. This explains his constant emphasis on maintaining church discipline, which seeks to keep the congregation as the body of Christ pure. The presence of Christ in the sacrament demands this. If the congregation is nourished with the life-giving flesh of Christ, it is a gross sacrilege if public sinners partake of the sacrament. The body of Christ may not be desecrated by a *promiscua exhibitio* (being offered to everyone).[70]

At this point the tension also emerges between the *corpus Christi* (body of Christ), as the congregation celebrating the Lord's Supper, and the *corpus christianum*, the Christian commonwealth, the ideal that Calvin strove for with all his might. Calvin tried to ease this tension with his doctrine of the distinction between the twofold government, the spiritual and the political. The first government seeks to nurture the conscience toward piety and the service of God.

68. CO 2:1005.
69. CO 2:1006. Here Calvin appeals to Chrysostom: we are renewed in our souls in communion with the flesh of Christ just as we are nourished in our bodies by the bread. "Christ makes us his body not only through faith but [also] in reality."
70. CO 2:907.

The second serves to develop the obligations of humanity and civil justice.[71] The Lutheran doctrine of the two kingdoms is transformed by Calvin to bring to expression the twofold character of the rule of Christ. The kingdom of Christ takes two forms. Even the civil government has a pastoral responsibility to fulfill and must oversee the progress and protection of the proclamation of the gospel.[72]

These two tasks may not be mixed, nor can they be separated from each other. Ecclesiastical office and civil service are related to each other like body and soul. The pair of ideas that plays a role in Calvin's explanation of the Christian life and reflection on the future life also dominates his reasoning here. It brings into the picture an eschatological element by which the tension between the two governments is pushed into the future. Temporal life has a higher goal. It is also maintained, however, by a political government that stands in the service of the gospel but whose objective task is, in a certain sense, independent of the question whether it carries out its duty to the gospel.

In any case, no private body or individual has the right to resist the civil government. This does not mean that the government stands outside the law or that it is autonomous. Laws form the nerve tissues of the state and the souls of civil governments. A magistrate is accountable to God, to whom the highest authority belongs. The *magistrates populares* (magistrates of the people) can make use of their powers to restrain the tyranny of princes.[73] Calvin is thinking here of the three estates (*tres ordines*), which, "as things now stand," are present in various kingdoms. They can act as legal bodies when they hold their chief assemblies. Otherwise, obedience and submission are mandatory. Of course, obedience to human authorities may not lead to the disobedience of God. In such a case one ought to take up his cross or go into exile. We should rather suffer anything than turn aside from piety. "And so that our courage might not grow faint, Paul spurs us on further with the warning, 'Christ bought us at so great a price as our redemption cost him, so that we would not be slaves to the wicked desires of human beings—much less be subject to their impiety' (1 Corinthians 7:23)."[74]

CHAPTER BIBLIOGRAPHY

Baron, Hans. *Calvins Staatsanschauung und das konfessionelle Zeitalter.* Munich: R. Oldenbourg, 1924.

71. CO 2:622f., 1092f.
72. CO 2:1094.
73. CO 2:1116.
74. CO 2:1118.

Barth, Karl. *Die Theologie Calvins 1922: Vorlesung Göttingen Sommersemester 1922.* Zurich: Theologisch Verlag, 1993.

Bauke, Herman. *Die Probleme der Theologie Calvins.* Leipzig: Hinrichs, 1922.

Benedetto, Robert, ed. *Interpreting John Calvin—Ford Lewis Battles.* Grand Rapids: Baker, 1996.

Beyerhaus, Gisbert. *Studien zur Staatsanschauung Calvins: Mit besonderer Berücksichtigung seines Souveränitätsbegriffs.* Berlin: Trowitzsch & Sohn, 1910.

Bohatec, Josef. *Calvins Lehre von Staat und Kirche mit besonderer Berücksichtigung des Organismusgedankens.* Aalen: Scientia Verlag, 1968.

Brunner, Peter. *Vom Glauben bei Calvin: Dargestellt auf Grund der Institutio, des Catechismus Genevensis und unter Heranziehung exegetischer und homiletischer Schriften.* Tübingen: J. C. B. Mohr (Paul Siebeck), 1925.

Bucer, Martin. *In sacra quatuor Euangelia, ennarationes perpetuae.* Basel: Herwagen, 1536.

———. *Martini Buceri Scripta Anglicana fere omnia.* Basel: Perna, 1577.

Cramer, Jan A. *De Heilige Schrift bij Calvijn.* Utrecht: A. Oosthoek, 1926.

Dee, Simon P. *Het geloofsbegrip van Calvijn.* Kampen: Kok, 1918.

Doumergue, Émile. *Jean Calvin: Les hommes et les choses de son temps.* Vol. 4, *La pensée religieuse de Calvin.* Lausanne: G. Bridel, 1910.

———. *Jean Calvin: Les hommes et les choses de son temps.* Vol. 5, *La pensée ecclésiastique et la pensée politique de Calvin.* Lausanne: Georges Bridel & Co., 1917.

Emmen, Egbert. *De Christologie van Calvijn.* Amsterdam: H. J. Paris, 1935.

Fischer, Alfons. *Calvins Eschatologie in der Erstausgabe der "Christianae Religionis Institutio" 1536.* Bamberg: Wissenschaftlicher Verlag Bamberg, 1995.

Fröhlich, Karlfried. *Gottesreich, Welt und Kirche bei Calvin: Ein Beitrag zur Frage nach dem Reichgottesglauben Calvins.* Munich: E. Reinhardt, 1930.

Ganoczy, Alexandre. *Calvin, théologien de l'église et du ministère.* Paris: Editions du Cerf, 1964.

Ganoczy, Alexandre, and Stefan Scheld. *Die Hermeneutik Calvins: Geistesgeschichtliche Voraussetzungen und Grundzüge.* Wiesbaden: F. Steiner, 1983.

Girardin, Benoit. *Rhétorique et théologie: Calvin, Le Commentaire de l'Épitre aux Romains.* Paris: Editions Beauchesne, 1979.

Groot, Douwe J. de. *Calvijns opvatting over de inspiratie der Heilige Schrift.* Zutphen: N. V. Nauta, 1931.

Hauck, Wilhelm-Albert. *Christusglaube und Gottesoffenbarung nach Calvin.* Gütersloh: C. Bertelsmann, 1939.

Hoogland, Marvin P. *Calvin's Perspective on the Exaltation of Christ in Comparison with the Post-Reformation Doctrine of the Two States.* Kampen: Kok, 1966.

Höpfl, Harro. *The Christian Polity of John Calvin.* New York: Cambridge University Press, 1982.

Jacobs, Paul. *Prädestination und Verantwortlichkeit bei Calvin.* Vol. 1, *Beiträge zur Geschichte und Lehre der Reformierten Kirche.* Neukirchen: Kr. Moers, 1937.

Jansen, John F. *Calvin's Doctrine of the Work of Christ.* London: J. Clark, 1956.

Köhler, Walther. *Dogmengeschichte als Geschichte des christlichen Selbstbewusstseins: Das Zeitalter der Reformation.* Zurich: M. Niehan, 1959.

Kolfhaus, Wilhelm. *Christusgemeinschaft bei Johannes Calvin.* Neukirchen: K. Moers, 1939.

———. *Vom christlichen Leben nach Johannes Calvin.* Neukirchen: Kreis Moers, 1949.

Koopmans, Jan. *Het oudkerkelijk dogma in de Reformatie: Bepaaldelijk bij Calvijn.* Wageningen: H. Veenman & Zonen, 1938.

Krusche, Werner. *Das Wirken des Heiligen Geistes nach Calvin.* Göttingen: Vandenhoeck & Ruprecht, 1957.

Lange van Ravenswaay, Jan Marius J. *Augustinus totus noster: Das Augustinverständnis bei Johannes Calvin.* Göttingen: Vandenhoeck & Ruprecht, 1990.

Leith, John H. "Calvin's Theological Method and the Ambiguity in His Theology." In *Reformation Studies: Essays in Honor of R. H. Bainton,* edited by Franklin H. Littell, 106–14. Richmond: John Knox Press, 1962.

Lelièvre, Charles. *La Maîtrise de l'esprit: Essai critique sur le principe fondamental de la théologie de Calvin.* Cahors: A. Coueslant, 1901.

Linde, Simon van der. *De leer van den Heiligen Geest bij Calvijn: Bijdrage tot de kennis der reformatorische theologie.* Wageningen: Veenman, 1943.

Locher, Gottfried W. *Testimonium internum: Calvins Lehre vom Heiligen Geist und das hermeneutische Problem.* Zurich: EVZ-Verlag, 1964.

Lülsdorff, Raimund. *Die Zukunft Jesu Christi: Calvins Eschatologie und ihre katholische Sicht.* Paderborn: Bonifatius, 1996.

McDonnel, Kilian. *John Calvin, the Church, and the Eucharist.* Princeton: Princeton University Press, 1967.

McKee, Elsie A. *Elders and the Plural Ministry: The Role of Exegetical History in Illuminating John Calvin's Theology.* Geneva: Droz, 1988.

———. *John Calvin on the Diaconate and Liturgical Almsgiving.* Geneva: Droz, 1984.

Millet, Olivier. *Calvin et la dynamique de la parole: Étude de rhétorique réformée.* Paris: H. Champion, 1992.

———. "*Docere/Movere*: Les catégories rhéthoriques et leurs sources humanistes dans la doctrine calvinienne de la foi." In *Calvinus Sincerioris Religionis Vindex: Calvin as Protector of the Purer Religion,* edited by Wilhelm H. Neuser and Brian G. Armstrong, 35–51. Kirksville, MO: Sixteenth Century Journal Publishers, 1997.

Milner, Benjamin C. *Calvin's Doctrine of the Church.* Leiden: Brill, 1970.

Moehn, Wilhelmus H. T. *God roept ons tot zijn dienst: Een homiletisch onderzoek naar de verhouding tussen God en de hoorder in Calvijns preken over Handelingen 4:1–6:7.* Kampen: Kok, 1996.

Mooi, Remko J. *Het kerk: En dogmahistorisch element in de werken van Johannes Calvijn.* Wageningen: H. Veenman & Zonen, 1965.

Mueller, William A. *Church and State in Luther and Calvin.* Nashville: Broadman, 1954.

Mülhaupt, Erwin. *Die Predigt Calvins, ihre Geschichte, ihre Form und ihre religiösen Grundgedanken.* Berlin: W. de Gruyter, 1931.

Neuser, Wilhelm H. "Calvins Verständinis der Heiligen Schrift." In *Calvinus Sacrae Scripturae Professor,* edited by Wilhelm H. Neuser, 41–71. Grand Rapids: Eerdmans, 1994.

———. "Die Theologie Calvins." In *Handbuch der Dogmen- und Theologiegeschichte,* vol. 2, *Die Lehrentwicklung im Rahmen der Konfessionalität,* edited by Carl Andresen, 238–85. Göttingen: Vandenhoeck & Ruprecht, 1980.

Niesel, Wilhelm. *Die Theologie Calvins.* Munich: C. Kaiser, 1957.

Nijenhuis, Willem. "Calvin." In *TRE (Theologische Realenzyklopädie),* edited by Gerhard Krause et al., vol. 7, pages 568–92. New York: W. de Gruyter, 1981.

Olson, Jeannine E. *Calvin and Social Welfare: Deacons and the Bourse française.* Selinsgrove, PA: Susquehanna University Press, 1989.

Oort, Johannes van. "Calvinus patristicus: Calvijns kennis, gebruik en misbruik van de patres." In *De kerkvaders in Reformatie en Nadere Reformatie,* edited by Johannes van Oort, 67–81. Zoetermeer: Boekencentrum, 1997.

————. "John Calvin and the Church Fathers." In *The Reception of the Church Fathers in the West: From the Carolingians to the Maurists*, edited by Irena Backus, vol. 2, pages 661–700. Leiden: Brill, 1997.

Opitz, Peter. *Calvins theologische Hermeneutik*. Neukirchen-Vluyn: Neukirchener Verlag, 1994.

Otten, Heinz. *Prädestination in Calvins theologischer Lehre*. Neukirchen-Vluyn: Neukirchener Verlag, 1968.

Pannier, Jacques. *Le témoignage du Saint-Esprit: Essai sur l'histoire du dogme dans la théologie réformée*. Paris: Librairie Fischbacher, 1893.

Parker, T. H. L. (Thomas Henry Lewis). *Calvin's New Testament Commentaries*. Louisville, KY: Westminster/John Knox Press, 1993.

————. *Calvin's Old Testament Commentaries*. Louisville, KY: Westminster/John Knox Press, 1993.

————. *Calvin's Preaching*. Louisville, KY: Westminster/John Knox Press, 1992.

————. "John Calvin." In *A History of Christian Doctrine*, edited by H. Cunliffe-Jones, 387–99. New York: T&T Clark, 2006.

————. *Supplementa Calviniana: An Account of the Manuscripts of Calvin's Sermons Now in Course of Preparation*. London: Tyndale, 1962.

Pelikan, Jaroslav. *The Christian Tradition: A History of the Development of Doctrine*. Vol. 4, *Reformation of Church and Dogma (1300–1700)*. Chicago: University of Chicago Press, 1984.

Peter, Rodolphe. "Genève dans la prédication de Calvin." In *Calvinus ecclesiae Genevensis custos*, edited by Wilhelm H. Neuser, 23–48. Frankfurt: Lang, 1984.

Polman, A. D. R. (Andries Derk Rietema) *De praedestinatieleer van Augustinus, Thomas van Aquino en Calvijn: Een dogmahistorische studie*. Franeker: T. Wever, 1936.

Quistorp, Heinrich. *Die letzten Dinge im Zeugnis Calvins: Calvins Eschatologie*. Gütersloh: C. Bertelsmann, 1941.

Reuter, Karl. *Das Grundverständnis der Theologie Calvins: Unter Einbeziehung ihrer geschichtlichen Abhängigkeiten*. Neukirchen-Vluyn: Neukirchener Verlag, 1963.

————. *Vom Scholaren bis zum jungen Reformator: Studien zum Werdegang Johannes Calvins*. Neukirchen-Vluyn: Neukirchener Verlag, 1981.

Richel, Pieter J. *Het kerkbegrip van Calvijn*. Utrecht: Libertas Drukkerijen, 1942.

Rimbach, Harald. *Gnade und Erkenntnis in Calvins Prädestinationslehr: Calvin im Vergleich mit Pighius, Beza und Melanchthon*. New York: P. Lang, 1996.

Rist, Gilbert. "Modernité de la method théologique de Calvin." *Revue de théologie et de philosophie* 18 (1968): 19–33.

Ritschl, Otto. *Dogmengeschichte des Protestantismus*. Vol. 3, *Die reformierte Theologie des 16. und des 17. Jahrhunderts in ihrer Entstehung und Entwicklung*. Göttingen: Vandenhoeck & Ruprecht, 1926.

Scheibe, Max. *Calvins Prädestinationslehre: Ein Beitrag zur Würdigung der Eigenart seiner Theologie und Religiosität*. Halle a. S.: M. Niemeyer, 1897.

Schroten, Hendrik. *Christus, de Middelaar, bij Calvijn: Bijdrage tot de leer van de zekerheid des geloofs*. Utrecht: P. den Boer, 1948.

Shepherd, Victor A. *The Nature and Function of Faith in the Theology of John Calvin*. Macon, GA: Mercer University Press, 1983.

Smits, Luchesius. *Saint Augustin dans l'oeuvre de Jean Calvin*. Vol. 1, *Étude de critique littéraire*. Paris: Van Gorcum, 1957.

————. *Saint Augustin dans l'oeuvre de Jean Calvin*. Vol. 2, *Tables des references augustiniennes*. Paris: Van Gorcum, 1958.

Spijker, Willem van 't. *Gemeenschap met Christus: Centraal gegeven van de gereformeerde theologie*. Kampen: In opdracht van de Theologische Universiteit van de Christelijke Gereformeerde Kerken in Nederland uitgegeven door Kok, 1995.

———. *Luther en Calvijn: De invloed van Luther op Calvijn blijkens de Institutie*. Kampen: Kok, 1985.

———. "Prädestination bei Bucer und Calvin: Ihre gegenseitige Beeinflussung und Abhängigkeit." In *Calvinus Theologus*, edited by Wilhelm H. Neuser, 85–111. Neukirchen-Vluyn: Neukirchener Verlag, 1976.

Stauffer, Richard. "Quelques aspects insolites de la théologie du premier article dans la prédication de Calvin." In *Calvinus Ecclesiae Doctor*, edited by Wilhelm H. Neuser, 47–68. Kampen: Kok, 1980.

Tamburello, Dennis E. *Union with Christ: John Calvin and the Mysticism of St. Bernard*. Louisville, KY: Westminster John Knox Press, 1994.

Torrance, Thomas F. *The Hermeneutics of John Calvin*. Edinburgh: Scottish Academic Press, 1988.

Wallace, Ronald S. *Calvin's Doctrine of the Christian Life*. Edinburgh: Oliver & Boyd, 1959.

Wendel, François. *Calvin et l'humanisme*. Paris: Presses Universitaires de France, 1976.

———. *Calvin: Ursprung und Entwicklung seiner Theologie*. Neukirchen-Vluyn: Neukirchener Verlag, 1968.

Wernle, Paul. *Der evangelische Glaube nach den Hauptschriften der Reformatoren*. Vol. 3, *Calvin*. Tübingen: J. C. B. Mohr (Paul Siebeck), 1919.

Willis, E. David. *Calvin's Catholic Christology: The Function of the So-called Extra Calvinisticum in Calvin's Theology*. Leiden: Brill, 1966.

Wolf, Hans H. *Die Einheit des Bundes: Das Verhältnis von Altem und Neuem Testament bei Calvin*. Neukirchen: Verlag der Buchhandlung des Erziehungsvereins, 1958.

Zachman, Randal C. *The Assurance of Faith: Conscience in the Theology of Martin Luther and John Calvin*. Louisville, KY: Westminster John Knox Press, 2005.

Zillenbiller, Anette. *Der Einheit der katholischen Kirche: Calvins Cyprianrezeption in seinen ekklesiologischen Schriften*. Mainz: P. Zabern, 1993.

11

Calvin's Influence

THE CHURCH OF GENEVA AS A MODEL

Calvin's strong personality radiated an influence that can hardly be overestimated. It had such a powerful effect first of all in the city of Geneva that, from the time of his return in 1541, he managed to build it into a *civitas christiana* (Christian commonwealth). With its confession and structure, the church of Geneva became a model for a great number of churches in Europe. The impression that Calvin left after his death was described by the magistracy in the city council minutes of June 8, 1564, with the term "majesty": "God had stamped him with a character of great majesty."[1]

Calvin himself recognized no higher authority than that of the Word of God, and he submitted himself to it without hesitation. With the talent of a genius, he poured all his energy into the formation of a commonwealth that did justice to the majesty of the Bible, as he understood it, and thus also to God's own authority, as he viewed it. The preaching of the Word became the most important means to that end. From 1549 onward, Calvin preached twenty times a month. Considering this high frequency and the way in which Calvin related his preaching to the current situation, this became a powerful means for exercising his influence. To be sure, Calvin never entered the pulpit unprepared; he always immersed himself in the text ahead of time. But he then left it to the current moment to address his material in a discerning way to his audience. The power of the preaching lay in the Word, and the effect

---

1. Ernst Staehelin, *Johannes Calvin: Leben und ausgewählte Schriften* (Elberfeld: Friderichs, 1863), 2:372.

was determined in large part by Calvin's ability to connect it with the situation inside and outside Geneva, especially in France. After the mid-1550s, his congregation consisted for the most part of asylum seekers with a French background. In their situation, the preaching played a comforting role.

Along with that came his personal influence, which emerged not only in his pastoral work and individual care of souls but especially in the course of affairs in Geneva. His influence on the magistracy sometimes took the form of control. He attended the meetings of the magistracy, regularly accompanied by the other preachers. At first he had difficulty persuading the council, but after 1555 his authority grew noticeably. Later his viewpoint came to be accepted more as a matter of course, since it not only had a principled spiritual quality about it, but also displayed real insight. Thus he more and more won over the confidence of the city. Right down to his closest acquaintances, Calvin managed to surround himself with people who cherished the same ideals as he did. The huge influx of refugees created a change in the makeup of the congregation as such. Especially during his last twenty years, Calvin felt himself to be a Frenchman among his compatriots. Here they could confess their faith in total freedom, something of which they spoke very highly in their correspondence.[2] Hence the congregation radiated far beyond Geneva.

An important factor here was the presence of a number of refugee congregations in the city.[3] There was no need for a separate French congregation. The asylum seekers from France far outnumbered the original congregational members. In addition, there was an Italian refugee congregation and a Spanish colony that joined with this church. Many of them never had the opportunity to return to the land of their birth, unlike the members of the English congregation, which was formed by a large number of Protestants forced to leave England in 1553. Most of the latter saw their sojourn in Geneva come to an end in 1559, and their influence on the advance of the Reformation in England can be clearly traced.[4]

Calvin also exercised a direct influence by means of the Academy of Geneva. Although many of the students were from France and found their way back there again, the distribution of graduates already in Calvin's own lifetime was much wider than that.[5] One can speak of a European impact that

2. Wihelmus H. T. Moehn, "God roept ons tot zijn dienst" (Ph.D. diss., University of Utrecht, 1996), 336ff.

3. William E. Monter, *Calvin's Geneva* (New York: Wiley, 1967), 165–90.

4. Christina Garret, *The Marian Exiles: A Study in the Origins of Elizabethan Puritanism* (Cambridge: Cambridge University Press, 1938), 23f.; Dan G. Danner, *Pilgrimage to Puritanism: History and Theology of the Marian Exiles at Geneva, 1555 to 1560* (New York: Lang, 1999), 33ff.

5. Karin Maag, *Seminary or University? The Genevan Academy and Reformed Higher Education, 1560–1620* (Brookfield, VT: Ashgate Publishing Co., 1995), 30.

emanated from Calvin's university. It is difficult to calculate all the pieces of advice that Calvin provided those who sought it from him in Geneva. Considering how Calvin reports the way he tended to spend his days, the number was huge.

CORRESPONDENCE

A special means that the Genevan reformer used to the full was an intensive correspondence that he carried on with people throughout Europe. Calvin himself valued these letters highly, as can be seen from the care he took to entrust his papers to Beza. In his own archive he preserved both the letters he received and copies of those he sent out. Just before his death, he gave this material to Beza, so that the latter could publish letters "that could be of benefit to the churches."[6]

In 1575 the first edition of Calvin's letters appeared, selected by Beza.[7] It comprised four hundred letters, approximately half of which were addressed to persons or authorities in France, and the rest to Germans, Poles, Englishmen, Italians, and people of other nationalities. Three-fourths were in Calvin's own hand. The *Thesaurus epistolicus*, which was included in the *Corpus reformatorum*, contains a total of 4,302 letters, of which 1,369 are from Calvin himself.[8]

Calvin covered a wide area with this correspondence, stretching across the whole of Europe. Regardless of whom he was writing to or what he was writing about, he always energetically championed the cause of the Reformation and the unity of the churches. Beza was right in publishing his biography of Calvin along with the letters: in the letters one comes to know Calvin close-up.[9] His letters rise above the level of just friends who know each other, as was often the case in humanistic circles. They are, rather, an expression of what animated his own life: *doctrina* and *disciplina* in the service of the kingdom of Christ.[10]

---

6. CO 20:353.

7. *Joannis Calvini Epistolae et Responsae quibus interiectae sunt insignium in Ecclesia Dei virorum aliquot etiam Epistolae.*

8. By comparison, the collection of surviving letters to and from Bullinger numbers approximately 12,000! The *Thesaurus epistolicus Calvinianus* (CO 10b–20) contains 267 letters between Calvin and Bullinger: 161 from Bullinger to Calvin, and 106 from Calvin to Bullinger.

9. Jean-Daniel Benoît, "Calvin the Letter-Writer," in *John Calvin: A Collection of Distinguished Essays*, ed. G. E. Duffield (Grand Rapids: Eerdmans, 1966), 96; Daniel Ménager, "La correspondance de Calvin," in *Calvin et ses contemporains: Acts du colloque de Paris 1995*, ed. Olivier Millet (Geneva: Droz, 1998); Bernard Roussel, "Jean Calvin conseiller de ses contemporains: de la correspondence à la legend," in Millet, *Calvin et ses contemporains*.

10. Beza's selections of 1575 especially make that clear.

DEDICATIONS

A category all its own was formed by the large number of dedications with which Calvin provided his published works and which clearly show us that he consciously tried to exercise his influence in areas that, in his estimation, were open to the Reformation.[11] He began using this means in the private sphere in an attempt to give his works some publicity. Hence he dedicated his commentary on the Letter to the Romans to Simon Grynaeus,[12] and his defense against Pighius, *Defensio sanae et orthodoxae doctrinae adversus calumnias A. Pighii*, to Melanchthon.[13] After 1548 he tried to influence the development of the Reformation in England by attaching the name of the duke of Somerset to his commentary on 1 Timothy.[14] Poland, too, captured Calvin's interest, as evidenced by the dedication honoring King Sigismund August (1549) in the exposition of the Letter to the Hebrews.[15] The significance of Edward VI for the restoration of the church in England was brought to Calvin's attention by Jan Utenhove, an elder in the Dutch refugee congregation in London. Calvin dedicated two explanations of sections of Scripture to the young prince: Isaiah and the Catholic Epistles (1550).[16] The extent of Calvin's interest can also be seen from the dedications to King Christian III and Prince Frederick of Denmark, in 1552 and 1554, respectively.[17]

Sometimes Calvin received indications of thanks and appreciation; at other times, his encouraging gestures got no response. Occasionally, his intent seemed not to be welcomed, as in the case of Queen Elizabeth of England, to whom he had sent his revised commentary on Isaiah (1559).[18] She did not appreciate his gesture because in Geneva, John Knox was proclaiming the view that the rule of a country by a woman was illegal. Even before that, Calvin had appeared less than happy with his choice of important names that he could connect to his work. In 1554, the Saxons reacted negatively: Calvin had a mistaken view of the Lord's Supper and, in addition, in this commentary on Genesis had called into question the exegetical qualities of Luther.[19]

11. Jean-François Gilmont, "Les dédicataires de Calvin," in Millet, *Calvin et ses contemporains*, 117–34.

12. CO 10b:402–6; Rodolphe Peter and Jean-François Gilmont, eds., *Bibliotheca Calviniana: Les oeuvres de Jean Calvin publiees au XVIe siecle* (Geneva: Droz, 1991–), 1:76.

13. CO 6:229–32; Peter and Gilmont, *Bibliotheca Calviniana*, 1:124.

14. CO 13:16–18; Peter and Gilmont, *Bibliotheca Calviniana*, 1:276.

15. CO 13:281–86; Peter and Gilmont, *Bibliotheca Calviniana*, 1:301–2.

16. CO 14:30–37; Peter and Gilmont, *Bibliotheca Calviniana*, 1:399–401.

17. CO 14:292–96; Peter and Gilmont, *Bibliotheca Calviniana*, 1:442. CO 15:14–17; Peter and Gilmont, *Bibliotheca Calviniana*, 1:502.

18. CO 17:413–15; Peter and Gilmont, *Bibliotheca Calviniana*, 1:699f.

19. CO 15:196–201; Peter and Gilmont, *Bibliotheca Calviniana*, 1:522f.

Calvin, however, was not deterred from continuing down the same path. In 1559 Gustav I of Sweden was sent two copies of Calvin's lectures on the twelve minor prophets, and their receipt was rather formally confirmed. Sweden was not open to a Reformed voice.[20] In Denmark, too, the interest shown by Geneva was not reciprocated.[21] Therefore, Calvin dedicated a second edition of his commentary on Acts in 1560 to Prince Radziwill in Poland.[22] He used the opportunity to criticize the ideas of Biandrata, who was active in Poland—something that the Poles did not take to very kindly. The prince then defended Calvin's former opponent.

In 1563 Calvin dedicated his lectures on Jeremiah and Lamentations to Elector Frederick III of the Palatinate.[23] He briefly outlined the conception of the Lord's Supper being taught in Geneva. Caspar Olevianus had suggested to him the possibility of contributing in this way to the clarification of these positions in Heidelberg. The Lutherans, however, were not pleased with Calvin's interference in the current controversy, and Bullinger informed him that a dedication to the prince was not very expedient. Frederick did not wish to pass for a Zwinglian or Calvinist. In the piece, remarkably, Calvin himself indicates that the appellation "Calvinist" does not seem appropriate to him either.

The final dedication that Calvin wrote was for the commentary on Genesis and the other books of Moses (1563), dedicated to Henry of Navarre.[24] In these lines he extols in detail the piety of Henry's mother, Jeanne d'Albret, who was devoted to the cause of the Reformation. Ten-year-old Henry ought to pattern himself on her and to beware of the vanities that threaten those who are young. In this way, Calvin was without a doubt looking beyond the House of Bourbon and addressing the Reformation adherents in France itself.

As in this last case, in most of these dedications the goal is clear. Calvin is conscious of his own calling. He is not only a preacher in Geneva; his idea of the church is as broad as his conception of the unity and connection of the people of God throughout the world. His intent is that especially people of stature, the princes, remember that truth and piety go hand in hand. In these dedications, his view of the responsibility of the authorities is given a very concrete application. Whatever influence Calvin possessed he placed in the service of the kingdom of Christ.

In this connection, he focused his attention particularly on the development of the church in France. The first edition of the *Institutes* had been intended

20. CO 17:445–48; Peter and Gilmont, *Bibliotheca Calviniana*, 1:717–19.

21. CO 14:292–96; Peter and Gilmont, *Bibliotheca Calviniana*, 1:442. CO 14:14–17; Peter and Gilmont, *Bibliotheca Calviniana*, 1:502.

22. CO 18:155–61; Peter and Gilmont, *Bibliotheca Calviniana*, 2:741f.

23. CO 20:72–79; Peter and Gilmont, *Bibliotheca Calviniana*, 2:1026.

24. CO 20:116–22; Peter and Gilmont, *Bibliotheca Calviniana*, 2:1016.

for it, which also contained an apology (defense) in the address to Francis I, whose help was being enlisted against the persecutors. From Geneva, Calvin continually tried to influence the ecclesiastical and political situation in the land of his birth, an aspiration that inspired his conduct during the religious colloquies.

Following the death of Francis I, however, the situation worsened noticeably. Between 1547 and 1550 more than five hundred people were convicted of "heretical blasphemies" by Francis's successor, Henry II (1547–1559). The Peace of Cateau-Cambrésis between France and Spain (1559) led to an entirely new development within France. In Paris, evangelicals organized their own ecclesiastical life when their first synod met there in 1559. Shortly after that, Henry II was killed during a jousting tournament. His young and weak successor was Francis II, who was virtually under the control of Catherine de Medici and became a plaything in the hands of the various factions. In her choice of means, Catherine appeared to display little in the way of political ethics. When the party of Duke Francis and Cardinal Charles de Guise tried to take the young king under its wing, this was viewed as a declaration of war against the Protestants, who were thought to comprise a third of the population of France. In 1561 a petition was submitted to the king on behalf of 2,150 congregations, asking that they be allowed to use their own churches.[25] They formed a part of the nation that could not be ignored, not only so far as their numbers were concerned but especially with regard to their composition, which included people from the circles of the higher estates.

The representatives from the Bourbons, Antoine de Navarre and Louis I, Prince of Condé, were recognized as the leaders. They claimed the regency over Francis II. In March 1560 a conspiracy was uncovered against the Guises in Amboise, and its bloody suppression actually introduced a period of the religious wars that would last for over thirty years. Calvin remained in close contact with the leaders of the Protestants, and Beza participated in activities in France itself in which particularly Admiral Caspar de Coligny was involved.

During this time, a change within French Protestantism can be detected that is usually designated by the term "politicization." A colloquy in Poissy (1561) did not lead to a tolerable compromise, as Catherine claimed was the intent. In 1562 the Guises instigated the massacre at Vassy, after which the conflict could no longer be stopped. Mass murder erupted throughout the country. The royal army finally tried to restore order after a series of victories provided the regent with the opportunity to dictate the Treaty of Amboise (1563). The factions, however, seemed to have entrenched themselves in their

---

25. David Potter, ed. and trans., *The French Wars of Religion: Selected Documents* (New York: St. Martin's Press, 1997), 30.

political views and objectives to such a degree that a real form of tolerance appeared impossible for the time being. Another war broke out that was concluded in 1570 with the Peace of Saint-Germain, which promised freedom of religion. La Rochelle became one of the well-known places of freedom.

The Saint Bartholomew's Day Massacre (August 24, 1572), in which thousands of Protestants were slain, led to an intensified resumption of the conflict. Only the Edict of Nantes, signed on April 13, 1598, finally granted freedom of conscience to the Protestants. Around a hundred *places de sûreté* (places of safety) served as a pledge of their recognition. Meanwhile, the number of evangelical adherents had dramatically declined. The wars of religion had radicalized the problem of religious differences, the last thing that Calvin ever intended.

One of the last publications from Calvin's hand, the lectures on Daniel (1561), was dedicated to the "Christians in France."[26] He explained that he had left France twenty-six years earlier and that it had not been easy for him, since the truth, along with pure religion and the doctrine of eternal salvation, had also gone into exile. This did not mean, however, that he had forgotten the land of his birth. He had made every effort to put his absence to good use: through study and publications, as well as through personal letters, he had wanted to make himself useful to his people. He forecast an even more intense struggle than his readers thought they should expect and stated that in this way God, in his wisdom, wanted to put the faith of his people to the test.[27] Calvin recalled that up to now he had tried to prevent any occasion for irregularity; now, too, he rendered the opinion that *privati homines* (private persons) should not overstep the bounds of their authority, even if the fires of persecution had been blazing for thirty years. In these circumstances, one ought also to remain patient in soul and expect that a "rock hewn without hands" would bring the kingdom of Christ close at hand.[28] From the first edition of the *Institutes* onward, in fact, Calvin never deviated from his position: there can be lawful resistance against the government only when it is undertaken by those with the authority to do so. He did not consider private individuals in that category and decidedly rejected radical measures like those contemplated or even taken in some French congregations.[29] In Geneva itself the magistracy did everything it could to keep the city from being viewed as a place where plots against the king of France were being hatched.[30] The appearance of neutrality had to be preserved.

---

26. CO 18:614–24; Peter and Gilmont, *Bibliotheca Calviniana*, 2:847.
27. CO 18:615.
28. CO 18:619f.
29. Richard Nürnberger, *Die Politisierung des französischen Protestantismus: Calvin und die Anfange des protestantischen Radikalismus* (Tübingen: Mohr, 1948), 82f.
30. Ibid., 92f.

CONFESSIO GALLICANA

Meanwhile, in the years 1555–62, around ninety preachers were sent out from Geneva to France.[31] Their activity resulted in the founding of numerous congregations, which, considering the circumstances of the time, required their own organization. This was set up during the synod held in Paris in 1559 under the leadership of François de Morel. Already two years earlier, at a meeting in Poitiers, a draft church order had been drawn up, the *Articles Polytiques pour l'Église Réformée selon le S. Evangile*.[32] On this occasion, it was argued that it would be advantageous for "all the churches of France" to assemble in order "with one accord to formulate a confession of faith and a church discipline." In this way they could avoid serious discord in both doctrine and discipline. The churches ought to unite under the same yoke of order and church government.[33]

The most important objectives of the church order were the same as those considered indispensable in the church in Geneva: *doctrina* and *disciplina* under the yoke of Christ. The circumstances, however, were completely different. France at this time could not offer the peaceful context for a movement to develop that one could find in the city by the lake under Calvin's leadership.

At first, Calvin did not support the developments being promoted in Paris, for he thought that a synod at this time would only provoke the king. He also let it be known that he was not pleased with their rush to draw up a confession.[34] De Morel had asked Calvin for advice, but Calvin did not reply until it became clear that the synod would actually meet.[35] When the synod had already been in session for three days deliberating about the church order, a draft confession by Calvin arrived and was approved, with a few changes. De Morel communicated to Calvin that the synod had unanimously decided to keep the confession in the church archives and present it to the magistrates only when it became necessary.[36]

This confession, the *Confessio Fidei Gallicana* (Gallican Confession), served primarily to express the unity of the churches, reproducing in outline form the more detailed theology of Calvin found in the last edition of the *Institutes* from that same year (1559). This summary served as the foundation not only for life

31. Robert M. Kingdon, *Geneva and the Coming of the Wars of Religion in France, 1555–1563* (Geneva: Droz, 1956), 79–92, 135ff.

32. Pierre Dez, "Les articles polytiques de 1557 et les origines du régime synodal," *Bulletin de la société de l'histoire du Protestantisme français* 103 (1957): 1–9; Émile G. Léonard, *Histoire generale du protestantisme* (Paris: Presses universitaires de France, 1961–64), 2:93f.

33. Theodore Beza, *Histoire ecclésiastique des Églises réformées au royaume de France*, ed. G. Baum and E. Cunitz (1883–89; repr., Nieuwkoop: B. de Graaf, 1974), 1:109.

34. CO 17:526.

35. CO 17:506, 525f.

36. CO 17:540.

in the local congregation but also for the establishment and maintenance of the churches as a group: the churches should recognize each other by the pure preaching of the Word.

DISCIPLINE ECCLESIASTIQUE

The new church order, too, created a structure that ensured doctrinal unity. The *Discipline ecclesiastique* comprised forty articles, which regulated relationships among the churches in a way that did justice both to the independence of the local congregation and to the unity of the churches as a group.[37] The relation between office and congregation was laid out so that the authority of the three offices of minister, elder, and deacon with respect to the congregation would function to give guidance to the priesthood of believers. As in Calvin's view, the congregation takes on its purest form at the Lord's Supper. Pastoral care and church discipline are aimed at the holiness that must be visible in the lives of believers. The consistory constitutes a permanent body; classis and synod have only an ad hoc function. The church order avoids episcopal tendencies by stipulating that a president of classis or synod concludes his assignment as soon as the meeting at which he presides is adjourned.[38]

The freedom of the churches is guaranteed in the opening words of the first article: no church shall lord it over another. On the other hand, mutual solidarity can be seen in the stipulation that no individual congregation should undertake something with serious consequences without consulting the provincial synod. Indeed, the church order in no way exhibits the character of immutable law; the articles can be changed as the needs of the church dictate—which is another task of the synod. The decision to read the church order in the consistory before each celebration of the Lord's Supper and at all synodical meetings was intended to keep the structure of the churches from weakening and to keep the church order up to date. The church order was adapted, expanded, and improved in such a way that a hundred years later, at the last synod before the Revocation of the Edict of Nantes (1685), the forty articles of 1559 had actually grown into an impressive handbook of 252 articles, divided into fourteen chapters.

Soon after the church order of 1559 was enacted, powerful opposition arose, especially in the higher, influential evangelical circles in France. It came

---

37. François Méjan, *Discipline de l'Église réformée de France* (Paris: Éditions Je sers, 1947), 300–304.
38. CO 21:816: After Calvin's death in 1564, Beza proposed that the president of the consistory be elected annually as an example for the churches in France, where possibly episcopal tendencies might have been emerging.

to expression in a treatise by Jean Baptiste Morély (*Traicté de la discipline et police Chrestienne*),[39] who thereby became the leader of the opposition to the presbyterial-synodical order of the French churches. Central to his view was the inspiration of the congregation through "prophecy": everyone who has received the Spirit can interpret Scripture. The consequences of the priesthood of all believers as propagated by Luther had not been fully developed by either Luther or Calvin. Morély appealed to the *claritas* of the gospel, which would drive out every form of heresy. The congregation itself must be the judge of doctrine: it must choose its own ministers and exercise its rights in a democratic manner. The consistory may merely advise, and the broader assemblies, the provincial and general synods, form only an *Église imaginativ* (a church of the imagination).

Attempts were made to nip Morély's opposition in the bud when, on August 23, 1563, he was excommunicated in Geneva as a schismatic. His book was also condemned by various synods in France for its pernicious teaching.[40] An official refutation was prepared on behalf of the French churches by Antoine de la Roche Chandieu. Chandieu, who had been closely connected with drafting the church order, defended it against its critics in *La confirmation de la discipline ecclésiastique observée des églises reformées du royaume de France* (1566).[41] With a strong emphasis on the concept of office, he dismissed the proposed democratization of the church out of hand. Evaluation of doctrine falls under the authority of those who are authorized and trained to explain Scripture competently. Unmistakable here is the aristocratic character that the church acquires in Chandieu's and Beza's representations.[42] Beza, especially, continued to function as defender of the ecclesiastical structure that was first drawn up in France. It was, in fact, Calvin's conception not only implemented now as the model of a city reformation, as was the case in Geneva, but also concretized within a territory in which the church sought to preserve its identity in the face of resistance and persecution.

Calvin's pattern became an identifying mark for the churches in the Netherlands and Scotland that felt closely connected to Geneva. The solidarity of this Calvinism could be seen at the Synod of La Rochelle (1571), where once again the ideas of Morély were rejected. Beza presided at this first national synod in France, which was convened with the consent of the king. Among the leading

39. Original, 1562; repr., Geneva: Slatkine, 1968.
40. Robert M. Kingdon, *Geneva and the Consolidation of the French Protestant Movement, 1564–1572: A Contribution to the History of Congregationalism, Presbyterianism, and Calvinist Resistance Theory* (Madison: University of Wisconsin Press, 1967), 62–75.
41. Beza's reading of this work enabled it to be published in Geneva.
42. Robert M. Kingdon, "Calvinism and Democracy," in *The Heritage of John Calvin: Heritage Hall Lectures, 1960–70*, ed. John H. Bratt (Grand Rapids: Eerdmans, 1973).

guests were Admiral De Coligny, the queen of Navarre, and prominent leaders of the Huguenot resistance movement. Louis of Nassau represented the resistance to Philip II in the Lowlands. His presence was significant because it represented a decision within Dutch Protestantism to orient itself toward the form of Calvinism found in France.

THE NETHERLANDS

Calvin exerted an influence on the Reformation in the Netherlands first of all through the personal contacts he made in his letters and above all through his instruction at the Academy of Geneva.[43] He felt something of a kinship with the Dutch, even being able to write to Bullinger at one point that "I myself am also a Lowlander."[44] Menso Poppius, who in 1550 was at work in the northern part of the Netherlands, corresponded with Calvin, among others, about questions related to church discipline,[45] but Calvin was also in written contact with others. Brothers Philips and Jan van Marnix were among the first to matriculate at the Academy of Geneva. Especially the former, Philips van Marnix of St. Aldegonde (1540–98), became known in connection with the struggle for the liberation of the Netherlands led by William of Orange, whom Philips served as a counselor. He also played an important role in the organization of Dutch ecclesiastical life according to the Reformed pattern.[46]

There is also a second line through which Calvin's influence on the development of the Reformation in the Netherlands can be traced: the Dutch refugee congregations in London, Emden, Frankfurt, and Heidelberg, where people had sought protection and the Reformed church was in the process of being constructed.[47] One cannot easily overstate the significance of the

---

43. Frederik L. Rutgers, *Calvijns invloed op de reformatie in de Nederlanden: Voor zoveel die door hemzelven is uitgeoefend* (Leeuwarden: De Tille, 1980), 5–17; Harman de Vries, *Genève pépinière du calvinisme hollandaise*, 2 vols. (Fribourg: Fragnière frères, 1918–24); Guillaume Fatio, *Genève et les Pays-Bas* (Geneva: Journal de Geneve, 1928).

44. "Sum enim Belga ipse quoqui"; CO 18:205. See also E. M. Braekman, "*Sum enim Belga ipse quoque*: Calvin et les ressortissants de Pays-Bas," in Millet, *Calvin et ses contemporains*, 83–96.

45. Rutgers, *Calvijns invloed*, 134–37.

46. Aloïs Gerlo and Rudolf de Smet, *Marnixi epistulae: De briefwisseling van Marnix van Sint-Aldegonde; Een kritische uitgave*, vol. 1, *1558–1576* (Brussels: University Press, 1990), 45–62, 74–90, 114–37, 172–76.

47. Aart A. van Schelven, *De Nederduitsche vluchtelingenkerken der XVIe eeuw in Engeland en Duitschland in hunne beteekenis voor de Reformatie in de Nederlanden* (The Hague: M. Nijhoff, 1909); Heinz Schilling, *Niederländische Exulanten im 16. Jahrhundert: Ihre Stellung im Sozialgefüge und im religiösen Leben deutscher und englischer Städte* (Gütersloh: G. Mohn, 1972); Philippe Denis, *Les églises d'étrangers en pays Rhénans (1538–1564)* (Paris: Les belles lettres, 1984); Andrew Pettegree, *Foreign Protestant Communities in Sixteenth-Century London* (New York: Oxford University Press, 1986); Owe Boersam, "Vluchtig voorbeeld: De nederlandse, franse en italiaanse vluchtelingenkerken in

"mother church" in Emden for the congregations in the northern Netherlands. A large number of writings were disseminated from Emden among the
"churches under the cross."[48] The congregation in Antwerp, certainly one of
the most prominent, was led by Gaspar van de Heyden, who had completed
his training in Emden.

Calvin's influence was felt indirectly in the southern part of the Netherlands
through activity generated in France and Strasbourg, which sent out preachers to help in establishing new congregations. Using pseudonyms, these congregations in the Netherlands tried to maintain contact with each other. They
followed the French model of forming synodical assemblies to give direction
to their ecclesiastical life. However, in the early 1560s, a kind of ecclesiastical
organization developed that, even more so than in France, underscored the
importance of the local church.[49] At a meeting in Wesel in 1568, a church
order was drafted for which "the best Reformed churches" were consulted.
After being sent to these churches for advice, the order was provisionally
adopted until a general synod could make a further decision.[50]

Worthy of note is the stipulation concerning "prophecy," a form of direct
participation by the congregation in the interpretation of Scripture. It was
defined in a manner distinct from the way it had been understood in the Dutch
refugee congregation in London. When in 1571 the Synod of Emden drew up
a church order that would serve the churches in the Netherlands when freedom arrived, the provisions concerning "prophecy" were not included.[51]
Apparently, they identified themselves wholly with the French churches,
which had distanced themselves from Morély's way of thinking.

Church unity in the Netherlands was founded upon two confessions: the
Confessio Belgica, which Guido de Brès had drafted in 1561, and the *Confessio
Gallicana* (1559), on which de Brès had based much of the Belgic Confession,

Londen, 1568–1585" (ThD diss., Theologische Academie, Kampen, 1994); Raingard Esser, *Niederländische Exultanten im England des 16. und frühen 17. Jahrhunderts* (Berlin: Duncker & Humblot, 1996).

48. Andrew Pettegree, *Emden and the Dutch Revolt: Exile and the Development of Reformed Protestantism* (New York: Oxford University Press, 1992).

49. Frederik R. J. Knetsch, "Church Ordinances and Regulations of the Dutch Synods 'Under
the Cross' (1563–1566) compared with the French (1559–1563)," in *Humanism and Reform: The
Church in Europe, England, and Scotland, 1400–1643; Essays in Honour of James K. Cameron*, ed.
James Kirk (Oxford: Blackwell Publishers, 1991), 202.

50. Walter Stempel et al., *Weseler Konvent, 1568–1968: Eine Jubiläumsschrift*, Schriftenreihe des
Vereins für Rheinische Kirchengeschichte 29 (Düsseldorf: Presseverband der Evangelischen
Kirche im Rheinland, 1968); J. F. G. Goeters, *Beschlüsse des reformierten Weseler Konvents (1568)*,
Schriftenreihe des Vereins für Rheinische Kirchengeschichte 30 (Düsseldorf: Presseverband der
Evangelischen Kirche im Rheinland, 1968).

51. Elwin Lomberg, ed., *Emder Synode, 1571–1971: Beiträge zur Geschichte und zum 400-
jährigen Jubiläum* (Neukirchen-Vluyn: Neukirchener Verlag, 1973).

thus giving expression to the relationship with the French churches. The Walloon (French-speaking) congregations also made use of the Genevan Catechism, while the Dutch-speaking churches employed the Heidelberg Catechism, which had been translated in the meantime into Dutch by Petrus Dathenus and published together with his Dutch rhymes of the French psalms in 1566.

Orientation to the French churches also meant that the Dutch churches could not directly enjoy the protection of the religious Peace of Augsburg (1555). King Philip II of Spain developed a unique kind of regime in the Netherlands, which he regarded as his hereditary domain. Prince William of Orange tried to form an alliance with the German Protestants in the struggle against Philip, and the churches stood firmly behind his opposition to Spain. To the prince's disappointment, however, the churches did not respond to his request for active political involvement, in accordance with the principle that would be formulated at a synod at Dort (Dordt, Dordrecht) in 1574: "Ministers and elders shall see to it that in their consistories, classes, and synods, they deal only with ecclesiastical matters."[52] Thus, as in Calvin's view, church and politics were certainly not separated, but they were distinguished from each other for the sake of the freedom of God's Word. In this way, they could preserve the autonomy and freedom of the churches in times of oppression and opposition. Even after freedom dawned in 1572, the churches under Reformed civil government did not want to give up their autonomy, which often led to a strained relationship between consistory and magistracy. In a situation in which the government had a free hand politically and militarily, the church refused to give up its independence. The Calvinist view of the difference between ecclesiastical and temporal authority is part of the legacy of the Reformation in the Netherlands.

SCOTLAND

The reformation in Scotland took place under the energetic leadership of John Knox (1513–72) and according to the model of Geneva. Knox had come under the Protestant preaching of George Wishart, who was burned in St. Andrews in 1546. In 1547 Knox himself preached in the castle where murderers of the Catholic bishop had taken up residence. After a time of imprisonment on the French galleys, he worked in England during the reign of Edward VI. When Queen Mary came to the throne, Knox moved on to Frankfurt, where a dispute

52. Willem van 't Spijker, "Stromingen onder de reformatorisch-gezinden te Emden," in *De Synode van Emden, oktober 1571: Een bundel opstellen ter gelegenheid van de vierhonderdjarige herdenking,* ed. D. Nauta, J. P. van Dooren, and Otto J. de Jong (Kampen: Kok, 1971), 50–74.

over liturgy broke out in the refugee congregation. He next settled in Geneva, where he got to know and appreciate Calvin intimately.[53]

In 1557 Knox published his *First Blast of the Trumpet against the Monstrous Regiment of Women*, a treatise that made trouble for Calvin and created a lasting barrier to positive relations between Queen Elizabeth I and the Scottish reformation. Knox's combative spirit was not appreciated by everyone in the circles around Calvin, and the French church denounced his attitude as dangerous.[54] In 1559 he returned to Scotland, where in his fiery preaching he advocated an alliance against Rome and France.

In 1560 the first Scottish church order appeared, *The First Book of Discipline*,[55] which underscored the necessity of preaching the gospel and administering baptism and the Lord's Supper. Ministers of the church were to be chosen by the congregation and examined by the "best reformed church" in the region. Temporary offices were those of *exhorter* and *reader*,[56] and superintendants were assigned the provisional function of establishing churches and appointing ministers. Alongside the administration of Word and Sacrament, the church order expressly mentions church discipline: the church cannot be brought to purity apart from discipline.[57] In this first reformational Scottish church order, one can clearly see the influence of Bucer and Calvin.

In 1578 the first church order was replaced by a second one, which came about through the influence of Knox's successor, Andrew Melville (1545–1622). This *Second Book of Discipline* formulated the principles of presbyterial-synodical church law in a more compact manner: a fourfold office structure of minister, teacher, elder, and deacon, who participate in the four ecclesiastical assemblies: presbytery, provincial synod, general synod, and an ecumenical synod of Reformed churches. Here, too, there is a strong emphasis on the difference between ecclesiastical and civil jurisdiction.

The *First Book of Discipline* regulated the *disciplina* of the church in close connection with *doctrina*,[58] which was established in the *Scots Confession*, also of 1560. This confession followed Calvin's catechism and the confession of faith of the English church in Geneva. It also contains elements from the French confession of faith and even from the *Liturgia sacra* of Valerandus Pollanus.

---

53. W. Stanford Reid, "John Calvin, John Knox, and the Scottish Reformation," in *Church, Word, and Spirit: Historical and Theological Essays in Honor of Geoffrey W. Bromiley*, ed. James E. Bradley and Richard A. Muller (Grand Rapids: Eerdmans, 1987), 141–51.

54. CO 17:541.

55. *The First Book of Discipline* (1621; repr., with introduction and commentary by James K. Cameron, Edinburgh: St. Andrew, 1972).

56. Ibid., 105ff., 111ff.

57. Ibid., 165–73; Michael F. Graham, *The Uses of Reform: "Godly Discipline" and Popular Behavior in Scotland and Beyond, 1560–1610* (Leiden: Brill, 1996).

58. *First Book of Discipline*, 87–89.

Nevertheless, it has a character of its own, practical and direct in its formulations. With this confession, the Scottish church took its place within the continental Reformed tradition then being developed. The same is true of the
liturgy *The Book of Common Order*, to which the name of John Knox is also connected. It came into existence under the approving eye of Calvin himself, was
used by the English refugees in Geneva during the time that Knox led this congregation,[59] and was adopted by the General Assembly in 1562.[60] The Church
of Scotland was not a carbon copy of the one in Geneva, but there is no mis-
taking that it was designed in entirely the same spirit.

ENGLAND

In an indirect way, Calvin's influence from Scotland also affected the ongoing
reformation in England.[61] Already during the time of Thomas Cranmer and
King Edward VI, Calvin managed to make and maintain contact with the evangelically inclined leaders.[62] After the death of the king and Queen Mary's
behavior toward the Protestants, the English exiles in Geneva were able to
acquaint themselves firsthand with Calvin's activity. In his typically unique way,
Martin Bucer had brought up matters of faith and church order during his stay
in Cambridge (1549–51), both in his lectures and his treatise *De regno Christi*,
which he dedicated to King Edward.[63] Calvin's voice, however, was not the only
one heard in England; other continental reformers exerted an influence as well.
Bullinger's significance was, in the long run, at least as great.[64]

During the reign of Elizabeth I, Calvin's impact became controversial.[65]
The queen wished to follow a via media (middle road), which would secure

59. *The forme of prayers and ministration of the sacraments, &c. vsed in the Englishe Congregation
at Geneua: and approued, by the famous and godly learned man, Iohn Caluyn* (Geneva: John Crespin,
1556); cf. Stephen A. Hurlbut, *The Liturgy of the Church of Scotland since the Reformation*, 4 vols.
(Washington, DC: St. Albans, 1944–52).

60. W. D. Maxwell, *John Knox's Genevan Service Book, 1556: The Liturgical Portions of the
Genevan Service Book Used by John Knox While a Minister of the English Congregation of Marian Exiles
at Geneva, 1556–1559* (1931; repr., Westminster: Faith Press, 1965).

61. Andrew Pettegree, "The Reception of Calvinism in Britain," in *Calvinus Sincerioris Religionis Vindex: Calvin as Protector of the Purer Religion*, ed. Wilhelm H. Neuser and Brian G. Armstrong (Kirksville, MO: Sixteenth Century Journal Publishers, 1997), 267–89.

62. Letters in *Epistolae tigurinae de rebus potissimum ad Ecclesiae anglicanae reformationem perti-
nentibus conscriptae A. D. 1531–1558* (1848; repr., New York: Johnson Reprint Corp., 1968).

63. Basil Hall, "Martin Bucer in England," *Martin Bucer: Reforming Church and Community*,
ed. David F. Wright (Cambridge: Cambridge University Press, 1994), 144–60.

64. Helmut Kressner, *Schweizer Ursprünge des anglikanischen Staatskirchentums* (Gütersloh:
Bertelsmann, 1953); Gottfried W. Locher, *Die Zwinglische Reformation im Rahmen der europäischen
Kirchengeschichte* (Göttingen: Vandenhoeck & Ruprecht, 1979), 646–50.

65. Peter O. G. White, *Predestination, Policy and Polemic: Conflict and Consensus in the English
Church from the Reformation to the Civil War* (Cambridge: Cambridge University Press, 1992).

both episcopacy and the monarchy. However, the return to England of the asylum seekers after the death of Queen Mary strengthened the presbyterial element and led to a break between episcopalians and presbyterians. The latter tried to follow the pattern of Geneva in England. Early Puritanism, therefore, can be regarded as a movement with its origins in Calvin. It was strongly supported by Calvin's successor, Theodore Beza, and presented its first clearly formulated program in the Puritan Manifestoes, which Calvin's followers addressed to the parliament (beginning in 1572).[66] Thomas Cartwright (1535–1603) and Walter Travers (1548–1635) appealed to Calvin and to the model of the churches in France, the Netherlands, and Scotland. Travers describes the standard presbyterial system in his *Ecclesiasticae Disciplinae, et Anglicanae Ecclesiae ab illa aberratione, plana e verbo Dei et dilucida explicatio* (1574).[67] Puritanism certainly adopted major elements of Calvin's thought, especially when it came to ecclesiastical structure, and in the seventeenth century it was transplanted to America. There it later took on the basic features of democracy, which were able to blossom in the new world earlier than in the European context.

THE PALATINATE

Of great significance for the development of Reformed Protestantism in western Europe was the conversion of Frederick III of the Palatinate (1515–76) to Calvinism in 1559.[68] The Palatinate provided strong support for the resistance by both the Huguenots in France and the Calvinists in the Netherlands. Already during Beza's stay in the Palatinate to marshal support for fellow believers in France, Calvin was trying to find a basis there for further action.

The conversion of Frederick III in 1559 was the fruit of a strong personal conviction, which made such an impression at the Diet of Augsburg in 1566 that no one dared to condemn him as a violator of the Peace of Augsburg

66. Walter H. Frere and Charles E. Douglas, eds., *Puritan Manifestoes: A Study of the Origin of the Puritan Revolt, with a Reprint of the Admonition to the Parliament and Kindred Documents, 1572* (New York: B. Franklin, 1972).

67. Cartwright prepared an ET that same year: *A Full and Plaine Declaration of Ecclesiastical Discipline owt off the Word of God* (1574); repr. in Samuel J. Knox, *Walter Travers: Paragon of Elizabethan Puritanism* (London: Methuen, 1962), 25–40; Andrew F. S. Pearson, *Thomas Cartwright and Elizabethan Puritanism, 1535–1603* (1925; Gloucester, MA: Peter Smith, 1966), 135–44.

68. Owen Chadwick, "The Making of a Reforming Prince: Frederick III, Elector Palatine," in *Reformation, Conformity and Dissent: Essays in Honour of Geoffrey Nuttall*, ed. R. Buick Knox (London: Epworth, 1977), 44–69; Derk Visser, ed., *Controversy and Conciliation: The Reformation and the Palatinate, 1559–1583* (Allison Park, PA: Pickwick Publications, 1986).

(1555).[69] Following a dispute over the Lord's Supper in 1560, Frederick dismissed the Lutheran leaders in his territory and replaced them with Calvinist-minded preachers and professors. Among them were Zacharias Ursinus (1534–83), a disciple of Melanchthon and Peter Martyr Vermigli, and Caspar Olevianus (1536–87), originally a law student but thereafter a theologian who had also studied in Switzerland. Calvin advised Olevianus on how to organize a congregation according to the Genevan model by explaining the appointment of ministers, the administration of infant baptism, the celebration of the Lord's Supper, mutual censure, and the exercise of church discipline.[70] With respect to church discipline, he emphasized the principle that actions by the consistory ought not to interfere with procedures in the civil courts. It was also his wish that people not be dealt with too harshly in church discipline and that there be no difference between the discipline of laypersons and office-bearers. The latter should be subject to the same punishments as the former.[71] Calvin's actions in Geneva were always dictated by a principled distinction between spiritual discipline and temporal punishment. Even when the civil authority had switched over to the Reformation, that did not mean that civil jurisdiction might now claim authority over the church. The church maintained its own law.

HEIDELBERG

In the Palatinate city of Heidelberg, a difference now emerged that would prove influential in later developments within the Reformed tradition. Bullinger's view of church discipline was different from Calvin's and, later, Beza's, but it did not result in open conflict.[72] In Heidelberg, however, a quarrel broke out between the "consistorialists," as the leaders of an ecclesiastical discipline were called, and

69. Walter Hollweg, *Der Augsburger Reichstag von 1566 und seine Bedeutung für die Entstehung der Reformierten Kirche und ihres Bekenntnisses* (Neukirchen-Vluyn: Neukirchener Verlag des Erziehungsvereins, 1964); Volker Press, *Calvinismus und Territorialstaat: Regierung und Zentralbehorden der Kurpfalz 1559–1619* (Stuttgart: E. Klett, 1970), 221–66; idem, "Die 'Zweite Reformation' in der Kurpfalz," in *Die reformierte Konfessionalisierung in Deutschland: Das Problem der "Zweiten Reformation": Wissenschaftliches Symposion des Vereins für Reformationsgeschichte 1985*, ed. Heinz Schilling (Gütersloh: G. Mohn, 1986), 104–29; Andreas Edel, *Der Kaiser und Kurpfalz: Eine Studie zu den Grundelementen politischen Handelns bei Maximilian II (1564–1576)* (Göttingen: Vandenhoeck & Ruprecht, 1997), 165–249.

70. CO 18:235–37.

71. CO 18: 237: "Ea autem est consistorii ratio, ut civilis iurisdictionis cursum nihil moretur. Ac ne plebs queratur de immodico rigore, non tantum iisdem poenis subiacent ministri, sed si quid excommunicationis dignum admiserint simul etiam abdicantur."

72. Bullinger wrote to Dathenus on June 1, 1570: "Quid quod nulla unquam fuit concertatio de excommunicatione inter nostram Tigurinam et Genevensem Ecclesiam nobis praedilectam." Thomas Erastus, *Explicatio Gravissimae Quaestionis utrum Excommunicatio . . . mandato nitatur Divino, an excogitata sit ab hominibus* (London: John Wolfe, 1589), 365.

those who would not allow for a separate exercise of discipline involving the Lord's Supper. Thomas Lüber, usually known as Erastus, represented Bullinger's position and came into conflict with Dathenus and Olevianus, who thought along the same lines as Oecolampadius, Bucer, and Calvin.[73] Conciliation between the parties was not successful. Olevianus's position was taken over by the elector and was adopted in the church order (which included the Heidelberg Catechism between the liturgical forms for baptism and the Lord's Supper) as the future structure for the churches in the Palatinate.[74]

By order of the elector, the Heidelberg Catechism (1563) was composed "by his theologians and those to whom the supervision of the churches within his territory had been entrusted."[75] It adopted Calvin's doctrine of the Lord's Supper, which was later expanded with an addition by Frederick III concerning the "idolatry of the papal mass." The catechism refers to the doctrine of God's election, but it does not give it special attention. As in the first edition of the *Institutes* (1536), election is included in the confession about the church, under the work of Christ: Christ gathers, protects, and preserves for himself a community chosen for eternal life (Q. and A. 54). The doctrine of election serves here to comfort believers and all the elect with heavenly joy and blessedness in the midst of affliction and persecution. Along with Luther's catechism, the Heidelberg Catechism is among the most popular pieces of literature that the Reformation produced.

CALVINISM: UNITY IN DIVERSITY

The form in which Calvin's work took shape in Heidelberg is just one of several in which Calvinism entered history. In some areas, his influence seemed to be only temporary, even though he sent letters and established contacts there. What at first appeared to be promising developments in Poland, Bohemia,

---

73. Ruth Wesel-Roth, *Thomas Erastus: Ein Beitrag zur Geschichte der reformierten Kirche und zur Lehre von der Staatssouveranitat* (Lahr/Baden: Schauenburg, 1954); J. Wayne Baker, "In Defense of Magisterial Discipline: Bullinger's 'Tractatus de Excommunicatione' of 1568," in *Heinrich Bullinger, 1504–1575: Gesammelte Aufsätze zum 400. Todestag*, ed. Ulrich Gäbler and Erland Herkenrath (Zurich: Theologischer Verlag, 1975), 1:141–59; Robert C. Walton, "Der Streitzwischen Thomas Erastus und Caspar Olevian über die Kirchenzucht in der Kurpfalz in seiner Bedeutung für die internationale reformierte Bewegung," in *Monatshefte für evangelische Kirchengeschichte des Rheinlandes* 37/38 (1988/1989): 205–46.

74. Emil Sehling, ed., *Die evangelischen Kirchenordnungen des XVI. Jahrhunderts*, vol. 14, *Kurpfalz* (Tübingen: Mohr, 1969), 333–408. The consistorial organization with the regulations for church discipline appears on 409–24.

75. I. John Hesselink, "The Dramatic Story of the Heidelberg Catechism," in *Later Calvinism: International Perspectives*, ed. W. Fred Graham (Kirksville, MO: Sixteenth Century Journal Publishers, 1994), 273–88; Lyle D. Bierma, "*Vester Grundt* and the Origins of the Heidelberg Catechism," in *Later Calvinism*, 289–309; Fred H. Klooster, "Calvin's Attitude to the Heidelberg Catechism," in *Later Calvinism*, 311–31.

Spain, and Italy were suppressed by the Catholic Counter-Reformation movement. Calvin's significance in Hungary and Transylvania was partly eclipsed by
that of Bullinger.

Calvin himself rejected the use of the term "Calvinism" as a designation of
his ideas, most clearly in the letter to Frederick III at the front of his commentary on Jeremiah (1563).[76] It is undeniable, however, that Calvin set in
motion a movement that, at the very least, displays features reminiscent of his
work and indicative of his lasting influence. The Reformed tradition sees
Scripture as its vital center. Calvin was an exegete, and in following his lead,
biblical scholarship was able to develop further. His deepest conviction was
inspired by a sense of God's eternal love, and his knowledge of simultaneously
being called by that love to a task in the world drove the movement that radiated from Geneva. It was Calvin who, like Augustine, tried to link grace and
church together. For him, the secret of this relationship lay in the tandem of
Word and Spirit, and it was along this line also that Reformed Protestantism
proceeded further. It was open not only to orthodoxy but also to the spiritual
revitalization without which orthodoxy becomes rigid. Calvin also knew how
handle diversity, so long as the Word of God remained central. He sought to
maintain unity with all reformers, though he was not entirely successful.

These are the characteristic features that Calvinism displayed, even as it followed different paths through history. It was propagated in the form of
scholasticism as well as Puritanism or Reformed Pietism. It expressed itself in
the architectonics of a balanced covenant theology, while remaining no less
recognizable in the simplicity of faith set forth in the first question and answer
of the Heidelberg Catechism. For this diversity in development, an appeal to
Calvin has always seemed legitimate. "Calvinists" have never succeeded in presenting themselves as a single theological, confessional, or ecclesiastical entity,
although attempts have certainly been made. When the Frankfurt Assembly
was convened in 1577 as a Reformed reaction to the unified Lutheranism
expressed in the Formula of Concord, nothing more came out of it than an
edition of the *Harmonia Confessionum*, which offered a synopsis of current confessional writings.[77] Within this diversity, however, there was enough room for
the unity of "Calvinism" to operate as a vital force in history.

76. CO 20:72–79, esp. 73, 76.
77. *Harmonia Confessionum Fidei, Orthodoxarum, et Reformatarum Ecclesiarum, quae in praecipuis
quibusque Europae Regnis, Nationibus, et Provinciis, sacram Evangelii doctrinam pure profitentur . . .
Quae omnia, Ecclesiarum Gallicarum, et Belgicarum nomine, subiiciuntur libero et prudenti reliquarum
omnium, iudicio* (Geneva: Petrum Santandreanum, 1581); Jan N. Bakhuizen van den Brink, "Het
Convent te Frankfort, 27–28 september 1577, en de Harmonia Confessionum," *Nederlandsch
Archief voor Kerkgeschiedenis* 32 (1941): 235–80; Olivier Labarthe, "Jean-François Salvard, Min-
istre de l'évangile. Vie, oeuvre et correspondence," in Marie-Claude Junod, Monique Droin-
Bridel, and Olivier Labarthe, *Polémiques religieuses: Études et texts* (Geneva: Jullien, 1979), 345–480.

CHAPTER BIBLIOGRAPHY

Baker, J. Wayne. "In Defense of Magisterial Discipline: Bullinger's 'Tractatus de Excommunicatione' of 1568." In *Heinrich Bullinger, 1504–1575: Gesammelte Aufsätze zum 400. Todestag,* edited by Ulrich Gäbler and Erland Herkenrath, vol. 1, pages 141–59. Zurich: Theologischer Verlag, 1975.

Bell, M. Charles. *Calvin and Scottish Theology: The Doctrine of Assurance.* Edinburgh: Handsel, 1985.

Benoît, Jean-Daniel. "Calvin the Letter-Writer." In *John Calvin: A Collection of Distinguished Essays,* edited by G. E. Duffield, 67–101. Grand Rapids: Eerdmans, 1966.

Beza, Theodore. *Histoire ecclésiastique des Églises réformées au royaume de France.* Edited by G. Baum and E. Cunitz, 1883–89. Reprint, Nieuwkoop: B. de Graaf, 1974.

Boersam, Owe. "Vluchtig voorbeeld: De nederlandse, franse en italiaanse vluchtelingenkerken in Londen, 1568–1585." ThD dissertation. Kampen: Theologische Academie, 1994.

Braekman, E. M. "*Sum enim Belga ipse quoque*: Calvin et les ressortissants de Pays-Bas." In *Calvin et ses contemporains,* edited by Olivier Millet, 83–96. Geneva: Droz, 1998.

Bratt, John H., ed. *The Heritage of John Calvin.* Grand Rapids: Eerdmans, 1973.

Brink, Jan N. Bakhuizen van den. "Het Convent te Frankfort, 27–28 September 1577, en de Harmonia Confessionum." *Nederlandsch Archief voor Kerkgeschiedenis* 32 (1941): 235–80.

Brown, George K. *Italy and the Reformation to 1550.* New York: Russell & Russell, 1971.

Cameron, Euan. *The Reformation of the Heretics: The Waldenses of the Alps, 1480–1580.* New York: Oxford University Press, 1984.

Cameron, James K. *The First Book of Discipline.* 1621. Reprint, with an introduction and commentary. Edinburgh: St. Andrew Press, 1972.

Cartwright, Thomas. "A Full and Plaine Declaration of Ecclesiastical Discipline out of the Word of God." Reprinted in *Walter Travers: Paragon of Elizabethan Puritanism,* edited by Samuel J. Knox, 25–40. London: Methuen, 1962.

Chadwick, Owen. "The Making of a Reforming Prince: Frederick III, Elector Palatine." In *Reformation, Conformity and Dissent: Essays in Honour of Geoffrey Nuttall,* edited by R. Buick Knox, 44–69. London: Epworth, 1977.

D'Assonville, V. E. *John Knox and the Institutes of Calvin.* Durban: Drakensberg Press, 1968.

Dankbaar, W. F. *Hoogtepunten uit het Nederlandsche Calvinisme in de zestiende eeuw.* Haarlem: H. D. Tjeenk Willink & Zoon N. V., 1996.

Danner, Dan G. *Pilgrimage to Puritanism: History and Theology of the Marian Exiles at Geneva, 1555–1560.* New York: P. Lang, 1999.

Denis, Philippe. *Les églises d'étrangers en pays Rhénans (1538–1564).* Paris: Les belles lettres, 1984.

Denis, Philippe, and Jean Rott. *Jean Morély (ca. 1524–ca. 1594) et l'utopie d'une démocratie dans l'église.* Geneva: Droz, 1993.

Dent, Christopher M. *Protestant Reformers in Elizabethan Oxford.* New York: Oxford University Press, 1983.

Dez, Pierre. "Les articles polytiques de 1557 et les origines du régime synodal." *Bulletin de la société de l'histoire du Protestantisme français* 103 (1957): 1–9.

Duke, Alastair. *Reformation and Revolt in the Low Countries.* London: Ronceverte, 1990.

Edel, Andreas. *Der Kaiser und Kurpfalz: Eine Studie zu den Grundelementen politischen Handelns bei Maximilian II (1564–1576).* Göttingen: Vandenhoeck & Ruprecht, 1997.

Esser, Raingard. *Niederländische Exultanten im England des 16. und frühen 17. Jahrhunderts.* Berlin: Duncker & Humblot, 1996.

Fatio, Guillaume. *Genève et les Pays-Bas.* Geneva: Journal de Geneve, 1928.

Frere, Walter H., and Charles E. Douglas, eds. *Puritan Manifestoes: A Study of the Origin of the Puritan Revolt, with a Reprint of the Admonition to the Parliament and Kindred Documents, 1572.* New York: B. Franklin, 1972.

Garret, Christina. *The Marian Exiles: A Study in the Origins of Elizabethan Puritanism.* Cambridge: Cambridge University Press, 1938.

Gerlo, Aloïs, and Rudolf de Smet. *Marnixi epistulae: De briefwisseling van Marnix van Sint-Aldegonde; Een kritische uitgave.* Vol. 1, *1558–1576.* Brussels: University Press, 1990.

Gilmont, Jean-François. "Les dédicataires de Calvin." In *Calvin et ses contemporains,* edited by Olivier Millet, 117–34. Geneva: Droz, 1998.

Goeters, J. F. G. *Beschlüsse des reformierten Weseler Konvents (1568).* Düsseldorf: Presseverband der Evangelischen Kirche im Rheinland, 1968.

Graham, Michael F. *The Uses of Reform: "Godly Discipline" and Popular Behavior in Scotland and Beyond, 1560–1610.* New York: Brill, 1996.

Graham, W. Fred, ed. *Later Calvinism: International Perspectives.* Kirksville, MO: Sixteenth Century Journal Publishers, 1994.

Hall, Basil. "Martin Bucer in England." In *Martin Bucer: Reforming Church and Community,* edited by David F. Wright, 144–60. Cambridge: Cambridge University Press, 1994.

Hein, Lorenz. *Italienische Protestanten und ihr Einfluss auf die Reformation in Polen während der beiden Jahrzehnte vor dem Sandomirer Konsens (1570).* Leiden: Brill, 1974.

Hollweg, Walter. *Der Augsburger Reichstag von 1566 und seine Bedeutung für die Entstehung der Reformierten Kirche und ihres Bekenntnisses.* Neukirchen-Vluyn: Neukirchener Verlag, 1964.

Holt, Mack P. *The French Wars of Religion, 1562–1629.* New York: Cambridge University Press, 1995. 2nd ed. 2005.

Hughes, Sean F. "The Problem of 'Calvinism': English Theologies of Predestination c. 1580–1630." In *Belief and Practice in Reformation England: A Tribute to Patrick Collinson from His Students,* edited by Susan Wabuda and Caroline Litzenberger, 229–49. Brookfield: Ashgate, 1998.

Hurlbut, Stephen A. *The Liturgy of the Church of Scotland since the Reformation.* 4 vols. Washington, DC: St. Albans, 1944–52.

Janton, Pierre. *Concept et sentiment de l'église chez John Knox le réformateur écossais.* Paris: Presses universitaires de France, 1972.

Kendall, R. T. *Calvin and English Calvinism to 1649.* Carlisle: Paternoster Publishing, 1997.

Kingdon, Robert M. "Calvinism and Democracy." In *The Heritage of John Calvin: Heritage Hall Lectures, 1960–70,* edited by John H. Bratt, 177–92. Grand Rapids: Eerdmans, 1973.

———. *Geneva and the Coming of the Wars of Religion in France, 1555–1563.* Geneva: Droz, 1956.

———. *Geneva and the Consolidation of the French Protestant Movement, 1564–1572: A Contribution to the History of Congregationalism, Presbyterianism, and Calvinist Resistance Theory.* Madison: University of Wisconsin Press, 1967.

Kirk, James. *Patterns of Reform: Continuity and Change in the Reformation Kirk.* Edinburgh: T&T Clark, 1989.

Kley, Dale K. van. *The Religious Origins of the French Revolution: From Calvin to the Civil Constitution, 1560–1791.* New Haven: Yale University Press, 1996.

Klink, Hubrecht. *Opstand, politiek en religie bij Willem van Oranje 1559–1568: Een thematische biografie.* Heerenveen: Groen, 1997.

Knecht, Robert J. *The French Wars of Religion.* New York: Longman, 1989.

Knetsch, F. R. J. "Church Ordinances and Regulations of the Dutch Synods 'Under the Cross' (1559–1563) Compared with the French (1559–1563)." In *Humanism and Reform: The Church in Europe, England, and Scotland, 1400–1643: Essays in Honor of James K. Cameron,* edited by James Kirk, 187–205. Oxford: Blackwell Publishers, 1991.

Kressner, Helmut. *Schweizer Ursprünge des anglikanischen Staatskirchentums.* Gütersloh: Bertelsmann, 1953.

Kuyper, Abraham. *Het Calvinisme: Zes Stone-lezingen.* Kampen: J. H. Kok, 1899.

Labarthe, Olivier. "Jean-François Salvard, Ministre de l'évangile: Vie, oeuvre et correspondance." In *Polémiques religieuses: Études et texts,* edited by Marie-Claude Junod, Monique Droin-Bridel, and Olivier Labarthe, 345–480. Geneva: Jullien, 1979.

Lecerf, Auguste. *Études calvinistes.* Neuchâtel: Delachaux et Niestle, 1949.

Léonard, Émile G. *Histoire generale du protestantisme.* 3 vols. Paris: Presses universitaires de France, 1961–64.

Locher, Gottfried W. *Die Zwinglische Reformation im Rahmen der europaischen Kirchengeschichte.* Göttingen: Vandenhoeck & Ruprecht, 1979.

Lomberg, Elwin, ed. *Emder Synode, 1571–1971: Beiträge zur Geschichte und zum 400-jährigen Jubiläum.* Neukirchen-Vluyn: Neukirchener Verlag, 1973.

Maag, Karin. *The Reformation in Eastern and Central Europe.* Brookfield: Ashgate, 1997.

———. *Seminary or University? The Genevan Academy and Reformed Higher Education, 1560–1620.* Brookfield, VT: Ashgate Publishing Co., 1995.

Maxwell, W. D. *John Knox's Genevan Service Book, 1556: The Liturgical Portions of the Genevan Service Book Used by John Knox While a Minister of the English Congregation of Marian Exiles at Geneva, 1556–1559.* 1931. Reprint, Westminster: Faith Press, 1965.

McKee, Elsie A. *Elders and the Plural Ministry: The Role of the Exegetical History in Illuminating John Calvin's Theology.* Geneva: Droz, 1988.

———. *John Calvin on the Diaconate and Liturgical Almsgiving.* Geneva: Droz, 1984.

McNeill, John T. *The History and Character of Calvinism.* New York: Oxford University Press, 1954.

Méjan, François. *Discipline de l'Église réformée de France.* Paris: Éditions Je sers, 1947.

Ménager, Daniel. "La correspondance de Calvin." In *Calvin et ses contemporains: Acts du colloque de Paris 1995,* edited by Olivier Millet, 107–15. Geneva: Droz, 1998.

Moehn, Wilhelmus H. T. "God roept ons tot zijn dienst." Ph.D. diss., University of Utrecht, 1996.

Monter, William E. *Calvin's Geneva.* New York: Wiley, 1967.

Nijenhuis, Willem. "De grenzen der burgerlijke ongehoorzaamheid in Calvijns laatstbekende preken Ontwikkeling van zijn opvattingen aangaande het verzetsrecht." In *Historisch bewogen: Opstellen over de radical reformatie in de 16th en 17th eeuw,* edited by Albert Fredrik Milink, 67–97. Groningen: Wolters-Noordhoff, 1984.

Nürnberger, Richard. *Die Politisierung des französischen Protestantismus Calvin und die Anfänge des protestantischen Radikalismus.* Tübingen: J. C. B. Mohr, 1948.

Parker, Geoffrey. *The Dutch Revolt.* Ithaca: Cornell University Press, 1977.

Pearson, Andrew F. S. *Thomas Cartwright and Elizabethan Puritanism, 1535–1603.* 1925. Reprint, Gloucester: Peter Smith, 1966.

Penny, D. Andrew. *Freewill or Predestination: The Battle over Saving Grace in Mid-Tudor England.* Rochester: Boydell Press, 1990.

Peter, Rodlophe, and Jean-François Gilmont, eds. *Bibliotheca Calviniana: Les oeuvres de Jean Calvin publiees au XVIe siècle.* 3 vols. Geneva: Droz, 1991–2000.

Pettegree, Andrew. *Emden and the Dutch Revolt: Exile and the Development of Reformed Protestantism.* New York: Oxford University Press, 1992.

———. *Foreign Protestant Communities in Sixteenth-Century London.* Oxford: Clarendon, 1986.

———. *Marian Protestantism: Six Studies.* Brookfield: Ashgate, 1996.

———. "The Reception of Calvinism in Britain." In *Calvinus Sincerioris Religionis Vindex: Calvin as Protector of the Purer Religion,* edited by Wilhelm H. Neuser, 267–89. Kirksville, MO: Sixteenth Century Journal Publishers, 1997.

Pettegree, Andrew, A. Duke, and G. Lewis. *Calvinism in Europe, 1540–1620.* Cambridge: Cambridge University Press, 1994.

Potter, David, ed. and trans. *The French Wars of Religion: Selected Documents.* New York: St. Martin's Press, 1997.

Press, Volker. *Calvinismus und Territorialstaat: Regierung und Zentralbehörden der Kurpfalz 1559–1619.* Stuttgart: E. Klett, 1970.

———. "Die 'Zweite Reformation' in der Kurpfalz." In *Die reformierte Konfessionalisierung in Deutschland: Das Problem der "Zweiten Reformation": Wissenschaftliches Symposion des Vereins für Reformationsgeschichte 1985,* edited by Heinz Schilling, 104–29. Gütersloh: G. Mohn, 1986.

Prestwich, Menna, ed. *International Calvinism, 1541–1715.* New York: Oxford University Press, 1985.

Reid, W. Stanford, ed. *John Calvin: His Influence in the Western World.* Grand Rapids: Zondervan, 1982.

———. "John Calvin, John Knox, and the Scottish Reformation." In *Church, Word, and Spirit: Historical and Theological Essays in Honor of Geoffrey W. Bromiley,* edited by James E. Bradley and Richard A. Muller, 141–51. Grand Rapids: Eerdmans, 1987.

———. *Trumpeter of God: A Biography of John Knox.* New York: Scribner, 1974.

Ridley, Jasper. *John Knox.* New York: Oxford University Press, 1968.

Roussel, Bernard. "Calvin conseiller de ses contemporains: De la correspondence à la légend." In *Calvin e ses contemporains: Actes du Colloque de Paris,* edited by Olivier Millet, 195–212. Geneva: Droz, 1998.

Rutgers, Frederick L. *Calvijns invloed op de Reformatie in de Nederlanden.* Leeuwarden: De Tille, 1980.

Salmon, John H. M. *Society in Crisis: France in the Sixteenth Century.* New York: St. Martin's Press, 1975.

Sap, Jan W. *Wegbereiders der revolutie: Calvinisme en de strijd om de democratische rechtsstaat.* Groningen: Wolters-Noordhoff, 1993.

Schelven, Aart A. van. *Het Calvinisme gedurende zijn bloetijd.* 3 vols. Amsterdam: W. Ten Have, 1943–1965.

———. *De Nederduitsche vluchtelingenkerken der XVIe eeuw in Engeland en Duitschland in hunne beteekenis voor de Reformatie in de Nederlanden.* The Hague: M. Nijhoff, 1909.

Schilling, Heinz. *Niederländische Exulanten im 16. Jahrhundert: Ihre Stellung im Sozialgefüge und im religiösen Leben deutscher und englischer Städte.* Gütersloh: G. Mohn, 1972.

Schnucker, Robert V., ed. *Calviniana: Ideas and Influence of Jean Calvin*. Kirksville: Sixteenth Century Journal Publishers, 1988.

Scribner, Robert W., Rob Porter, and Mikulas Teich. *The Reformation in National Context*. New York: Cambridge University Press, 1994.

Sehling, Emil, ed. *Die evangelischen Kirchenordnungen des XVI. Jahrhunderts*. Vol. 14, *Kurpfalz*. Tübingen: Mohr, 1969.

Spijker, Willem van 't. *Democratisering van de kerk anno 1562*. Kampen: Kok, 1975.

———. "Stromingen onder de reformatorisch-gezinden te Emden." In *De Synode van Emden, oktober 1571: Een bundel opstellen ter gelegenheid van de vierhonderdjarige herdenking*, edited by D. Nauta, J. P. van Dooren, and Otto J. de Jong, 50–74. Kampen: Kok, 1971.

Staehelin, Ernst. *Johannes Calvin: Leben und ausgewählte Schriften*. 2 vols. Elberfeld: Friderichs, 1863.

Stempel, Walter, et al. *Weseler Konvent, 1568–1968: Eine Jubiläumsschrift*. Schriftenreihe des Vereins für Rheinische Kirchengeschichte 29. Düsseldorf: Presseverband der Evangelischen Kirche im Rheinland, 1968.

Strohm, Christopf. *Ethik im frühen Calvinismus: Humanistische Einflüsse, philosophische, juristische und theologische Argumentationen sowie mentalitätsgeschichtliche Aspekte am Beispiel des Calvin-Schülers Lambertus Danaeus*. New York: W. de Gruyter, 1996.

Troeltsch, Ernst. "Der Calvinismus." In *Die Soziallehren der christlichen Kirchen und Gruppen*, edited by Ernst Troeltsch, 605–795. Tübingen: Mohr, 1923.

Visser, Derk, ed. *Controversy and Conciliation: The Reformation and the Palatinate, 1559–1583*. Allison Park, PA: Pickwick Publications, 1986.

Vries, Harman de. *Geneve: Pépinière du Calvinisme hollandaise*. 2 vols. Fribourg: Fragnière frères, 1918–24.

Wallace, Dewey D. *Puritans and Predestination: Grace in English Protestant Theology, 1525–1695*. Chapel Hill: University of North Carolina Press, 1982.

Walton, Robert C. "Der Streit zwischen Thomas Erastus und Caspar Olevian über die Kirchenzucht in der Kurpfalz in seiner Bedeutung für die internationale reformierte Bewegung." *Monatshefte für evangelische Kirchengeschichte des Rheinlandes* 37/38 (1988/1989): 205–46.

Warfield, Benjamin B. *Calvin and Calvinism*. New York: Oxford University Press, 1931.

Welti, Manfred E. *Kleine Geschichte der Italienischen Reformation*. Gütersloh: G. Mohn, 1985.

Wesel-Roth, Ruth. *Thomas Erastus: Ein Beitrag zur Geschichte der reformierten Kirche und zur Lehre von der Staatssouveranität*. Lahr/Baden: Schauenburg, 1954.

White, Peter O. G. *Predestination, Policy and Polemic: Conflict and Consensus in the English Church from the Reformation to the Civil War*. Cambridge: Cambridge University Press, 1992.

Select General Bibliography

Calvin Bibliographies

Bihary, Michael, ed. *Bibliographia Calviniana: Calvin's Works and Their Translations, 1850–1997.* 3rd ed. Prague: s.n., 2000.

De Klerk, Peter; Paul Fields. "Calvin Bibliography." *Calvin Theological Journal* 7–, no. 2 (1972–present).

Erichson, Alfred. *Bibliographia Calviniana: Catalogus Chronologious Operum Calvini; Catalogus Systematicus Operum quae sunt de Calvino; cum Indice Auctorum Alphabetico.* Berlin: C. A. Schwetschke, 1900. Reprint, Nieuwkoop: B. De Graaf, 1960.

Greef, Wulfert de. *The Writings of John Calvin: An Introductory Guide.* Translated by Lyle D. Bierma. Grand Rapids: Baker, 1993. Originally published as *Johannes Calvijn zijn werk en geschriften.* Kampen: De Groot Goudriaan, 1989.

———. *The Writings of John Calvin, Expanded Edition: An Introductory Guide.* Translated by Lyle D. Bierma. Louisville, KY: Westminster John Knox Press, 2008. Originally published as *Johannes Calvijn: Zijn Werk en Geschriften.* 2nd ed. Kampen: Kok, 2006.

Kempff, Dionysius. *A Bibliography of Calviniana, 1959–1974.* Potchefstroom: Institute for Reformational Studies, 1983.

Niesel, Wilhelm. *Calvin-Bibliographie, 1900–1959.* Munich: C. Kaiser, 1961.

Peter, Rodolphe, and Jean-François Gilmont, eds. *Bibliotheca Calviniana: Les oeuvres de Jean Calvin publiées au XVIe siècle; Écrits, théologiques, litéraires et juridiques, 1532–1600.* 3 vols. Geneva: Droz, 1991–2000.

Tylenda, J. N. "Calvin Bibliography, 1960–1970." *Calvin Theological Journal* 6, no. 2 (1971): 156–93.

Calvin's Works

Armstrong, Brian G., et al., eds. *Ioannis Calvini opera omnia denuo recognita et adnotatione critica instructa notisque illustrata.* Geneva: Droz, 1992–.

Battles, Ford Lewis, and André Malan Hugo. *Calvin's Commentary on Seneca's "De Clementia" with Introduction, Translation, and Notes.* Leiden: E. J. Brill, 1969.

Bergier, Jean-François, and Robert M. Kingdon. *Registres de la Compagnie des Pasteurs de Genève.* Geneva: Droz, 1962–.

Busch, Eberhard, et al., eds. *Calvin-Studienausgabe.* Neukirchen: Neukirchener Verlag, 1994–.

Calvin, John. *Calvin d'après Calvin: Fragments extraits des oeuvres français du réformateur.* Edited by C. O. Viguet and D. Tissot. Geneva: J. Cherbuliez, 1864.

———. *Calvin, homme d'église: Oeuvres choisies du reformateur et documents sur les Églises reformees du XVIe siecle.* Geneva: Labor & Fides, 1971.

———. *Deux congrégations et exposition du catéchisme.* Edited by Rodolphe Peter. Paris: Presses Universitaires de France, 1964.

———. *Ioannis Calvini opera quae supersunt omnia.* Edited by Guilielmus Baum, Eduardus Cunitz, and Eduardus Reuss. 59 vols. Braunschweig: Schwetschke, 1863–1900.

———. *Joannis Calvini opera selecta.* Edited by Petrus Barth and Guilielmus Niesel. 5 vols. Munich: C. Kaiser, 1926–1952.

Gloede, Gunter, ed. *Reformatorenbriefe: Luther, Zwingli, Calvin.* Neukirchen: Neukirchener Verlag, 1973.

Herminjard, Aimé Louis. *Correspondance des Réformateurs dans les pays de langue française.* 9 vols. Geneva: H. Georg, 1866–1897.

Lambert, Thomas A., and Isabella M. Watt, eds. *Registers of the Consistory of Geneva in the Time of Calvin.* Vol. 1, *1542–1544.* Translated by M. Wallace McDonald. Grand Rapids: Eerdmans, 2000–.

Kingdon, Robert M., et al., eds. *Registres du Consistoire de Genève au Temps de Calvin.* Geneva: Droz, 1996–.

Mülhaupt, Erwin, ed. *Supplementa Calviniana: Sermons inédits.* Vols. 1–3, 5–8, 10–11. Neukirchen: Neukirchener Verlag, 1936–.

Parker, Thomas H. L., ed. *Johannis Calvini commentarius in Epistolam Pauli ad Romanos.* Leiden: Brill, 1981.

Peter, Rodolphe, ed. *Les lettres à Calvin de la collection Sarrau.* Paris: Presses Universitaires de France, 1972.

Schwarz, Rudolf, ed. *Johannes Calvins Lebenswerk in Seinen Briefen: Eine Auswahl von Briefen Calvins in Deutscher Übersetzung.* 2 vols. Neukirchen: Neukirchener Verlag, 1961–62.

Selderhuis, Herman, ed. *Calvini Opera Database 1.0.* DVD. Apeldoorn: Instituut voor Reformatieonderzoek, 2006.

Wevers, Richard F., ed. *Calvin's 'Institutes' Latin-English Search and Browser Programs.* CD-ROM. Grand Rapids: Meeter Center for Calvin Studies, 1999.

———, ed. *Concordance to Calvin's Institutio 1559: Based on the Critical Text of Petrus Barth and Guilelmus Niesel.* 6 vols. Grand Rapids: Meeter Center for Calvin Studies, 1992.

———, ed. *Institutes of the Christian Religion of John Calvin, 1539: Text and Concordance.* 4 vols. Grand Rapids: Meeter Center for Calvin Studies, 1988.

Calvin Biographies

Adam, Melchior. "Vita Calvini." In *Decades duae continentes vitas theologorum exterorum prinicpum, qui ecclesiam Christi superiori seculo propagarunt et propugnarunt,* 63–113. Frankfurt: Jonae Rosae, 1653.

Baum, Guilielmus, et al., eds. "Annales Calviniani." In *Calvini Opera,* vol. 21, pages 186–818. Braunschweig: Schwetschke, 1879.

Beza, Theodore, and Nicolas Colladon. "Vie de Calvin." In *Calvini Opera,* vol. 21, pages 21–172. Braunschweig: Schwetschke, 1879.

Bouwsma, William J. *John Calvin: A Sixteenth-Century Portrait.* New York: Oxford University Press, 1988.

Cadier, Jean. *Calvin: Sa vie, son oeuvre; Avec un exposé de sa philosphie.* Paris: Presses universitaires de France, 1967.

———. *Der Mann, den Gott bezwungen hat.* Translated by Matthias Thurneysen. Zollikon: Evangelischer, 1959.

Cottret, Bernard. *Calvin: A Biography.* Translated by M. Wallace MacDonald. Grand Rapids: Eerdmans, 2000.

———. *Calvin: Biographie.* Paris: Payot & Rivages, 1998.

Dankbaar, W. F. *Calvijn: Zijn weg en werk.* Nijkerk: W. F. Callenbach, 1982.

———. *Calvin: Sein Weg und sein Werk.* Neukirchen: Neukirchener Verlag, 1959.

Doumergue, Émile. *Jean Calvin: Les hommes et les choses de son temps.* 7 vols. Lausanne: G. Bridel, 1899–1927.

Kampschulte, Franz Wilhelm. *Johann Calvin: Seine Kirche und sein Staat in Genf.* 2 vols. Leipzig: Duncker & Humblot, 1869–1899.

Lang, A. *Johannes Calvin: Ein Lebensbild zu seinem 400. Geburtstag am 10. Juli 1909.* Leipzig: Verein für Reformationsgeschichte, 1909.

McGrath, Alister E. *A Life of John Calvin: A Study in the Shaping of Western Culture.* Oxford: Blackwell Publishers, 1990.

Neuser, Wilhelm H. *Calvin.* Berlin: W. de Gruyter. 1971.

Parker, T. H. L. *John Calvin: A Biography.* Philadelphia: Westminster Press, 1971. Reprint, Louisville, KY: Westminster John Knox Press, 2007.

Pierson, Allard. *Studiën over Johannes Kalvijn.* Amsterdam: P. N. Van Kampen, 1881.

Potter, George, and Mark Greengrass. *John Calvin.* New York: St. Martin's Press, 1983.

Staedtke, J. *Johannes Calvin. Erkenntnis und Gestaltung.* Göttingen: Musterschmidt-Verlag, 1969.

Staehelin, Ernst. *Johannes Calvin: Leben und ausgewählte Schriften.* 2 vols. Elberfeld: R. L. Friderichs, 1863.

Walker, Williston. *John Calvin: The Organiser of Reformed Protestantism, 1509–1564.* New York: G. P. Putnam's Sons, 1906. Reprinted with a bibliographical essay by John T. McNeill. New York: Schocken Books, 1969.

Wallace, Ronald S. *Calvin, Geneva and the Reformation: A Study of Calvin as Social Reformer, Churchman, Pastor and Theologian.* Grand Rapids: Baker, 1988.

Calvin's Theology

Bauke, Hermann. *Die Probleme der Theologie Calvins.* Leipzig: Hinricks, 1922.

Gamble, Richard, ed. *Articles on Calvin and Calvinism: A Fourteen-Volume Anthology of Scholarly Articles.* 14 vols. New York: Garland, 1992.

Ganoczy, Alexandre. "Grundzüge der Theologie Calvins." In *Ökumenische Kirchengeschichte.* Vol. 2, *Mittelalter und Reformation*, edited by Raymond Kottje and Bernd Moeller, 381–86. Mainz: Matthias-Grunewald, 1973.

Hillebrand, Hans J., ed. *The Oxford Encyclopedia of the Reformation.* 4 vols. New York: Oxford University Press, 1996.

Hunter, A. Mitchell. *The Teaching of Calvin: A Modern Interpretation.* London: James Clarke & Co., 1950.

Neuser, Wilhelm H. "Die Theologie Johann Calvins." In *Handbuch der Dogmen und Theologiegeschichte.* Vol. 2, *Die Lehrentwicklung im Rahmen der Konfessionalität*, edited by Carl Andresen, 238–71. Göttingen: Vandenhoeck & Ruprecht, 1980.

Niesel, Wilhelm. *Die Theologie Calvins.* 2nd ed. Munich: C. Kaiser, 1950.

———. *The Theology of Calvin.* Translated by Harold Knight. Grand Rapids: Baker, 1980.

Nijenhuis, Wilhelm. "Calvin's Theology." In *TRE* (*Theologische Realenzyklopädie*), edited by Gerhard Krause et al., vol. 7, pages 578–87. New York: W. de Gruyter, 1981.

Oberman, Heiko A. *The Dawn of the Reformation: Essays in Late Medieval and Early Reformation Thought.* Edinburgh: T&T Clark, 1986.

———. *Werden und Wertung der Reformation vom Wegestreit zum Glaubenskampf.* Tübingen: J. C. B. Mohr, 1977.

Partee, Charles. *The Theology of John Calvin.* Louisville, KY: Westminster John Knox Press, 2008.

Reuter, Karl. *Das Grundverständnis der Theologie Calvins unter Einbeziehung ihrer geschichtlichen Abhängigkeiten.* Neukirchen-Vluyn: Neukirchener Verlag, 1963.

———. *Vom Scholaren bis zum Reformator: Studien zum Werdegang Johannes Calvins.* Neukirchen-Vluyn: Neukirchener Verlag, 1981.

Schützeichel, Heribert. *Die Glaubenstheologie Calvins.* Munich: M. Hueber, 1972.

Stauffer, Richard. "Johannes Calvin." In *Gestalten der Kirchengeschichte.* Vol. 6. *Die Reformationszeit,* edited by Martin Greschat, 228–37. Stuttgart: Kohlhammer, 1981.

Wendel, François. *Calvin: Origins and Development of His Religious Thought.* Translated by Philip Mairet. Grand Rapids: Baker, 1997.

———. *Calvin: Sources et evolution de sa pensée religieuse.* Paris: Presses Universitaires de France, 1950.

Historiography on Calvin

Armogathe, Jean-Robert. "Les vies de Calvin au XVI et XVII siècle." In *Historiographie de la Réforme,* edited by Joutard Philippe et al., 45–59. Paris: Delachaux & Niestle, 1977.

Bolsec, Jérôme-Hermès. *Histoire de la vie, moeurs, actes, doctrine, constance et mort de Jean Calvin, jadis minister de Genève.* Lyon: J. Patrasson, 1577.

Büsser, Fritz. *Calvins Urteil über sich selbst.* Zurich: Zwingli-Verlag, 1950.

Perry, Elizabeth I. *From Theology to History: French Religious Controversy and the Revocation of the Edict of Nantes.* The Hague: M. Nijhoff, 1973.

Pfeilschifter, Frank. *Das Calvinbild bei Bolsec und sein Fortwirken im französischen Katholizismus bis ins 20. Jahrhundert.* Augsburg: FDL-Verlag, 1983.

Scholl, Hans. *Calvinus Catholicus: Die katholische Calvinforschung im 20. Jahrhundert.* Freiburg: Herder, 1974.

Schützeichel, Heribert. *Katholische Calvin-Studien.* Trier: Paulinus-Verlag, 1980.

Stauffer, Richard. *Calvins Menschlichkeit.* Zurich: EVZ-Verlag, 1964.

Zahn, Adolf. *Studien über Johannes Calvin: Die Urteile katholischer und protestantischer Historiker im 19. Jahrhundert über den Reformator.* Gütersloh: Bertelsmann, 1894.

Index

177